Palgrave Advances in Managing and Marketing Tourism, Hospitality, and Events

Series Editor
Marianna Sigala
Sheffield Business School
Sheffield Hallam University
SHEFFIELD, UK

Tourism is one of the largest, most diversified, complex, global but also most dynamic, continuously evolving, and resilient industries. Additionally, it is an important social and business practice affecting - but also being affected by - all aspects of human life and societies. In this context, this series brings together multidisciplinary research examining the continuous evolution, transformation, and contemporary practice of tourism as a business phenomenon. It places particular emphasis on how the various forces and factors from multi-disciplinary areas, such as politics, economics, and psychology, affect the various elements of the tourism ecosystem including tourism demand, tourism suppliers, and the various tourism stakeholders. A unique platform for understanding the evolution of tourism, hospitality and events, books in the series will examine and illustrate the actors and factors that are driving change within the industry as well as the processes and the outcomes of such transformational efforts. In this vein, the purpose of the series is to publish work that can help tourism researchers, scholars, professionals and policy makers alike stay updated about contemporary and emerging issues. Going beyond that, the series aims to empower readers to envision and shape the trends, challenges and transformations in the industry.

Ultimately, this series equips its readers with the knowledge and the capacity needed to re-imagine and lead tourism and hospitality futures within their professional and/or scholarly sphere.

Charalampos Giousmpasoglou
Evangelia Marinakou

The Contemporary Hotel Industry

A People Management Perspective

Charalampos Giousmpasoglou
Bournemouth University
Poole, UK

Evangelia Marinakou
Bournemouth University
Poole, UK

ISSN 2948-278X ISSN 2948-2798 (electronic)
Palgrave Advances in Managing and Marketing Tourism, Hospitality, and Events
ISBN 978-3-031-52802-6 ISBN 978-3-031-52803-3 (eBook)
https://doi.org/10.1007/978-3-031-52803-3

© The Editor(s) (if applicable) and The Author(s), under exclusive license to Springer Nature Switzerland AG 2024

This work is subject to copyright. All rights are solely and exclusively licensed by the Publisher, whether the whole or part of the material is concerned, specifically the rights of translation, reprinting, reuse of illustrations, recitation, broadcasting, reproduction on microfilms or in any other physical way, and transmission or information storage and retrieval, electronic adaptation, computer software, or by similar or dissimilar methodology now known or hereafter developed.

The use of general descriptive names, registered names, trademarks, service marks, etc. in this publication does not imply, even in the absence of a specific statement, that such names are exempt from the relevant protective laws and regulations and therefore free for general use.

The publisher, the authors and the editors are safe to assume that the advice and information in this book are believed to be true and accurate at the date of publication. Neither the publisher nor the authors or the editors give a warranty, expressed or implied, with respect to the material contained herein or for any errors or omissions that may have been made. The publisher remains neutral with regard to jurisdictional claims in published maps and institutional affiliations.

This Palgrave Macmillan imprint is published by the registered company Springer Nature Switzerland AG.
The registered company address is: Gewerbestrasse 11, 6330 Cham, Switzerland

Paper in this product is recyclable.

Preface

This book aims to provide a detailed account of the global hotel industry, focusing on managerial work and people management. The authors (Babis and Lia) are proud ASTER alumni, a Swiss-type Hotel School in Rhodes (Greece). Babis spent two decades as a senior manager in luxury hospitality establishments before he joined academia, and Lia decided to pursue an academic career after having worked in the hospitality and tourism industry. Both authors are experienced academics and maintain excellent professional networks in the local and international hospitality industry. It is not surprising, therefore, that they have both researched this topic extensively in the past 15 years.

The book explores the different aspects of managerial work in global hotel industry settings: general management, leadership, skills and competencies, education and training, and managing diversity. Based on the existing literature and the authors' previous research, the book suggests that senior managers (i.e., General Managers and Heads of Department) should adopt a people-centric management and leadership style while at the same time maintaining operational efficiency.

Understanding the managers' work from a people management perspective is critical for successful hotel operations; nevertheless, this area is under-researched. Similarly, diversity and inclusion are areas of people management to be critically explored in the hospitality industry context. Diversity management strategies should be further developed to be practiced in contemporary hospitality organisations. This book is unique in scale and depth; it is expected to provide valuable insights from both theoretical and practical perspectives.

Poole, UK   Charalampos Giousmpasoglou
                                                      Evangelia Marinakou

Acknowledgements

Babis and Lia would like to thank the people who contributed to the content of this book (roughly in order that they occur in the book): Henry Mintzberg, Michael Clitheroe, Ned Capeleris, Emily Goldfischer, Marlene Poynder, Tammy Markley, Dimitris Sikalias, EHL Hospitality Business School, The European Hotel Managers Association, and Panos Almyrantis.

We would also like to thank all the friends and former colleagues in hotels who helped us with their valuable comments and recommendations. Their passion for hospitality and hard work will always inspire younger generations to join this industry!

Contents

1	Introduction	1
2	An Overview of the Hotel Industry	9
3	The Nature of Managerial Work	39
4	Managerial Skills and Competencies	65
5	Leadership	95
6	Human Resources Management in Hotels	129
7	Hospitality Management Education	159
8	Diversity and Gender Issues in Hotel Management	187
9	Current Challenges and Future Perspectives	213
	Index	237

About the Author

Charalampos Giousmpasoglou is a principal academic at Bournemouth University (ranked in the Top 20 Universities globally for Hospitality and Tourism), UK. Babis has worked both in academia and in the industry; as a practitioner, he spent 20 years as a hotel manager in Greek luxury hospitality establishments. As an academic, he worked in Greece, Bahrain, and the UK in undergraduate and postgraduate hospitality and business administration-related programmes. His research interests focus on managerial work, hospitality management, and human resources management. On these research themes, he has written three books, book chapters, and journal articles and presented papers to several international conferences. Babis is a Senior Fellow member of the Higher Education Academy, UK; Academic Fellow in Chartered Institute of Personnel and Development (CIPD); and an Institute of Hospitality Member (MIH). He is also a member of the Global Hospitality Research Alliance (GHRA), among other professional groups. Babis is a reviewer and editorial board member in reputable academic journals such as the *International Journal of Contemporary Hospitality Management* and the *International Journal of Human Resources Management*.

About the Author

Evangelia Marinakou is a Principal Academic at Bournemouth University, UK. Before completing her PhD on Gender and Leadership from Strathclyde Business School, she had a career in the Greek hospitality industry. In her academic career journey, Lia has served as Head of Department at academic institutions in Greece, Switzerland, Bahrain, and the UK. Her experience in academic quality assurance is extensive and she contributes to programme revalidations and accreditations as an expert panel member at an international level. Her research interests include gender and diversity management, leadership, talent management, and human resource management in the hospitality industry context. In these research areas, she has written books, book chapters, and journal articles, and facilitated presentations in international conferences. She is also a founding member of Future Talent Council and a member of the Global Hospitality Research Alliance (GHRA), among other professional groups. Additionally, she has led European-funded projects with a focus on hospitality and tourism training. Lia is a visiting lecturer at universities in the UK, France, and Greece. She has also trained several industry professionals in Lifelong Learning programmes on emotional intelligence, employee motivation, and talent retention.

List of Figures

Fig. 2.1	Types of hotel ownership. (Source: Authors' creation)	19
Fig. 2.2	Typical hotel organisational chart. (Source: Authors' creation)	25
Fig. 2.3	Main department managers' positions for a large hotel. (Source: Authors' creation)	26
Fig. 3.1	The management function evolution in the twentieth century. (Source: Authors' creation)	44
Fig. 3.2	Mintzberg's managerial roles. https://www.bl.uk/people/henry-mintzberg. (Source: Adapted from Mintzberg (1989, p. 17))	48
Fig. 3.3	New approaches to management (post-1990s). (Source: Authors' creation)	52
Fig. 4.1	Three levels of management in hotel units. (Source: Authors' creation)	67
Fig. 4.2	Hotel managers' traits and personal characteristics. (Source: Authors' creation)	74
Fig. 4.3	Differences between skills and competencies. (Source: Adapted from McNeill (n.d.))	79
Fig. 5.1	Management vs Leadership. (Source: Authors' creation)	99
Fig. 5.2	Leadership theories summarised. (Source: Authors' creation)	100
Fig. 5.3	Transformational leadership components. (Source: Author's creation)	102

Fig. 5.4	Advantages and disadvantages of transactional leadership. (Source: https://www.leadershipahoy.com/transactional-leadership-what-is-it-pros-cons-examples/)	104
Fig. 5.5	Effective leadership in contemporary hotel management. (Source: Authors' creation)	119
Fig. 6.1	The HRM cycle in hotels. (Source: Authors' creation)	134
Fig. 6.2	Talent management in luxury hotels. (Source: Adapted from Marinakou and Giousmpasoglou [2019, p. 3870])	147
Fig. 7.1	Student life at *Ecole hôtelière de Lausanne*. (Source: photos courtesy of EHL Archives [© 2023 EHL. All rights reserved])	161
Fig. 8.1	Hospitality manager pay gap in the US. (Source: www.zippia.com)	201
Fig. 8.2	Glass ceiling dimensions in hotel management. (Source: Authors' creation)	202
Fig. 9.1	Future talent retention factors in hospitality. (Source: Adapted from People 1st [2021])	218
Fig. 9.2	Risks from unethical recruitment. (Source: Adapted from Sustainable Hospitality Alliance [2022])	223
Fig. 9.3	Required actions towards the industry's recovery. (Source: Author's creation)	224
Fig. 9.4	Examples of Hospitality Awards. (Source: Author's creation)	230

List of Tables

Table 2.1	Categorisation and classification of accommodation	15
Table 2.2	Hotel classification in the UK	21
Table 2.3	Hotel operational and guest-facing staff	28
Table 3.1	The evolution of management from the Ancient World to the industrial revolution	41
Table 3.2	Fayol's principles of management	46
Table 3.3	Influential studies on managerial work	49
Table 4.1	An integrated framework for the GMs' work roles, demands, and relationships in hotels	70
Table 4.2	Functions performed by hospitality managers	81
Table 4.3	A comparison of managerial competency frameworks in the hospitality industry	86
Table 6.1	Differences between training and development	139
Table 7.1	Top 20 hospitality programmes globally in 2023	162

List of Boxes

Box 2.1	Accor's Portfolio of Brands	19
Box 3.1	Ten Managerial Roles by Henry Mintzberg	48
Box 4.1	A day in the life of a luxury hotel GM	73
Box 4.2	International Hotel Managers' development—Ned's story	76
Box 5.1	Women in Leadership—The Carlyle Example	117
Box 6.1	Marriott uses a Careers Chatbot for Facebook Messenger	149
Box 6.2	Green Key Training—Geraniotis Hotel and Resort	153
Box 8.1	Accor Group's Commitment to People with Disabilities	192
Box 8.2	IHG diversity example	204

1. Introduction

Photo Credits: The authors

Managerial Work in Hotels

The hospitality and tourism industry is acknowledged as a significant force in value creation and as the third largest employer in the world economy (WTTC, 2022). The hotel sector, an integral part of this industry, is a dynamic and highly competitive area with continuously developing new hotels and alternative lodging options. Hotel managers are crucial to the expansion and competitiveness of the industry since they have to develop novel strategies for attracting guests and business. Therefore, it is crucial to comprehend what hotel management is and how it works.

Hotel Management is taught at business schools nowadays and viewed as a management specialisation. However, there has been an ongoing discussion for many years about the "uniqueness" of hotel management compared to other fields or industries (Hsu et al., 2017). While many academics would argue against such a contentious claim, most hospitality professionals would agree (Lashley & Morrison, 2010); the middle ground is where the truth lies. The work life in hotels is challenging and rewarding at the same time. Hotel managers must think and act in a complex and volatile environment that involves multiple stakeholders within and outside the business unit (hotel). Although hotel managers are expected to operate at various levels and in many different areas, People Management is undoubtedly the most challenging.

Hotels are labour-intensive businesses that depend on employees to deliver superior quality products and services to guests. The hotel industry is centred on people, and hotel managers are responsible for ensuring that employees and guests are satisfied. It can be challenging for hoteliers to fulfil their job requirements because of the complexity of expectations and interactions with the key stakeholders (staff, guests, owners/shareholders). An excellent illustration of this argument is the required modifications and changes during the COVID-19 pandemic: hotel managers functioned as change agents to ensure the hotel guests' safety while remaining connected to their staff members, who were retained or rehired whenever possible. On the other hand, when the owner or corporate office failed to support hotel unit managers, the employees were made redundant, and the hotel lost its business following the lockdowns (Giousmpasoglou et al., 2021).

Although many generic Hospitality and Tourism Management books exist, only a handful focus on Hotel Management, recognised as a distinctive specialisation in Higher Education (HE) programmes today. This book provides valuable insights into hotel managerial work from theoretical and practical perspectives. Hotel managers assume different roles to meet challenging job demands (Giousmpasoglou, 2019), especially in luxury establishments (4* and 5* hotels) where guest expectations are high for products and services. Managing a hotel can be challenging and rewarding, requiring exceptional communication and problem-solving skills and the willingness to work under diverse conditions. In summary, hotel managers must remain adaptable and forward-thinking to address the challenges while capitalising on existing and emerging opportunities in the hospitality and tourism industry.

The book focuses on contemporary hotel management issues from a People Management perspective and is organised into nine chapters. Understanding the hotel sector is the first step towards understanding managerial work in hotels (Chap. 2). Then, to comprehend what constitutes managerial work, we explore the evolution of managerial work studies from the early twentieth century until today (Chap. 3). Hotel job requirements can be understood through the required skills and competencies for hotel managers (Chap. 4). Successful hotel management is strongly related to Leadership and the leadership styles followed by hotel managers (Chap. 5). Furthermore, People Management requires specialised Human Resources Management (HRM) and Talent Management (TM) knowledge to facilitate practices, processes, policies, and strategies to successfully and effectively manage the hotel's employees (Chap. 6). In addition, the hotel managers' future generation creation goes through Hospitality Education (Chap. 7). Employee Diversity is another distinctive characteristic of the hotel sector; the knowledge of gender and broader diversity issues helps hotel managers create and maintain an inclusive working environment for all employees (Chap. 8). Lastly, the ability to accurately assess current and future challenges and opportunities is essential for hotel managers to make informed decisions (Chap. 9). The following section provides a summary of each book chapter.

Book Structure

Chapter 1: Introduction

The introductory chapter provides an overview of this book and its structure, including chapter summaries.

Chapter 2: An Overview of the Hotel Industry

Chapter 2 introduces the different types of accommodation lodges and hotels for commercial use (i.e., luxury, mid-priced, budget, resort, city, special interest, themed). The organisational structure, as well as the ownership status (i.e., corporate, independent, managed, and franchised) of the different hotel establishments, is also presented in this chapter. Furthermore, a discussion on the key challenges in today's hotel management such as the use of technology and environmental concerns provides a thorough presentation in the context of the global hotel sector.

Chapter 3: The Nature of Managerial Work

Chapter 3 delves into the fundamental theories and concepts defining managerial work's nature. The chapter opening provides a glimpse into the early management practices from ancient times to the Industrial Revolution. Then, the chapter focuses on management theories and schools of thought that have been shaped throughout the twentieth century. These theories range from the principles of Scientific Management to the innovative conceptualisation of managerial work roles by Henry Mintzberg and the modern approaches to management. In the closing section of the chapter, we explore the breakdown of managerial work into eight distinct functions: Organisational Behaviour, Human Resources Management, Ethics and Corporate Social Responsibility, Managing Diversity and Cross-Cultural Management, Managing Quality and Service Quality, Managing Change, Crisis Management, and Sustainability Management.

Chapter 4: Managerial Skills and Competencies

Chapter 4 starts by describing managerial work requirements in the hospitality industry context. The development of the hospitality industry has boosted the global demand for managers at all levels (entry, middle, and senior management). Therefore, it is imperative to understand the skills and competencies framework required for hotel managers to cope with the industry's current and future challenges.

Chapter 5: Leadership

Chapter 5 focuses on Leadership and its importance in hospitality. The goal of every organisation is to exceed the needs of the guests. Leaders emphasise the value of customer service in achieving repeat business, service excellence, and gaining a competitive advantage. Conversely, managers focus on operations and putting systems in place. Leaders are more proactive and strategic in understanding the dynamics of human resources and inspiring their followers. This chapter discusses the key leadership styles in hospitality management with particular reference to those characteristics that leaders require to be successful. It also presents ways to develop leaders and leadership skills required in today's turbulent global environment.

Chapter 6: Human Resources Management in Hotels

Chapter 6 investigates the Human Resources Management (HRM) function in hospitality settings. More specifically, the application of the fundamental HRM functions (namely Planning, Recruitment and Selection, Training and Development, Performance and Reward, and Employee Relations) as fundamental components of global Hospitality Management are critically discussed. Talent Management (TM) is also explored as a distinctive HRM function in Hotel Management. Examples and contemporary research findings are included in this chapter, as well as practical examples.

Chapter 7: Hospitality Management Education

The Swiss Hotel Schools, founded in the late nineteenth century, are the source of the long-standing legacy of hotel management education in Europe. The Swiss Hotel Management approach has been accused of its industry focus and vocational orientation. There is evidence today that the curricula in Further and Higher Education hospitality programmes are sometimes unable to keep up with the global hotel industry escalating needs. In order to properly prepare future hotel managers, the existing curriculum must be updated, and there must be closer industry and expert practitioner engagement. In addition, during the past forty years, integrating Information and Communication Technologies (ICT) into curriculum design has revolutionised the field of Hospitality Education. The most recent, far-reaching advancements in Artificial Intelligence (AI) present enormous difficulties and potential for hospitality education providers. Furthermore, well-planned internship programmes and hospitality courses give aspiring hoteliers the tools they need to succeed in this competitive field. This chapter presents the current situation in Hospitality Education and proposes ways to prepare future hospitality leaders.

Chapter 8: Diversity and Gender Issues in Hotel Management

Chapter 8 explores diversity and gender issues in the global hotel industry. Despite the profound benefits of an inclusive working environment, the global hotel industry is slow in adopting best practices in Diversity Management. In addition, the challenging working conditions and the masculine occupational culture are the key challenges for women to pursue a career in hotels. The latest developments, such as the #metoo movement, bring to the surface phenomena such as sexual harassment and gender segregation in the hotel industry, especially in senior management and board positions. The chapter presents success stories from existing hotels and proposes ways to benefit from the existing talent of women and other diverse groups.

Chapter 9: Current Challenges and Future Perspectives

With a particular emphasis on People Management, the last chapter examines the current issues facing hotel management and its prospects for the future. Irrespective of the size or sector, the protracted crises in the global, regional, and national economies, known as "Permacrisis," brought about profound changes for those working in the hotel industry. Staffing shortages, Talent Management, managerial resilience, employee work-life balance, and problems connected to Fair Work and labour exploitation were identified as the people management areas most impacted by this circumstance. It will take industry-wide initiatives and coordination in specific areas, such as labour mobility, technology use, skills development, and the promotion of the Fair Work agenda, to address this ongoing crisis in people management. A new generation of hotel professionals will emerge due to the much-needed industry transition, and they will need to develop a distinct set of competencies and abilities to pursue careers in this challenging field.

References

Giousmpasoglou, C. (2019). Factors affecting and shaping the general managers' work in small-and medium-sized luxury hotels: The case of Greece. *Hospitality & Society, 9*(3), 397–422.

Giousmpasoglou, C., Marinakou, E., & Zopiatis, A. (2021). Hospitality managers in turbulent times: The COVID-19 crisis. *International Journal of Contemporary Hospitality Management, 33*(4), 1297–1318.

Hsu, C. H., Xiao, H., & Chen, N. (2017). Hospitality and tourism education research from 2005 to 2014: "Is the past a prologue to the future?". *International Journal of Contemporary Hospitality Management, 29*(1), 141–160.

Lashley, C., & Morrison, A. (2010). *In search of hospitality*. Routledge.

WTTC. (2022). Global trends. https://wttc.org/Portals/0/Documents/Reports/2022/EIR2022-Global%20Trends.pdf

2

An Overview of the Hotel Industry

Photo Credits: *Kaleidico* (*Free to use under the Unsplash License*). (Source: https://unsplash.com/photos/man-wearing-gray-polo-shirt-beside-dry-erase-board-3V8xo5Gbusk)

Introduction

Hospitality has been extensively researched, with numerous conceptualisations from different disciplines. Hospitality has a broad dimension that challenges management-oriented conceptions of what hospitality is (Lugosi, 2008). Other approaches also exist, such as defining hospitality based on social and cultural norms or even the social and emotional components of the consumer experience. This chapter examines hospitality, including operating structures, hotel ownership, and significant management and operational challenges.

History of Hospitality

The term *hospitality* is derived from the French word "hospice," which means taking care of travellers (Walker, 2021). Others state that the word hospitality comes from the Latin "hospitalitas," which means to receive as a guest. Brotherton (1999, p. 168) defined hospitality as a "contemporaneous human exchange, which is voluntarily entered into and designed to enhance the mutual wellbeing of the parties concerned through the provision of accommodation and/or food and drink." Kelly (2015) proposed two types of hospitality definitions. The first type, *semantic* definitions of hospitality, includes four characteristics: (a) they are conferred on guests who are away from home; (b) they are interactive, involving the coming together of the provider and the receiver; (c) they comprise a blend of tangible and intangible factors; and (d) they involve the host providing for the guest's security and psychological and physiological comfort. The second type, *practice-based* definitions of hospitality, relates to the economic exchange between firms and customers. Hemmington (2007) defined hospitality in the business context with five criteria: (a) the host-guest relationship; (b) generosity; (c) theatre and performance; (d) little surprises; and (e) safety and security. Finally, Brotherton and Wood (2000 in Lugosi, 2008, p. 140) suggested that:

The hospitality industry is comprised of commercial organisations that specialise in providing accommodation, and/or food, and/or drink, through a voluntary human exchange, which is contemporaneous in nature, and undertaken to enhance the mutual wellbeing of the parties involved.

From Ancient Times to Industrial Revolution

Hospitality has evolved through a long and diverse journey throughout human history. The concept of hospitality is "as old as civilisation itself" (Walker, 2021, p. 30), encompassing a wide range of cultural, social, and economic practices. The concept of hospitality is mentioned in writings from ancient Greece dating back to 15,000 B.C. It all started when people travelled for different purposes, and locals allowed them to rest on kitchen floors or other spaces. There were no purpose-built facilities until the first establishments were found in monasteries. The Sumerians were the first to refer to hospitality 4500 years before the common era (B.C.E.). As they started making money from selling their crops, they had more time to be involved in other activities such as writing, making tools, and producing beer, among others. In tavernas, they served beer for locals to relax and interact with each other (O'Gorman, 2007). Between 4000 and 2000 B.C.E., civilisations in Europe, China, Egypt, and India had elements of hospitality (i.e., inns and taverns). Inns and taverns were found everywhere, either run by freemen or retired gladiators; rest houses for pilgrims in the eighth century were established on the European continent. For example, in Italy, the inns belonged to the city; in England, inns and taverns were called post houses. The more the quality of the inns improved, the more people started travelling, mainly wealthy people who had expectations from the inns they stayed.

In the late sixteenth century, the first taverns served a fixed-price, fixed-menu meal (Walker, 2021). By the fifteenth century, England and France had laws regarding accommodation operations (O'Gorman, 2007). With the Renaissance and the Age of Exploration, the scope of hospitality expanded as global trade and colonisation increased. Opening trade routes to the East and discovering the Americas led to the establishment of colonial outposts and inns catering to travellers and traders. In the mid-eighteenth century, inns began to appeal to wealthier patrons. The hotel industry began in Europe with chalets and small hotels that provided a variety of services to the aristocracy (Andrews, 2007). In 1768, one of the first modern hotels was established in Exeter. In the early nineteenth century, hotels proliferated throughout Western Europe and North America, and luxury hotels began to emerge in the late nineteenth century, particularly in the US.

The Birth and Evolution of the Modern Hospitality Industry

In 1919, Conard Hilton opened the first hotel in Texas, giving birth to hotel chains; in the following years, other renowned companies appeared, that is, Marriott (1927), Sheraton (1937), and Hyatt (1957) (Wood, 2017). The golden age of hospitality (1961–1980) started with value creation driven by wealthy people interested in Luxury. The post-1980s years is when we see the first luxury hotel brands developed, such as the Ritz Carlton, in 1983. Between 1981 and 2000, the industry grew tremendously, leading to ideas such as design-led boutique hotels. New models and digital distribution methods arose in the 1990s, revolutionising the hospitality and tourism business. This has resulted in the loss of traditional distribution channels such as Tour Operators, and the rise of digital platforms such as Airbnb (2008) and Online Travel Agencies (OTAs) such as Expedia and Booking.com and other distribution channels for the accommodation sector (Hollander, 2022). Many hotels nowadays depend on distribution channels for selling their room inventory, where OTAs may take up to 15% commission on each booking (Van Ginneken, 2017). They also heavily rely on online customer reviews through portals such as TripAdvisor, causing a progressive reduction in direct sales (Walker, 2021).

Hospitality has been a social phenomenon with roots in societies for thousands of years (O'Gorman, 2007). Hospitality involves the hosts sharing their home with strangers (travellers-guests) with the main concern for the guest's welfare, safety, and happiness. Today, hospitality is still about "entertaining friends or acquaintances in one's home" (Wood,

2017, p. 27); nevertheless, hospitality has been reduced to the expense of economic exchange. The primary function of hospitality is to establish a relationship between the host and the guest through exchanges of goods and services, both material and symbolic (Selwyn, 2000, p. 54). If viewed as a commercial exchange, hospitality is considered inhospitable as the behaviour is provided for financial motives to gain a commercial advantage (Ritzer, 2019). Interestingly, O'Connor (2005, p. 267) proposed that:

> *Only once an understanding of hospitality's origins and its place in human nature is achieved can one expect to discover what hospitality means today, and more importantly what it will mean to those entering the industry in the future.*

The Hotel Sector

The hotel sector is a subset of the hospitality industry that specialises in providing accommodation services to consumers. Various hotel types can be classified based on size, function, service, and pricing. Service levels are typically divided into three categories: restricted service, mid-range service, and full service. However, some customers may be more accustomed to the star rating system, where one is the lowest and five is the highest. The global hotel and resort industry market size grew steadily until the outbreak of the coronavirus (COVID-19) pandemic in 2020 when travel disruptions around the world hit it. However, this figure grew in 2022 and was forecast to reach 1.21 trillion US dollars by 2023 (Statista, 2023).

In the UK, the hospitality industry contributed £59.3 billion to UK GDP in 2019, creating 2.53 million jobs, including 223,000 businesses, of which 50,660 were accommodation businesses comprising 23% of the hospitality industry (Hutton, 2022, pp. 10–11). The hotel sector is vertically disintegrated (Roper, 2017), and hotel ownership, operation, and branding are not often separated. Knowles observes that a small group of large companies globally dominates the hotel industry. Economies of scale for hotels are found in increased purchasing power, economies of centralising services such as laundry, reservations, or marketing, the ability to raise finance, and lower administration and training costs.

Types of Accommodation

Today's hotels can be categorised in several ways, that is, size, price, location, rating, services, and amenities. Barrows (2008, p. 72) suggested that "many types of hotels can fall into more than one category." Table 2.1 demonstrates the categorisation and classification of accommodation.

Hotel Ownership

There are four types of ownership and management of hotels: franchise, privately owned and operated, leased, and managed. Private ownership has been the most common operating structure of hotels. Later, *leases* separated property ownership from operating the business (Van Ginneken, 2017). Many international hotel chains prefer other ownership types than leasing, as they may not be willing to take the business risk in such contracts (Van Ginneken, 2017). Lately, leases are based on turnover with a rent payment based on hotel revenue with a minimum fixed rent (De Souza et al., 2016). The hotel owner loses control over how the building will be managed and operated. There are many challenges in how the lease term will end, that is, what happens with the furniture and the tenant's investment in improvements.

Another owner-operator structure is the *management contract*, developed with the international expansion of hotel chains (Walker, 2021). For example, Hilton Hotels offer a management contract to owners who receive three-quarters of gross operating profit but are also responsible for any losses. The one hotel considered to be a pioneer in this model is the Hong Kong Hilton which still serves as inspiration for other agreements (Wood, 2017). This case is an inspiration for modern hotel contracts. In this agreement, the management company receives fees (usually a percentage of revenue—the base fee—and a percentage of profit—the incentive fee) from the owner for managing the hotel on the owner's behalf (Evanoff, 2016). Hotel owners increasingly seek management companies for equity contributions to help finance their property's development (such as renovations and expansions) (Van Ginneken, 2017).

The *asset-light business* is where companies' revenue is generated from management and franchise fees rather than their operations (Van

Table 2.1 Categorisation and classification of accommodation

Classified by	Name	Description
Price	Limited-service hotels	Offer guest rooms only, with low room rates and limited if no facilities.
	Full-service hotels	Offer a wide range of facilities and amenities such as meeting space, with average or slightly above the market-area average room rates.
	Luxury hotels	Are usually large hotels, with upscale décor and design, offering full range of facilities such as fine-dining, at high room rates.
	Economy / budget hotels	Economy or budget hotels offer clean and reasonably sized rooms at affordable prices. This sector has grown tremendously over the past 20 years. Such hotels usually have a standardised appearance and offer no-frills service.
Function	Conference and convention hotels	As the title states, these are accommodation facilities that meet the needs of groups that attend and/or organise conventions. Usually, such hotels are close to airports or accessible by efficient transport links. There are meeting rooms with all necessary facilities on top of other key facilities such as banqueting.
Location	City centre and suburban hotels	These accommodation types serve business or leisure travellers. They can be luxury, midscale, business, suites, economy, or residential and offer a range of services from butler services in luxury provision to car rental. City centre hotels are usually more expensive than those in the suburbs due to high land costs.
	Airport hotels	These hotels are ideal for travellers in transit or who want to stay near the airport they are departing from. The guests at these hotels vary from business travellers to groups or leisure travellers. They offer easy check-in and check-out service or shuttle buses to the airport. These are usually large hotels with facilities such as room service, but with smaller rooms and limited facilities. With the increasing demand for such hotels for the meetings industry, airport hotels have started offering conference rooms
	Freeway and interstate hotels and motels	Such hotels provide accommodation to road travellers offering a convenient place to stay at a reasonable price. Facilities are basic, including parking, vending machines, or satellite TV. Motels (motor hotels) are less expensive accommodation with a variety of facilities offered such as swimming pool, parking, etc.

(continued)

Table 2.1 (continued)

Classified by	Name	Description
Market Segment	Resort hotels	Are often a destination themselves, usually encompass all services, and can be found close to beaches, mountain scenery, or in other locations with leisure and recreational activities. They accommodate mainly the leisure customers. Within this category we find themed resorts, which are hotels tied to a theme with distinct identity, for example, the Disney hotel.
	Casino hotels and resorts	Have become a significant segment of the entertainment and leisure industry. Such hotels offer services such as shows, fine cuisine, health spas, and conference centres and are found in casinos.
	Boutique hotels	Span in all prices and usually have distinct design, soft attributes, and atmosphere, which are usually perceived as trendy.
	Business hotels	Business customers have increased and have become a valuable segment as they can afford high average room rates (the company paying) and they spend a lot on food and drinks. They also tend to visit the hotels with their spouses or their family for a holiday. They require meeting space, fast check-in and check-out, as well as very good Internet access. Such hotels provide corporate rates for company bookings.
	Condotels, timeshare, and mixed-use hotels	A condotel is a combination of a hotel and a condominium, as owners of the condos may rent them, giving the hotel operating company a commission. Guests have access to facilities such as a swimming pool, sauna, or gym. Timeshare is a vacation or fractional ownership where owners buy specific times at the hotel/resort, and access and ownership are designated in defined periods. Owners can also exchange vacations and travel the world by trading their timeshare with another at comparable resorts worldwide (this requires a fee payment).
	Campus accommodation	Student accommodation available during semesters; reasonably priced accommodation to tourists at other times.

Ownership	Independent hotels	Offer a more personalised and friendly approach to service, to differentiate from competition.
	Single-owner hotels	Usually managed and operated based on the owner's request and standards.
	Chain hotels	Have standardised services, providing reliability, trust, and inspire loyalty.
Other	Full-service / extended-stay hotels	These hotels can be full-service, economy, extended-stay, and all-suite hotels. They offer a wide range of services mainly for guests who stay longer, that is, business travellers.
	Bed and breakfast inns	This accommodation type is widely known B&Bs; they offer an alternative lodging experience where the owner usually lives in the same premises. They offer accommodation and breakfast at reasonable prices.
	Youth hostel	Usually with dormitory-style accommodation, common toilets with some common social space.
	Cruises/ ferries / trains	Increasingly viewed as a threat to the more traditional accommodation providers as they provide both transportation and accommodation, food and beverage, and sometimes entertainment.

Source: Adapted from Barrows (2008), Clarke and Chen (2007), and Walker (2021)

Ginneken, 2017). Sternlicht, in 1991, revolutionised the hotel industry by separating the hotel operations (Starwood Lodging Corp) from the Real Estate (Starwood Lodging Trust) so that he could avoid corporate taxation on income from the real estate (REIT) by agreeing to pass 95% of rental income back to shareholders. Fewer taxes meant more projected income; more projected income meant higher valuation; and higher valuation meant higher purchase prices (Wood, 2017). A good example here is *franchising*, which offers opportunities for hotel owners as the franchisor offers them the right to operate and manage the product under the company's name; in return, the franchisee pays a fee for royalty payments. In this format, chains grow fast with minimum investment; franchising contributes to the industry's disintegration as it separates ownership of intellectual property (the hospitality brand) and ownership and operation of the hotel property (Lashley & Morrison, 2000).

There are *two main approaches to hotel ownership and control*: the first is when there is an owner and the second where hotel companies move away from ownership (Fig. 2.1). Usually, in the first approach, the owner has some control of the property, which is managed by a general manager (Dev et al., 2010). In the second approach, hotel chains manage the properties with minimum investment on the property, but with control of their brand with strict brand standards (Van Ginneken, 2017). Recently, hotel owners have preferred collaborating with independent small companies rather than large brands. These companies specialise in managing hotels and are not affiliated with a specific hotel brand. On this note, owners may decide to outsource the management of certain services to companies other than the franchisor. For example, the restaurant and bar management in the Amsterdam 'W' hotel was outsourced to The Entourage Group rather than the Marriott (van Ginneken, 2017). Although luxury hotel chains are reluctant to franchise the brand, Gold (2015—in van Ginneken, 2017) presented the cases of the Sofitel, Intercontinental, and Conrad in the UK, as they have developed soft or *collection*-style brands that are available for franchising where there is a relatively loose relationship between the owner and the company as the franchisee benefits from marketing, loyalty programmes, and distribution networks offered by the franchisor. Gold (ibid.) argues that the connection with the local market helps keep the brand's reputation and grow the number of properties in their systems. This approach divides hotel

Business Model	Hotel Ownership	Parent Company Capital Intensity	Employees	Brand Ownership, Marketing & Distribution
Franchised	Third Party	Low	Third Party	Parent Company
Managed	Third Party	Low	Parent Company & Third Party	Parent Company
Owned, Leased & Managed Leased	Parent Company	High	Parent Company	Parent Company

Fig. 2.1 Types of hotel ownership. (Source: Authors' creation)

properties' ownership, management, and branding among different parties. In addition, human resources practices and people management vary depending on the control and agreements in place in each case.

> **Box 2.1 Accor's Portfolio of Brands**
>
> *Accor continues transforming and simplifying its structure by leveraging its leadership positions in the most buoyant hospitality markets and segments.*
>
> The Accor Group is a global hotel operator and leader in Luxury and lifestyle Hospitality that operates a unique portfolio of brands covering all segments, from economy to Luxury, in 110 countries. The Group is evolving its structure to capitalise on the transformation undertaken in recent years, consolidate its leadership positions, focus its efforts, strengthen its know-how, accelerate its growth, and continue to improve its profitability.
>
> According to the Chairman and CEO, Mr. Sébastien Bazin, the Group's organisational structure is simplified, and it is now based on two distinct business divisions:
>
> - The "Economy, Midscale & Premium" division will notably include ibis, Novotel, Mercure, Swissôtel, Mövenpick, and Pullman and will incorporate four major regions.
> - The "Luxury & Lifestyle" division will combine the brands from these segments and will be structured around four brand collections: Raffles & Orient Express, Fairmont, Sofitel & MGallery, and Ennismore.
>
> The Accor Group confirmed the renewal of its Chairman and CEO term to support the new structure and accelerate growth. The new structure was implemented in October 2022.
>
> Source: Adapted from Pfalz (2023) and Accor (n.d.)

Quality and Grading Schemes

In hotels, quality inspections are significant operational procedures ensuring that hotels meet certain standards and that guests receive a consistent level of service. Quality inspections assist in maintaining the hotel's reputation, contribute to guest satisfaction, and assure compliance with numerous legislation and industry standards. The first property inspection system was established by AAA in 1937 (AAA, 2020). Furthermore, the Mobil Corporation introduced the first hotel star rating system in 1958. They created the Mobil Travel Guide that promoted trips in the US. Certain criteria were used to allocate hotels to each category. Today, this guide is known as the *Forbes Travel Guide* and covers hotels worldwide. Despite efforts to establish a single international rating system, no such arrangement exists. Accommodation is either *Classified* (i.e., type of property) or *Graded* (i.e., quality of provision). Star classification is essentially a guide to the type of hotel, indicating the character of the accommodation and service it sets out to provide (WTO, 2014). Table 2.2 provides some information on the classification in the UK hotel sector.

There are over 100 hotel rating systems worldwide in official and unofficial systems (WTO, 2014). Hotel guests nowadays use social media and electronic word of mouth (e-WOM) to gather information about hotels from online platforms such as *TripAdvisor.com* and *Booking.com* (Fotis et al., 2012). Furthermore, it is common for OTAs to base their ratings on guest reviews of hotels they have visited. This practically means that potential customers utilise hotel reviews to confirm if the official hotel rating corresponds to the real provision of products and services. When choosing a type of service or facility, there are typically several factors to consider; thus, it is not always easy to gauge customer satisfaction based on the service level, quality of facilities, or practices followed by each hotel. For example, environmental sensitive guests would consider a hotel's performance in this area. Environmental awards, such as the Green Key International hotel excellence certification, provide information on the hotel's sustainable practices and environmental consciousness; the criteria hotels must meet to receive the Green Keys include waste management, water management, and the use of clean energy.

Table 2.2 Hotel classification in the UK

Classification	Description
ONE STAR 1*	Hotels and inns generally of small scale with acceptable facilities and furnishings. All bedrooms with hot and cold water, adequate bath and lavatory arrangements, meals provided for residents, but their availability for non-residents may be limited.
TWO STAR 2*	Hotels offering a higher standard of accommodation and some private bathrooms and showers. A wider choice of food is provided but the availability of meals to non-residents may be limited.
THREE STAR 3*	Well-appointed hotels with more spacious accommodation, a large number of bedrooms with private bathrooms and showers. Fuller meal facilities are provided, but luncheon and weekend meal services to non-residents may be restricted.
FOUR STAR 4*	Exceptionally well-appointed hotels offering a high standard of comfort and service with a majority of bedrooms with private bathrooms and showers.
FIVE STAR 5*	Luxury hotels offering the highest international standards. These properties are usually large, with spacious rooms and the best facilities.

Source: Adapted from https://www.theaa.com/hotel-services/ratings-and-awards

Recently, "7-star" hotels were introduced to highlight the provision of special facilities and services. For example, Dubai's Burj Al Arab has been given the 7-star label, offering Rolls Royce shuttle service, a butler for every room and even helicopter transfer from the airport. This can be viewed as a hotel marketing trend that promotes the lavish and extraordinary services and facilities these properties provide. Such rating may be confusing or arbitrary as standards and criteria may differ by country (Koutoulas & Vagena, 2023). Even the legislation differs between countries, which confuses travellers looking for reliable information to make a purchase decision. In any case, the fulfilment of the criteria is monitored by auditors or inspectors (UNWTO, 2015). To receive a permit to operate in certain countries, hotels must register for classification or grading purposes; Tourism Ministries or Boards typically control these registers. Some argue that this approach generates red tape and inhibits innovation. Private organisations are also involved, including the Automobile Association (AA) with its rating of accommodation (www.theaa.com) or the Michelin Guide (www.michelinguide.com/). Public sector organisations such as national and regional tourist boards also classify and grade accommodation for legal purposes.

Hospitality Professional Bodies and Associations

Hospitality professional bodies and associations play a crucial role in the hospitality industry by providing support, education, networking opportunities, and representation for professionals in various industry sectors, including hotels, restaurants, travel, tourism, and event management. These organisations help elevate industry standards, promote best practices, and foster collaboration among professionals. They also contribute to advancing sustainable practices in hotel management and providing continuing professional development and lifelong learning to diverse hospitality businesses. The following are some indicative examples:

- **International Hotel & Restaurant Association** (IH&RA—https://www.ih-ra.org/): The IH&RA is the only international trade association exclusively devoted to promoting and defending the interests of the hotel and restaurant industry worldwide. It is a non-profit organisation and is officially recognised by the United Nations. IH&RA monitors and lobbies all international agencies on behalf of the hospitality industry.
- **The American Hotel & Lodging Association** (AH&LA—www.ahla.com/): AH&LA is the largest hotel association in the US, representing all segments of the industry nationwide, including major chains, independent hotels, management companies, REITs, bed and breakfasts, and industry partners.
- **UK Hospitality** (https://www.ukhospitality.org.uk/): The single, authoritative voice of hospitality represents everything from pubs, restaurants, hotels, nightclubs, attractions, leisure and events, and contract catering. UK Hospitality was formerly known as the *British Hospitality Association* (BHA), incorporating *The Restaurant Association* (RA).

- **The Institute of Hospitality** (IoH—www.instituteofhospitality.org): IoH is a professional membership body for hospitality employees around the globe. As a registered charity, they are committed to delivering continuing professional development and lifelong learning across the diverse hospitality family since 1938.
- **European Hotel Managers Association** (EHMA—https://www.ehma.com/): EHMA was established in Rome in 1974. It is a non-profit Association of Hotel General Managers operating first-class and luxury hotels across Europe. The founding members firmly believed that service is the principal tenet of quality hospitality.
- **United Nations World Tourism Organisation** (UNWTO—www.unwto.org): As the leading international organisation in the field of hospitality and tourism, UNWTO promotes tourism as a driver of economic growth, inclusive development, and environmental sustainability and offers leadership and support to the sector in advancing knowledge and tourism policies worldwide.

Organisational Structure

The organisational structure of a hotel is determined by its ownership, size, and type of business. Larger hotels have a more complex organisational structure because interdepartmental cooperation is required under the control of a general manager. The organisational structure is critical to the smooth operation of a hotel. A hotel's organisational structure, according to Lacalle (2022), is a plan or high-level overview established by a hotelier to help clearly outline the duties and responsibilities of each department, creating order throughout all aspects of the hotel. Organisational structures and charts are intended to facilitate hotel administration and operations, but they should also allow for flexibility in decision-making through empowering employees (Evanoff, 2016). To fulfil organisational objectives and deliver great service, hotel jobs necessitate cooperation, coordination, and effective leadership. Organisational charts provide an overview of the business and lay out the role of people in different positions, and if they are effectively designed, they may increase productivity and efficiency. Hotels need organisational charts for several reasons:

- convey the roles and responsibilities of every entity,
- help in decision-making,
- tell employees about whom they will communicate, and
- help in multiple managerial programmes.

In a study of hotels, Rutherford (2002) proposed that hotels were built around the *chef* ("king of the kitchen") and the *maître d' hotel* ("master of the hotel"). The hotel structure was based on line managers and staff, hierarchically organised by the general manager. Eddystone and Nebel (2002) excluded the engineering department and the facilities management responsibility from the hotel structure, whereas Conklin (2002) proposed and added the need to combine three inter-related partners (the customers, employees, and the general manager), hence introduced the human element in the hotel organisational structure.

The most frequent approach to structuring a hotel is separating departments by function. For larger hotels, jobs should be grouped to ensure efficient coordination and control (Walker, 2021). In general, departments may be grouped as 'front of the house' (where employees have guest contact) and 'back of the house' (where employees have little or no guest contact). Organisational charts demonstrate the delegation of authority and chain of command specifying reporting relationships in the organisation. According to Ivancevich et al. (1996), a common challenge for hoteliers is to develop an organisational structure committed to quality, which should be consistent with the hotel's strategy and directed towards achieving the organisation's objectives. An example of a medium-sized hotel organisational chart is presented in Fig. 2.2.

Globalisation, continuous change, and staff shortages require hotels to respond and adapt. Overall, there is a tendency towards flatter businesses with fewer management levels. Flatter structures provide flexibility and guarantee that systems, procedures, policies, and people adjust to changing circumstances, allowing for greater autonomy and customising work relationships (Brookes & Roper, 2010).

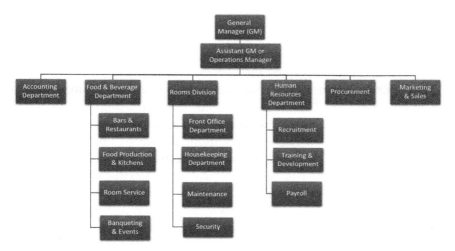

Fig. 2.2 Typical hotel organisational chart. (Source: Authors' creation)

Owners and Managers

The owner and the general manager (GM) set the hotel's standards, policies, budgets, and strategies. The general manager is also responsible for the day-to-day operation of the hotel as well as the design and execution of the business strategy. The general manager's job entails various tasks, responsibilities, roles, skills, and competencies discussed in Chap. 4. GMs are responsible for managing all the departments and their managers, defining and implementing policies, and coordinating activities demonstrating hard and soft skills such as decision-making, leadership, empathy, and interpersonal skills, among others. In Small and Medium Hotel Enterprises (SMHEs), typically independent or family businesses, the owner is usually the hotel's GM. In larger hotels, the GM works with and for the managing director or the CEO and is the liaison to the hotel's owner or corporate parent (Giousmpasoglou, 2019).

Assistant / Departmental Managers

They usually support the general manager's work, mainly in the hotel's daily operations. The Assistant General Manager, or the Operations Manager, supervises the departmental managers and communicates responsibilities, policies, and decisions. Departmental managers are responsible for their departments and their teams. For example, a Food & Beverage (F&B) manager is responsible for all the F&B outlets, and the Front Office (FO) Manager oversees the front desk (reception), concierge, and reservation teams. Figure 2.2 demonstrates the key departmental managers in a large hotel.

Furthermore, authority delegation in hotels refers to assigning and distributing decision-making responsibilities and tasks from managers to various levels of employees within the hotel. Delegating authority effectively ensures smooth operations, efficient management, and guest satisfaction (Walker, 2021). Finding the right balance between delegation and oversight is crucial to maintaining high service and quality standards (Fig. 2.3).

Operational and Guest-Facing Staff

Hotel operational and guest-facing staff are essential components of a hotel's workforce, responsible for ensuring the smooth functioning of various hotel departments and providing excellent guest experiences.

Fig. 2.3 Main department managers' positions for a large hotel. (Source: Authors' creation)

These staff members play different roles, from behind-the-scenes operations to direct guest interactions. Guest-facing staff working at different hotel departments, such as waiting staff and receptionists, in most cases, are the ones who deal directly with customers. In addition, operational roles collectively contribute to the overall functioning of a hotel and play a crucial part in delivering exceptional guest experiences (Walker, 2021). Effective coordination and communication among different operational and guest-facing teams are vital for the success of any hotel establishment. Some key roles typically found in these categories are provided in Table 2.3.

Hotel Management Challenges

Hotel management faces multiple challenges that hoteliers and managers must navigate to ensure their establishments' smooth operation and success. Internal and external environment events such as natural disasters, economic crises, and poor communication pose unique challenges for managers and threaten the hotel's existence. The COVID-19 pandemic, for example, created significant difficulties for the hotel sector, which experienced the worst economic fall of any sector; in 2021, the sector's proportion of the GDP plummeted from 3% in 2019 to 2% (Hutton, 2022, p. 18). Some common challenges faced by hotel managers are outlined in this section.

Increased Competition and Guest Expectations

The hotel industry is highly competitive, and new hotels or other types of accommodation are constantly entering the market (Wood, 2017). Due to the increased competition and the plethora of options available, guests have higher expectations, especially regarding service quality, technology, and personalised experiences. As guests have access to more information, they are more demanding, have higher expectations, and can make more informed decisions (Mohsin et al., 2019).

Table 2.3 Hotel operational and guest-facing staff

Guest-facing staff (front of the house)	Operational staff (back office)
Front Desk Staff: Greet guests, handle check-in/check-out procedures, assist with inquiries, provide information about the hotel and its services, and address guest concerns.	**Housekeeping Staff:** Responsible for cleaning and maintaining guest rooms, public areas, and ensuring overall cleanliness and hygiene throughout the hotel.
Concierge: Assist guests with various requests, including restaurant reservations, tour bookings, transportation arrangements, and other personalised services.	**Maintenance Staff:** Responsible for the upkeep and maintenance of the hotel's physical infrastructure, including plumbing, electrical systems, HVAC, and other facilities.
Bellhops/Porters: Assist guests with luggage, provide directions, and offer general assistance upon arrival and departure.	**Kitchen Staff:** Includes chefs, cooks, and kitchen assistants responsible for preparing and serving food in the hotel's restaurants, room service, and banquet events.
Waitstaff: Serve guests in restaurants, lounges, and during events, taking orders, delivering food and beverages, and ensuring a positive dining experience.	**Engineering Staff:** Handle the technical aspects of the hotel, including managing equipment, systems, and facilities to ensure proper functioning.
Bartenders: Prepare and serve drinks in the hotel's bars and lounges, engaging with guests and creating a welcoming atmosphere.	**Security Personnel:** Ensure the safety and security of guests, staff, and hotel premises through surveillance, access control, and emergency response protocols.
Spa and Wellness Staff: Provide services such as massages, facials, and fitness training in the hotel's spa and wellness facilities.	**Procurement and Inventory Staff:** Responsible for managing inventory levels of supplies, amenities, and other materials needed for hotel operations.
Entertainment and Activities Staff: Organise and lead recreational activities, events, and entertainment programmes for guests.	
Sales and Marketing Staff: Engage with guests to promote hotel amenities, special offers, and events and work on attracting new customers.	

Source: Authors' creation

Meeting and exceeding these expectations can be challenging, as hotels must constantly adapt and innovate. This puts pressure on existing hotels to differentiate themselves and attract guests. High-quality guest experience through research on guests' expectations could help hotel managers address competition. Ultimately, increased competition in the hotel industry can drive innovation and improvements across the sector, benefiting customers with more choices and enhanced experiences. Hotels that adapt and respond effectively to this competition are more likely to survive and grow in the evolving marketplace.

Revenue Management

Maximising revenue while maintaining competitive pricing is a complex task. Hotel managers must analyse market trends, adjust room rates dynamically, and implement effective sales and marketing strategies (Ivanov, 2014). On the other hand, the increased prices of consumables and energy due to events such as the war in Ukraine impact inflation and cause additional structural problems for hotel managers. Thus, hotels must successfully handle the rising operational costs, including labour, energy, and supplies. Managing and optimising expenses while maintaining service quality is a constant challenge. Hotel managers must constantly be alert and revise revenue strategies to address such economic changes. Furthermore, hotels have considerable labour costs because they rely on people to deliver and maintain quality service. Flexible work arrangements and remote work may be some ways to deal with increased labour costs.

Seasonal Demand and Market Fluctuations

Hotels are greatly affected by seasonal demand and market fluctuations, impacting occupancy rates and revenue. Managing staffing levels, inventory, and marketing efforts during high and low demand require careful planning and forecasting. Seasonality also creates challenges in People Management, as people may not be interested in working on a seasonal basis (Walker, 2021). Retaining employees during slower periods (low season) is also challenging. Furthermore, building strong customer relationships can lead to loyalty and increase and prolong demand. A comprehensive understanding of these dynamics, strategic planning, and technology use can help hotels navigate these challenges and optimise their performance throughout the year.

Workforce Management and Employee Retention

Managing a diverse workforce with different skill sets, languages, and cultural backgrounds can be challenging. Hiring and retaining qualified staff, training them, and ensuring good communication and teamwork are crucial for success (Marinakou & Giousmpasoglou, 2019). The hospitality and tourism industry faces high employee turnover, necessitating using migrants, temporary and agency workers, and part-time employees to fill different positions and roles. The hotel sector traditionally has faced employee retention and recruitment problems, demonstrating the highest staff turnover rates in the UK, reaching 6% in 2022 (The Caterer, 2022). Consequently, staff shortages remain a considerable challenge for hotels, especially after the COVID-19 pandemic. For example, in June 2022, the UK hospitality sector had over 174,000 jobs available (ONS, 2022). Employee retention is also discussed in Chap. 9.

Technology Integration

The rapid advancement of technology poses both opportunities and challenges for hotel management. Integrating new systems, such as property management platforms, online booking engines, and guest review platforms, requires careful planning and staff training (Walker, 2021). Managers in hospitality face multiple challenges from the development and increase in service automation, artificial intelligence (AI), and robotics. Employment in hospitality has witnessed a new trend of replacing interpersonal encounters with technology, including service robots (Lee et al., 2018). Such systems and robots are furnished with artificial intelligence and interact, communicate, and deliver various services to hospitality customers (Wirtz et al., 2018). Examples of such technology implementation include hotel chains like the Hilton and Marriott International (Hospitality Technology 2020). Hilton Worldwide has introduced the concierge robot Connie, powered by IBM's Watson artificial intelligence platform (Hopf et al., 2019). Belanche et al. (2020) claim that customers appreciate the investment in robots. Hospitality customers expect to interact with employees and get a personalised service, a service contact that robots cannot provide as they cannot substitute for humans (yet) (Tussyadiah, 2020).

This new trend poses challenges in managing people in hospitality, as hotel managers should take extra precautions on recruitment and the use of technology. Within the next two decades, half of the jobs could be replaced by technology. On the other hand, Belanche et al. (2020) state that 390,000 new jobs will be created due to automatisation and digitalisation in Germany by 2030. Recent studies suggest that hotel customers prefer to be served by humans rather than innovative technology. At the core of hospitality are the shared experiences between the guest and the host; service providers should make the guest feel welcomed, valued, and cared for (Kim et al., 2021). While technology may beat humans in terms of efficiency, consistency, and reliability, empathy and creativity are human competencies that provide assurance and a friendly exchange while meeting consumers' demands and service expectations (Tai et al., 2021). Employees react promptly and adjust their service appropriately and creatively to satisfy customers and go beyond their expectations providing exceptional service, which is critical in customer satisfaction.

Online Reputation Management

Hotel Online Reputation Management (ORM) refers to monitoring, influencing, and maintaining a hotel's digital image and perception across various online platforms (Fotis et al., 2012). In today's interconnected world, potential guests often rely on online reviews, social media, and other digital sources to decide where to stay. Many channels are available to guests who can comment on their experience in different ways, that is, TripAdvisor. As a result, a hotel's online reputation significantly impacts its success and bookings. Negative reviews can also impact bookings and revenue, so monitoring and responding to guest feedback is important (Fernandes & Fernandes, 2018). A good practice for hotels is to create or adopt protocols to respond to positive and negative reviews. Hotel ORM requires consistent effort and a focus on delivering excellent guest experiences. Combining positive reviews and a strong online reputation can increase bookings, guest loyalty, and help the hotel achieve a competitive advantage.

Sustainability and Environmental Concerns

Hotels are under increasing pressure to implement environmentally friendly practices and decrease their carbon footprint. Implementing eco-friendly practices, such as managing waste and reducing energy consumption, can take considerable effort. ESG (environmental, social, and governance) are now investment criteria embedded in the US and growing in Europe, with the UK leading the way. Booking.com propose that 83% of global travellers in their study think sustainable travel is vital, and 61% said that the pandemic made them want to travel "in a more sustainable way." In this study, accommodation providers report they have at least one sustainable measure or practice in place but do not promote such practices to their guests (Booking.com, 2021). Arun et al. (2021) said that "green hotels and green initiatives in hotels are quickly becoming the norm," putting pressure on hotel managers to pay attention to such environmental issues and create awareness among employees, who have also started paying attention for employment at hotels with positive environmental footprint (Casey & Sieber, 2016). Hotel managers must ensure employees are trained, informed, and motivated to implement green strategies successfully.

Security and Safety

Ensuring the safety and security of guests and staff is a top priority. Hotels must implement robust security measures, including surveillance systems, access control, and emergency preparedness plans. Problems and perceptions of crime have grown in recent decades in hospitality. For example, a big issue for hotels is human trafficking, as hotel staff should be trained to identify and face such crime issues. Anthony Capuano, the

Marriott International President and CEO, said that at Marriott a human trafficking awareness programme has been offered since 2016 aiming to train all on-property staff by 2025 in 8200 locations and 138 countries worldwide (Mogan, 2023). Overall, safety and security are ongoing concerns for management teams in hotels. These teams must regularly assess and update security protocols and measures based on changes in technology, regulations, and the threat landscape to maintain a safe and secure environment for everyone in the hotel.

Chapter Summary

Evidently, there are sectoral and organisational variations in hospitality provision as not all hotels deliver the same experience to customers and employees, nor does it require the same performance in the service delivery. Each hotel service type, category, classification require different performance from employees with implications to recruitment, selection, training, as well as compensation strategies. Different structures and service provision are found to address different market needs. The study of hospitality and hotel management should embrace both the commercial provision and the social aspect of the service delivery. It seems that the norm nowadays is modern-day management agreements which balance the interests of all parties involved (Evanoff, 2016). Regardless of the ownership model or hotel structure, parties try to protect the business interests, retain as much as they can control the business, and maintain their competitive advantage. The hotel sector is resilient, proven by the recovery from COVID-19, but it needs agile tools to manage change and the people to lead the sector.

References

AAA. (2020). *AAA Diamond program*. Retrieved https://approved.aaa.biz/aaa-diamond-program

Accor. (n.d.). *Accor continues to transform and simplify its structure by leveraging its leadership positions in the most buoyant hospitality markets and segments*. Retrieved http://surl.li/kldmb

Andrews, S. (2007). *Introduction to Tourism and Hospitality Industry*. Tata McGraw-Hill Education.

Arun, T. M., Kaur, P., Bresciani, S., & Dhir, A. (2021). What drives the adoption and consumption of green hotel products and services? A systematic literature review of past achievement and future promises. *Business Strategy and the Environment, 30*. https://doi.org/10.1002/bse.2768

Barrows, C. W. (2008). *Introduction to the hospitality industry*. Wiley.

Belanche, D., Casalo, L. V., & Flavian, C. (2020). Frontline robots in tourism and hospitality: Service enhancement or cost reduction? *Electronic Markets, 31*, 477–492.

Booking.com. (2021). *Sustainable travel report 2021*. https://insights.ehotelier.com/insights/2021/05/19/why-sustainability-in-the-hospitality-industry-must-be-our-top-priority/

Brookes, M., & Roper, A. (2010). The impact of entry modes on the organisational design of international hotel chains. *The Service Industries Journal, 30*(9), 1499–1512.

Brotherton, B. (1999). Towards a definitive view of the nature of hospitality and hospitality management. *International Journal of Contemporary Hospitality Management, 11*, 165–173.

Casey, D., & Sieber, S. (2016). Employees, sustainability and motivation: Increasing employee engagement by addressing sustainability and corporate social responsibility. *Research in Hospitality Management, 6*(1), 69–76.

Clarke, A., & Chen, W. (2007). *International hospitality management: Concepts and cases*. Taylor & Francis group.

Conklin, M. (2002). *As I see it: Hotel organisation structure*. In D. G. Rutherford (Ed.), *Hotel management and operations* (3rd ed.). John Wiley & Sons.

de Souza, A. G., Salazar, S. V., de Moraes, F. A. W., Leite, P. Y., & Ivanova, M. (2016). Entry modes: Lease contract. In M. Ivanova, S. Ivanov, & V. P. Magnini (Eds.), *The Routledge handbook of Hotel Chain Management* (pp. 185–192). Routledge.

Dev, C. S., Thomas, J. H., Buschman, J., & Anderson, E. (2010). Brand rights and hotel management agreements—Lessons from Ritz-Carlton Bali's lawsuit. *Cornell Hospitality Quarterly, 51*(2), 215–230.

Eddystone, C., & Nebel, I. I. I. (2002). Organisation design. In D. G. Rutherford (Ed.), *Hotel management and operations* (3rd ed., pp. 73–85). John Wiley & Sons.

Evanoff, M. (2016). The international hotel management agreement: Origins, evolution, and status. *Cornell Hospitality Report, 16*(11), 3–15.

Fernandes, T., & Fernandes, F. (2018). Sharing dissatisfaction online: Analyzing the nature and predictors of hotel guests negative reviews. *Journal of Hospitality Marketing & Management, 27*(2), 127–150.

Fotis, J., Buhalis, D., & Rosides, N. (2012). Social media use and impact during the holiday travel planning process. In M. Fuchs, F. Ricci, & L. Cantoni (Eds.), *Information and Communication Technologies in Tourism 2012* (pp. 13–24). Springer-Verlag.

Giousmpasoglou, C. (2019). Factors affecting and shaping the general managers' work in small-and medium-sized luxury hotels: The case of Greece. *Hospitality & Society, 9*(3), 397–422.

Hemmington, N. (2007). From service to experience: Understanding and defining the hospitality business. *The Service Industries Journal, 27*(6), 747–755.

Hollander, J. (2022). *Modern history of the hospitality industry: The last 100 years*. Retrieved https://hoteltechreport.com/news/modern-history-hospitality-industry

Hopf, V., Velten, L., & Rowson, B. (2019). *Robotism or pessimism: HR managers face a challenge*. In B. Rowson & C. Lashley (Eds.), *Experiencing hospitality* (pp. 203–228). Nova Science Publishers.

Hutton, G. (2022). *Hospitality industry and Covid-19*. House of Commons Library. https://researchbriefings.files.parliament.uk/documents/CBP-9111/CBP-9111.pdf

Ivancevich, J. M., Lorenzi, P., Skinner, S. J., & Crosby, P. B. (1996). *Management: Quality and competitiveness*. Richard D. Irwin.

Ivanov, S. (2014). *Hotel revenue management: From theory to practice*. Zangador.

Kelly, R. (2015). *What is the lived experience of hospitality for adults during their hospital stay?*. Unpublished Masters' Thesis, Auckland University of Technology.

Kim, S., Kim, J., Badu-Baiden, F., Giroux, M., & Choi, Y. (2021). Preference for robot service or human service in hotels? Impacts of the COVID-19 Pandemic. *International Journal of Hospitality Management, 93*. https://doi.org/10.1016/j.ijhm.2020.102795

Koutoulas, D., & Vagena, A. (2023). The present and future of hotel star ratings through the eyes of star rating operators. *Journal of Tourism Futures*, Vol. ahead-of-print No. ahead-of-print. https://doi.org/10.1108/JTF-04-2022-0120

Lacalle, E. (2022). *The typical organisational structure of a hotel*. https://www.mews.com/en/blog/hotel-organizational-structure

Lashley, C., & Morrison, A. J. (Eds.). (2000). *Franchising hospitality services*. Routledge.

Lee, W. H., Lin, C. W., & Shih, K. H. (2018). A technology acceptance model for the perception of restaurant service robots for trust, interactivity, and output quality. *International Journal of Mobile Communications, 16*(4), 361–376.

Lugosi, P. (2008). Hospitality spaces, hospitable moments: consumer encounters and affective experiences in commercial settings. *Journal of Foodservice, 19*, 139–149.

Marinakou, E., & Giousmpasoglou, C. (2019). Talent management and retention strategies in luxury hotels: Evidence from four countries. *International Journal of Contemporary Hospitality Management, 31*(10), 3855–3878.

Mogan, L. C. (2023). Marriott CEO: Human trafficking is a huge problem for hotels—Here's what we're doing about it. http://surl.li/kldep

Mohsin, A., Rodrigues, H., & Brochado, A. (2019). Shine bright like a star: Hotel performance and guests' expectations based on star ratings. *International Journal of Hospitality Management, 83*, 103–114.

O'Connor, D. (2005). Towards a new interpretation of hospitality. *International Journal of Contemporary Hospitality Management, 17*(3), 267–271.

O'Gorman, K. D. (2007). The hospitality phenomenon: Philosophical enlightenment? *International Journal of Culture, Tourism and Hospitality Research, 1*, 189–202.

ONS. (2022, March 7–12). *Business insights and conditions survey*. Wave, 52. www.ons.gov.uk

Pfalz, L. (2023). Accor announces new organizational structure with two main divisions. https://www.travelpulse.com/news/hotels-and-resorts/accor-announces-new-organizational-structure-with-two-main-divisions

Ritzer, G. (2019). Inhospitable hospitality? In B. Rowson & C. Lashley (Eds.), *Experiencing hospitality* (pp. 73–90). Nova Science Publishers.

Roper, A. (2017). Vertical disintegration in the corporate hotel industry. *Current Issues in Tourism, 20*(1), 1–6.

Rutherford, D. G. (2002). *Hotel management and operations* (3rd ed.). John Wiley & Sons.

Selwyn, T. (2000). *An anthropology of hospitality*. In C. Lashley & A. Morrison (Eds.), *In Search of Hospitality: Theoretical perspectives and debates*. Butterworth-Heinemann.

Statista. (2023). Hotel industry worldwide—Statistics & facts. https://www.statista.com/topics/1102/hotels/#topicOverview

Tai, Y., Wang, Y., & Luo, C. (2021). Technology- or human-related service innovation? Enhancing customer satisfaction, delight, and loyalty in the hospitality industry. *Service Business, 15*, 667–694.

The Caterer. (2022). *Average of 6% of hospitality staff leave jobs each month, report claims.* https://www.thecaterer.com/news/hospitality-high-staff-turnover-fourth-report

Tussyadiah, I. P. (2020). A review of research into automation in tourism: launching the annals of tourism research curated collection on artificial intelligence and robotics in tourism. *Annals of Tourism Research, 81.* https://doi.org/10.1016/j.annals.2020.102883

UNWTO. (2015). *Hotel classification systems: Recurrence of criteria in 4- and 5-star hotels.* https://www.e-unwto.org/doi/book/10.18111/9789284416646

Van Ginneken, R. (2017). Trends and issues in hotel ownership and control. In R. C. Wood (Ed.), *Hotel accommodation management* (pp. 15–30). Routledge.

Walker, J. (2021). *Introduction to hospitality.* Global Edition: Pearson.

Wirtz, J., Patterson, P. G., Kunz, W. H., Gruber, T., Lu, V. N., Paluch, S., & Martins, A. (2018). Brave new world: Service robots in the frontline. *Journal of Service Management, 29*(5), 907–931.

Wood, R. C. (Ed.). (2017). *Hotel accommodation management.* Routledge.

WTO. (2014). *Online guest reviews and hotel classification systems: An integrated approach.* World Tourism Organization.

3

The Nature of Managerial Work

Photo Credits: *Hunters Race* (*Free to use under the Unsplash License*). (Source: https://unsplash.com/photos/person-standing-near-the-stairs-MYbhN8KaaEc)

Introduction

This chapter aims to provide critical insights into the nature of managerial work by exploring management approaches and practices from ancient to modern times. This is a necessary step for developing a deeper understanding of managerial work in hotels. The focus is on studies in the post-WWII era that shaped management and managerial work as we know them today.

There are two fundamental questions about managerial work (Hales, 1986): what managers do and why they do it. These questions have been the focus of a debate spanning almost three decades, from the early 1970s until the late 1990s. The controversy stems from the necessity to create a theoretical framework that describes the managerial work's common characteristics in an acceptable academic fashion. The only study that provided such a framework was Mintzberg's (1973) Role Model, which triggered many similar studies with considerably smaller contributions (Hales & Nightingale, 1986). Post-2000 studies are characterised by the application of specialised functions (i.e., human resources management, crisis management, and corporate social responsibility) across various sectors and contexts, including the hospitality sector.

Management from the Ancient Years to the Industrial Revolution

Management in public or private organisations has been in place for thousands of years (Table 3.1). Management techniques have been employed since the early stages of the first organised human communities. About 5000 years ago, the Sumerians developed the script (*cuneiform*) to manage the first growing cities (Mark, 2022). Their main contribution was to invent writing because their priests kept business and legal records on clay tablets (Torrington & Weightman, 1994). Ptahhotep's Instructions are the oldest completely preserved text; they were allegedly written by the ruler's vizier (highest official) around 2400 BC and describe how superiors, equals, and inferiors should behave (Witzel, 2016). Furthermore, translations from early Egyptian papyri, dating back to

Table 3.1 The evolution of management from the Ancient World to the industrial revolution

Year	Individual or group	Contribution
Ancient World		
5000 BC	Sumerians	Written documents; records; taxation
4000 BC	Egyptians	Planning; control; organising
2600 BC	Egyptians	Decentralisation
1800 BC	Babylonians	Business; law; minimum wage; responsibility
1600 BC	Egyptians	Centralisation
1500 BC	Hebrews	Management by exception; chain of command
1100 BC	Chinese	Planning; organising; directing; controlling
600 BC	Nebuchadnezzar	Production control and wage incentives
500 BC	Chinese	Job specialisation
400 BC	Xenophon	Recognition of management as a separate activity
175 BC	Cato	
900 AD	Alfarabi	Job descriptions
1100 AD	Ghazali	Traits of leader Traits of a manager
Medieval period		
1340 AD	Venetians	Double entry booking
1395 AD	Francisco Di Marco	Cost accounting practice
1410 AD	Soranzo brothers	Journal entries and ledgers
1436 AD	Venetians	Assembly line production techniques; inventory and cost Control; personnel management
1468 AD	Friar Johannes Nider	
1500 AD	Sir Thomas More	Rules of trade; business ethics
1525 AD	Machiavelli	"Sin" of poor management; job specialisation politics and power in achieving control; mass consent; leadership qualities
Industrial revolution		
1767 AD	Sir James Stewart	Source of authority and impact of automation
1776 AD	Adam Smith	*Wealth of the Nations*, specialisation, control
1799 AD	Eli Whitney	Scientific method, quality control, span of management
1800 AD	James Watt	
1810 AD	Matthew Boulton	Standard operating procedures
1820 AD	Robert Owen	Planning, work methods, incentive wages
1832 AD	James Mill	Personnel management, training, workers' housing
1835 AD	Charles Babbage Marshall Laughlin	Human movement at work Scientific approach to work organisation Relative importance of management aspects at work

Source: Adapted from Cole (2004) and Witzel (2016)

1300 BC, recognised the importance of organisation and administration in bureaucratic states (Rutgers, 1999). In about 500 BC, Sun Tzu wrote a military textbook on the "Art of War" (Griffith, 1963). It sets out the basis of military campaigning and, in the process, identified many key management tactics described from the military perspective, such as planning, control, directing, and leadership (Reddington, 2008). In addition, formal records of production management techniques have been found in ancient China, where Mencius (372-289 BC) dealt with models and systems and pointed to the advantages of the division of labour, putting the concepts rediscovered over 2000 years later into perspective (Easterby-Smith et al., 2002).

Ancient Greece and Rome saw yet more aspects of management developed that would be familiar in today's organisations. Around 400 BC, Socrates defined management as a skill separate from technical knowledge and experience (Witzel, 2016). Plato also recognised management as a separate art and promoted principles of specialisation (Pindur et al., 1995). In *The Republic*, Plato (2003) describes how carefully selected young men should be trained so that they would develop the appropriate personalities and skills necessary to serve as leaders. Aristotle contended that before becoming a leader, an individual should first learn how to take orders (Kraut, 2022). Alexander the Great (356-323 BC) was the first leader who used large-scale systematic strategic planning and organising approaches in his successful campaigns to conquer the known world of his time. The Greek legacy of the effective military organisation was developed further by the Romans, whose empire rested on the success of its army (Talbot, 2003). Diocletian, a Roman emperor in AD 284, initiated organisational hierarchies when he reorganised his empire into 101 provinces and grouped them into 13 *dioceses* (Bury, 1923); this marked the beginning of the delegation of authority and chain of command. Although ancient Rome's management records were incomplete, the complexity of the administration influenced the development of managerial techniques. Using the scalar principle and the delegation of authority, Rome efficiently expanded into an empire (Pindur et al., 1995).

There is little recorded material on management after the fall of Rome and during the period that followed (known as the "Dark Ages"). A bright exemption may be that of the Venetian merchants and the management techniques used to promote trade. Among the most impressive aspects of Venetian management are those found in the records from the "Arsenal of Venice," a state-owned shipyard operational since 1436. Its purpose was to build naval ships to protect the merchant fleet operating out of Venice (Iordanou, 2019). The shipyard's surviving body of records demonstrates that Venetians were aware of managerial practices and functions such as cost and inventory control, personnel management, and ship production standardisation in the assembly line (Witzel, 2016).

According to Gephart Jr. (1996), *modern management* thought emerged from what Max Weber calls the pre-modern (feudal or patriarchal) society. In pre-modern or traditional society, authority and legitimacy were based on rules of inheritance transmitted from generation to generation. In pre-modern organisations and societies, the ruler or patriarch commanded obedience by right of inheritance and social position; thus, authority was essentially an aspect of personal property (Weber, 1930). With the rise and secularisation of the Protestant ethic, the rational quest for profit became institutionalised in society, and the modern capitalist bureaucracy instantiated capitalist rationality in its very form: a rule-based hierarchy of authority with rigidly specified positions and duties, ongoing in nature, and composed of agents selected freely based on technical qualifications. These agents were agents of the organisation per se, and thus there was a separation of ownership and control of the office holder from the office itself (Weber, 1968).

Managerial Work Research in the Twentieth Century

The twentieth century has been the historical period in which management as an occupational activity gained much of its recognition, especially in the last quarter of the century. Management studies for a long time focused on what it would achieve as an overall activity. In addition, the growth of large managerial bureaucracies at the dawn of the twentieth century encouraged several attempts at developing key principles or elements of management which distinguished it from other activities and

Fig. 3.1 The management function evolution in the twentieth century. (Source: Authors' creation)

justified distinctive occupational status and training programmes (Whitley, 1989). It can be argued that the twentieth century was, without any doubt, the time when the world experienced the emergence of the most influential theories in management thinking expressed through various management schools of thought (Fig. 3.1): Classical Management thinking; the Human Relations movement; Behavioural Management movement; the Quantitative Management Movement; the Systems and Contingency approach; and finally the diverse Modern Management approaches. It is not the scope of this book to provide an account of these management approaches. Instead, the discussion below will focus on studies and approaches that shaped managerial work from the early twentieth century until today.

The Classical Management School

The *classical management school* includes two main approaches: *Scientific* and *Administrative* management. The Scientific Management approach focused on ways to improve labour productivity. Frederick W. Taylor was one of the early practical management theorists who spent his life working on the problem of achieving greater efficiency on the shop floor and trying to find the "one best way" of working (Jensen, 2017). Taylor believed that management should be a scientific process and that the best way to improve productivity was by systematically studying work processes. Taylor suggested that managers should carefully analyse tasks and then design the most efficient way to complete them. He also advocated for a piece-rate pay system, in which workers were paid based on the number of units they produced (Witzel, 2016). US manufacturing companies and car makers embraced Taylor's ideas during the 1920s and

1930s. Henry Ford was one of the great advocates of scientific management. When he introduced the assembly line in 1914, he achieved an impressive drop in the time required to assemble a car from over 700 hours to 93 minutes (Boddy, 2014). Taylor's ideas also found fertile ground outside the US in many industrial economies of that time, particularly in China. Today, a century after the release of Taylor's original doctrine, many of these ideas are still applied in manufacturing and services, especially those making clothing and consumer electronic goods, the fast-food industry, and the low-cost hospitality and tourism providers.

On the other hand, the Administrative approach was distilled in the work of Henri Fayol (1949), who categorised the managerial activities into a few basic tasks and procedures which applied to all administrative positions in hierarchical structures. Fayol's POC^3 model (Forecast and Plan, Organise, Command, Co-ordinate, and Control) was the cornerstone of the managerial work for over half of the twentieth century. Fayol maintained that all activities involved with industrial projects could be separated into six sections: Technical (production, manufacture, and adaptation); Commercial (buying, selling, exchange, and market information); Financial (obtaining capital and making optimum use of available funds); Security (protection of property and persons); Accounting (statistical analysis); and Managerial (planning, organisation, command, coordination, and control). Fayol carried the management process beyond the basic hierarchical model developed by Taylor. Under Fayol's system, the command function continued to operate efficiently and effectively through coordination and control methods summarised in his 14 *Principles of Management* (Table 3.2), several of which are part of management philosophy today (Cole, 2004). While Fayol is regarded as one of the founders of management thinking, his account of the functions of management tells us little about management and managing (Collins, 2000).

The Behavioural Management Movement

Since the end of the Second World War, a growing number of studies focused on managerial behaviour (i.e., Carlson, 1951; Martin, 1956; Sayles, 1964; Stewart, 1967) and raised doubts about whether the classical

Table 3.2 Fayol's principles of management

1. Division of work	Reduces the span of attention or effort for any one person or group. Develops practice and familiarity.
2. Authority	The right to give orders. Should not be considered without reference to responsibility.
3. Discipline	Outward marks of respect in accordance with formal or informal agreements between the firm and its employees.
4. Unity of command	One man one superior!
5. Unity of direction	One head and one plan for a group of activities with the same object.
6. Subordination	The interest of one individual or one group should not prevail over the general good. This is a difficult area of management.
7. Remuneration	Pay should be fair to both the employee and the firm.
8. Centralisation	Is always present to a greater or lesser extent, depending on the size of the company and the quality of its managers.
9. Scalar chain	The line of authority from top to bottom of the organisation.
10. Order	A place for everything and everything in its place; the right man in the right place.
11. Equity	A combination of kindliness and justice towards employees.
12. Stability of personnel tenure	Employees need to be given time to settle into their jobs, even though this may be a lengthy period in the case of managers.
13. Initiative	Within the limits of authority and discipline, all levels of staff should be encouraged to show initiative.
14. Esprit de corps	Harmony is a great strength of an organisation; teamwork should be encouraged

Source: Adapted from Cole (2004, p. 15)

approach was the right way to define and understand management. The *Behavioural Management Movement* was an approach that emphasised the importance of understanding human behaviour and motivation in the workplace. It emerged in the 1950s and 1960s as a reaction to the more traditional management approaches based on bureaucracy and formal authority principles. The key idea behind the behavioural management movement is that by understanding and influencing the behaviour of employees, managers can improve organisational performance (Cole, 2004). Under the behaviourist perspective, workers are seen as individuals and members of a social group, with attitudes and behaviours that are the key to effectiveness—in other words, employees are seen as valuable resources for the organisation. This approach uses various techniques to motivate and influence employees, such as positive reinforcement, feedback, and goal setting (Steers et al., 2004). Several directions have emerged in this movement, making it hard to categorise it under a single heading; this led to numerous limitations in the Behavioural Approach studies regarding the research focus and treatment of evidence that was eventually to influence further developments in the field (Hales, 1986). The major limitation of behavioural management studies is the difficulty in predicting human behaviour due to its complexity. Furthermore, it is difficult to implement complex behavioural concepts, which make managers reluctant to adopt them (Pindur et al., 1995).

Critical Studies on Managerial Work

The seminal work of Henry Mintzberg (1973) on managerial work (Box 3.1) has triggered a plethora of research into managerial jobs and behaviour (Table 3.3), attempting to provide a suitable theoretical framework. Some of the most quoted studies are those of Stewart (1967, 1976), Stewart et al. (1980), Kotter (1982), Luthans et al. (1985), Carroll and Gillen (1987), Hirsh and Bevan (1988), and Whitley (1989). Most of the above studies were criticised for being "acontextual and atheoretical" (Fondas & Stewart, 1994). A common problem for most of these studies is that the researchers have developed their concepts/frameworks by ignoring other studies in the field. During this debate, a paradox emerged in managerial work research. Despite strong criticisms of Mintzberg's Role Model by scholars such as Fondas and Stewart (1994), Luthans et al. (1985), and Martinko and Gardner (1985), the overall findings were surprisingly similar. The effort to create a common acceptable framework on the nature of managerial work looked like a jigsaw puzzle with uneven and missing parts for a long time. A credible model of managerial work was again offered by Mintzberg (1994), with its conceptual elegance and the capacity to accommodate some extant evidence.

Box 3.1 Ten Managerial Roles by Henry Mintzberg

In the early 1970s, a ground-breaking study from Henry Mintzberg (1973) reversed the image of the manager who rationally plans all his/her activities based on carefully collected information, directing, commanding people, and coordinating work activities. Mintzberg was the first to develop a conceptual framework for the manager's job by attempting to describe what managers do and why they do it; he identified ten managerial roles under three categories (Fig. 3.2). In addition, he drew a completely different picture of managers working in a chaotic environment spending most of their time talking to others—in and out of the workplace—influencing people, collecting information from various sources such as gossip and rumours, and generally trying to maintain a very delicate balance like jugglers do.

This study has triggered a radical change in managerial work research. As Hales (1986) states, researchers have abandoned the search for definite characteristics of managerial work and focused their attention on indicating its diversity and variation to provide analytical tools for handling that diversity. At first, it seemed that management was turning out to be something different from what had previously been thought. The inhuman mechanistic manager described by classical management writers such as Taylor, Fayol, and Weber is now replaced by the Machiavellian "fixer," a ruthless manipulator who negotiates anything. There were two seemingly contrasting images of management as, on the one hand, a matter of systematic, rational, neutral, and pre-planned control and coordination and, on the other, a matter of rather frenetic, opportunistic, "seat-on-the-pants," political and interactive style of "getting things done" (Watson & Harris, 1999).

1. Interpersonal	2. Information	3. Decision-making
• **Figurehead:** performing symbolic duties as a representative of the organisation. • **Leader:** establishing the atmosphere and motivating the subordinates. • **Liaiser:** developing and maintaining webs of contacts outside the organisation.	• **Monitor:** collecting all types of information that are relevant and useful to the organisation. • **Disseminator:** transmitting information from outside the organisation to those inside. • **Spokesman:** transmitting information from inside the organisation to outsiders.	• **Entrepreneur:** initiating change and adapting to the environment. • **Disturbance Handler:** dealing with unexpected events. • **Resource Allocator:** deciding on the use of organisational resources. • **Negotiator:** negotiating with individuals and dealing with other organisations.

Fig. 3.2 Mintzberg's managerial roles. https://www.bl.uk/people/henry-mintzberg. (Source: Adapted from Mintzberg (1989, p. 17))

Table 3.3 Influential studies on managerial work

Author	Year	Study focus
Carson	1951	A four-week observation of ten executives in Sweden incorporating checklists and questionnaires
Burns	1957	A five-week study of 76 top managers, from 6 medium-sized Scottish factories using self-record diaries
Sayles	1964	Field observations of 75 lower and middle managers in the division of a large US corporation
Steward	1967	A four-week study of 160 UK-based managers using self-recording diaries
Mintzberg	1973	Intensive observation ("shadowing") of five US chief executives using also diaries and analysis of managers' records, incorporating a review of other relevant studies
Child & Ellis	1973	Self-administered questionnaires in 787 managers from 78 organisations in 6 UK industries
Silverman & Jones	1976	Tape-recorded informal interviews and observation of managers and management trainees in large UK public sector organisations
Stewart	1976	Self-recorded diaries over three weeks; observation; informal and formal interviews (Pilot interviews: 180 managers in diverse jobs. Main interviews: 274 middle and senior managers)
Stewart et al.	1980	Interviews and observations of 41 District NHS Administrators
Stewart et al.	1982	Open-ended interviews and observation of 98 managers, by level and function—6 pairs of managers in 6 different jobs
Kotter	1982	Study of 15 high-level US general managers over a range of corporations/used questionnaires, observation, diaries, interviews, and printed information
Martinko & Gardner	1985	Critical Literature Review in Structure Observation Studies of managers and supervisors
Luthans et al.	1985	A two-week observation study of 52 managers in three diverse organisations using the Leader Observation System (LOS) tool
Hales	1986	Critical Literature Review: "*What do managers do*"
Carroll & Gillen	1987	An evaluation of classical management functions usefulness in describing managerial work
Hirsh & Bevan	1988	Research conducted in more than 40 UK organisations to explore managerial skills and establish a common language to describe these skills

(*continued*)

Table 3.3 (continued)

Author	Year	Study focus
Whitley	1989	Theoretical work which places emphasis on tasks and skills in managerial work—also discusses implications for management education
Fondas & Stewart	1994	Theoretical work in managers' roles
Mintzberg	1994	A variety of interviews and observations with various managers were used as examples to describe a model for the intergraded job of managing
Hales	1999	Critical Literature Review: "Why do managers do what they do?"

Source: Authors' creation

In a critical literature review, Hales (1986) suggested that Mintzberg's role concepts could provide one sustainable theoretical framework. He argued (ibid.) that the Role Model was useful for analysing both the influence of expectations in managerial behaviour and the effect of individual actions and preferences on behaviour; he also argued that the Role Model could facilitate comparisons among managers. The following decade (the 1990s) offered little to the study of managerial work as the interest of researchers focused on the characteristics and dynamics of the management process (Hales, 1999). Based on current studies and debates on managerial work, we can conclude that this research stream ended in the 1990s without providing a solid unitary model accepted by academics and practitioners. Table 3.3 summarises the most influential studies on managerial work conducted in the second half of the twentieth century.

Modern Approaches to Managerial Work

Modern management studies have undergone a dramatic devolution since the late 1980s, as management has been divided into various schools of thought, each with its unique approach. This process was accelerated by the radical socio-economic changes in the 1990s, which shook the foundations of every established management theory that existed until then. Suddenly there was a need for new competencies and ways of managing people and organisations. Peter Drucker (1998, p. 152), one of the greatest management thinkers of the twentieth century, notes:

> *In a fast-changing world, what worked yesterday probably doesn't work today...as we advance into the knowledge economy, the basic assumptions underlying much of what is taught and practised in the name of management are hopelessly out of date.*

It is argued that the modern management movement is more a synthesis of diverse management theories often conflicting with each other rather than a unified, holistic approach. Consequently, the study of managerial work poses numerous difficulties, mainly due to its concentration on distinct management tasks (i.e., operations, finance, marketing, human resources management, etc.). Current management theory is so dynamic and fast-changing that it would be unrealistic to propose that all existing theories could be presented. It would also be difficult to distinguish what constitutes a management fashion or an established theory (Collins, 2000). Figure 3.3 showcases eight distinct areas that encompass the new approaches to management. These areas have a significant impact on both managerial work and people management.

Finally, there is a need to distinguish between *management* as a function, *managers* as an occupational group appointed by the organisations to fulfil/execute the management function, and *managing* as a directing activity conducted by managers (Watson & Harris, 1999).

- *Management*: this can be viewed as an outcome that must be achieved. It is a functional requirement of the work organisation as it has been shaped in the twentieth-century capitalist societies.
- *Managers*: any employee formally assigned to perform management functions is referred to as a manager. It is a modern form of occupation that has grown with the growth of the modern bureaucratised work organisation in the twentieth century.
- *Managing*: a set of processes, practices, and activities designed to direct or steer an organisation's future in its environment. Conflict and

Fig. 3.3 New approaches to management (post-1990s). (Source: Authors' creation)

rivalry are often prominent in managerial work, which may appear messy, confused, fragmented, and chaotic (Mintzberg, 1994). However, in this hectic, fragmented, and stressful environment, the managers are thriving by using their distinctive and unique style to perform the activity of "managing."

Organisational Behaviour

Organisational Behaviour (OB) studies focus on how people behave and interact at work and how organisations interact with their environments. It is an interdisciplinary field that draws from psychology, sociology, economics, anthropology, and management theories (Mullins & McLean, 2019). Some key topics in organisational behaviour include motivation, leadership, communication, group dynamics, power and influence, decision-making, and organisational culture. Organisational behaviour research can also involve studying factors such as job satisfaction, stress, and performance (Baldwin et al., 2020). Furthermore, studying organisational culture has a central role in organisational behaviour. Organisational culture includes the shared values, beliefs, and practices that shape the behaviour of individuals and groups within an organisation (Schein, 2010). A positive organisational culture can lead to higher levels of employee engagement, job satisfaction, and productivity, while a negative culture can lead to high employee turnover and low morale.

OB studies are important for practitioners because they help managers and leaders better understand motivating employees, building effective teams, and creating a positive workplace culture (Seppälä & Cameron, 2015). By understanding the factors that influence employee behaviour within organisations, managers can support productive and engaging work environments that lead to better performance and increased job satisfaction (Cross & Carbery, 2022).

Human Resources Management

Human Resources Management (HRM) is an integrated set of practices, processes, programmes, and systems in an organisation that focuses on effective employee allocation, support, and development. Human Resources Management evolved from Personnel Management to become an organisation's strategic function today (Storey et al., 2019). These processes include the following key HRM functions: HR planning; Recruitment and Selection; Onboarding (induction); Training and Development; Performance Appraisal; Compensation; Health and Safety; Compliance; and Employee Relations (Armstrong & Taylor, 2020). Any successful organisation requires employees and systems to support them, making human resources management one of its most critical functions. Effective HRM requires a deep understanding of the organisation's strategy and goals, as well as the needs and aspirations of its workforce. By aligning HR practices with the organisation's strategic objectives, HRM can help to drive performance, improve employee engagement, and support the organisation's overall success (Paauwe & Boon, 2018). The design and implementation of the HR strategies, systems, and practices are not limited to the HR Department; they are shared across the organisation's managers and supervisors, regardless of their seniority. This makes HRM an integral part of managerial work, especially in labour-intensive industries like Hospitality and Tourism (Boella & Goss-Turner, 2019).

Ethics and Corporate Social Responsibility

Business Ethics is the sum of moral principles and standards that guide the established behaviour and code of practice in the business world. *Corporate Social Responsibility* (CSR) refers to a company's or an organisation's commitment to act in the best interest of society and the environment in an ethical manner. CSR practices typically focus on how organisations can integrate social and environmental concerns into their business practices and the impact of such practices on stakeholders such as employees, customers, communities, and the environment (Carroll & Brown, 2018). CSR aims to help organisations understand how to operate socially, responsibly, and sustainably while still achieving their goals. There are five key areas in CSR: environmental sustainability, social sustainability, ethical behaviour, corporate philanthropy, and corporate governance.

Furthermore, *Creating Shared Value* (CSV) is the strategic process through which corporations can turn social problems into business opportunities (Menghwar & Daood, 2021). CSV's strategic approach is solving societal issues and its close relationship with strategic CSR function. The understanding and adoption of CSR practices can be viewed as an integral part of managerial work that can improve and transform workplaces, achieve employee satisfaction, and contribute to the betterment of society (Franco et al., 2020).

Managing Diversity and Cross-Cultural Management

Managing Diversity at work involves creating an inclusive environment where employees from different backgrounds and perspectives feel valued and respected (Ravazzani, 2016). The creation of an inclusive work environment requires the facilitation and combination of strategies, policies, and practices that include the following (Kirton & Greene, 2021): the establishment of a diversity policy; the creation of a truly diverse workforce; the provision of diversity training; the adoption of an open communication culture; the avoidance of any discrimination type; and the embracement of the organisation's diversity culture by all employees and key stakeholders.

Cross-cultural Management is a distinctive diversity management function in organisations; it can be defined as managing the differences between individuals and groups from different cultures (Browaeys & Price, 2019). It involves developing strategies and practices to bridge the gap between cultural differences and enable individuals and teams to work together effectively (Romani et al., 2018). Cross-cultural management is becoming increasingly important in globalisation, as organisations operate in multicultural environments. Effective cross-cultural management can help managers overcome communication barriers, build trust and relationships with clients and employees from different cultural backgrounds, and improve performance and productivity (Giousmpasoglou, 2014). Some key aspects of cross-cultural management include understanding cultural differences, developing cultural sensitivity and awareness, and adapting to cultural norms and practices. It also involves developing effective communication strategies that can accommodate diverse perspectives and styles of communication (Thomas & Peterson, 2016). Cross-cultural management can be challenging, but it is essential for managers working in a globalised business environment and/or with culturally diverse teams. By embracing cultural diversity and leveraging it as a source of strength, organisations can create a more inclusive and innovative workplace that can better meet the needs of a diverse customer base.

Managing Quality and Service Quality

Quality Management ensures that products, services, and processes meet or exceed customer expectations. It is an essential aspect of any business as it helps to improve customer satisfaction, increase efficiency, reduce costs, and increase profitability (Ross, 2017). The quality management movement appeared after WWII ended and was very popular in manufacturing. In the 1970s, *Total Quality Management* (TQM) emerged as an approach to management that focuses on continuously improving the quality of products, services, and processes by involving all employees in the organisation collectively. It is a customer-focused approach to quality that seeks to meet or exceed customer expectations through continuous improvement (Oakland et al., 2020). Implementing a TQM system requires the following: customer focus; continuous improvement; employee involvement; process involvement; and data-driven decision-making.

The focus of TQM approaches to manufacturing created the need for a new quality management approach for the service industries. The seminal work of Parasuraman et al. (1991) and their SERVQUAL model signposted the introduction of the Service Quality Movement. Although the SERVQUAL model was mainly focused on the hospitality industry, the following two decades saw its application in other service sectors such as retail, banking, education, and health care. *Service Quality Management* can be defined as the process of ensuring that the services provided by an organisation meet or exceed customer expectations (Zeithaml et al., 2002). It involves designing, implementing, and monitoring systems, processes, and standards that enable an organisation to deliver high-quality services consistently. It is argued that effective Service Quality Management is essential for organisations that want to build strong customer relationships, maintain a competitive edge, and achieve long-term success (Dhar, 2015). Additionally, service quality management profoundly affects managerial work: managers must constantly strive to achieve customer satisfaction through employee satisfaction (Jeon & Choi, 2012).

Managing Change

The sweeping economic and sociocultural changes during the past three decades, in conjunction with globalisation, led organisations to develop strategies, processes, and structures to help them cope with the volatile external environment. The management function that helps organisations survive, adapt, and stay competitive, especially during times of uncertainty, is called *Change Management* (Kotter et al., 2011). This function involves the structured approach to transition an organisation or a team, from a current state to a desired future state. This transition can include processes, technologies, organisational structures, or culture changes. The goal of change management is to minimise the negative impact of changes on employees and key stakeholders while maximising the benefits of the change (Hayes, 2022). It involves identifying the need for change, planning and implementing the change, and evaluating the results to ensure its success. When an organisation does not have the capacity and resources to design and facilitate a change management programme (especially in restructuring and downsizing cases), it involves external consultants who are experts in this field. The external approach has been criticised, especially for the impact on the organisation's employees (Ashkenas, 2013). The most challenging aspect of the organisational transformation process is employee resistance to change (Ford et al., 2008). It is argued that clear communication and employee involvement are essential to minimise the uncertainty and anxiety among affected employees. In addition, the management team can play a catalytic role during the transformation process, acting as a change agent (Furnham, 2002).

Change management can be challenging, requiring strong leadership, effective communication, and a willingness to adapt to new ways of doing things; when implemented appropriately, it can help organisations, leaders, and managers achieve their goals and stay competitive in an ever-changing business environment.

Crisis Management

Regional and global crises have plagued the world since the early 2000s due to natural disasters (such as tsunamis, earthquakes, and volcanic eruptions) or other causes (such as political turmoil, terrorism attacks, recessions, wars, and health threats). Any major event that can cause negative effects that threaten the viability of organisations, companies, or industries and is characterised by cause ambiguity can therefore be defined as a crisis (Paraskevas & Quek, 2019). In response, organisations developed crisis management strategies; crisis management refers to preparing for, managing, and recovering from crises (Drennan et al., 2014).

It is first important to analyse the different response stages involved to understand better and manage a crisis. Wang and Ritchie (2010) proposed three distinct phases: proactive pre-crisis planning, strategy implementation, and evaluation and feedback. Despite its challenging nature, any crisis can be seen as an opportunity for innovation and change, that is, simplifying processes, redefining labour needs and skills, re-training employees, downsizing, reviewing the marketing mix or market segments, and using social media (Lai & Wong, 2020). Crisis management has become integral to managerial work; managers (regardless of their seniority) are the first to respond to a crisis and implement existing plans or create new ones if needed (Giousmpasoglou et al., 2021). In addition, effective crisis management requires a coordinated effort from all levels of an organisation and collaboration with external stakeholders such as emergency services, government agencies, and the media.

Sustainability Management

Sustainability Management is managing an organisation's social, environmental, and economic impact to promote long-term sustainability. This process involves identifying and managing risks and opportunities related to sustainability issues such as climate change, resource depletion, social inequality, and ecosystem degradation (Epstein & Buhovac, 2014). Among the activities included in sustainability management are monitoring and reporting performance, setting targets, developing strategies, and engaging stakeholders (Ortiz-de-Mandojana & Bansal, 2016). It also involves integrating sustainability considerations into decision-making processes and embedding sustainability principles into an organisation's culture (Oriade et al., 2021).

Sustainability management is important for organisations because it helps them to reduce their environmental footprint, enhance their reputation among stakeholders, attract customers who are increasingly concerned about sustainability, and reduce costs by improving efficiency and reducing waste (Hansen & Brown, 2020). It also helps organisations identify and manage risks related to sustainability issues, such as regulatory changes or reputational damage (Sroufe & Gopalakrishna-Remani, 2019). Overall, sustainability management is about balancing economic, social, and environmental considerations to create a sustainable future for all stakeholders linked to an organisation (Seuring & Gold, 2013).

Chapter Summary

This chapter offers an overview of management and managerial work studies, focusing on the work conducted in the twentieth century. The discussion begins by exploring the early forms of management as an administrative function, from ancient times to the industrial revolution. The Scientific Management approach, which emerged in the early twentieth century, marks the starting point of modern management theories. Later, the Behavioural Studies and the Human Relations School, particularly after WWII, emphasised the individual's needs. In the 1970s, a new stream of research on managerial work emerged, which concluded in the late 1990s without a unanimous agreement on what managers do and why. Despite this, Henry Mintzberg's work in this field remains influential and widely accepted among researchers and practitioners.

Studies of managerial work have moved in recent years to focus on specific management functions, like human resources management, crisis management, and sustainability management. As new management fashions and trends develop, such as the demise of inflexible hierarchies and the emergence of the "managerless" organisation (Hill, 2021), the list is almost guaranteed to grow. The different approaches outlined thus far all share that the demands placed on managers have grown in recent years and become more complex and unpredictable. According to the studies and debates discussed above, managerial work is very political and hardly ever involves direct formal planning based on all available information. On the other hand, the effect or outcome of this messy and ambiguous activity is that work is coordinated by a general plan in the manager's mind; thus, a certain degree of control can be achieved.

References

Armstrong, M., & Taylor, S. (2020). *Armstrong's handbook of human resource management practice*. Kogan Page Publishers.

Ashkenas, R. (2013). Change management needs to change. https://hbr.org/2013/04/change-management-needs-to-cha

Baldwin, T., Bommer, B., & Rubin, R. (2020). *Organizational behavior: Real solutions to real challenges*. McGraw-Hill.

Boddy, C. R. (2014). Corporate psychopaths, conflict, employee affective well-being and counterproductive work behaviour. *Journal of Business Ethics, 121*(1), 107–121.

Boella, M. J., & Goss-Turner, S. (2019). *Human resource management in the hospitality industry: A guide to best practice*. Routledge.

Browaeys, M. J., & Price, R. (2019). *Understanding cross-cultural management* (4th ed.). Pearson.

Bury, J. B. (1923). *History of the later Roman empire: From the death of Theodosius I. to the death of Justinian*. The Macmillan Company.

Carlson, S. (1951). *Executive behaviour*. Strömbergs.

Carroll, A. B., & Brown, J. A. (2018). Corporate social responsibility: A review of current concepts, research, and issues. *Corporate Social Responsibility, 2*, 39–69.

Carroll, S., & Gillen, D. (1987). Are the classical management functions useful in describing managerial work? *Academy of Management Review, 12*(1), 38–51.

Cole, G. A. (2004). *Management theory and practice* (6th ed.). Thomson Learning.

Collins, D. (2000). *Management fads and buzzwords: Critical-practical perspectives*. Psychology Press.

Cross, C., & Carbery, R. (2022). *Organisational behaviour*. Bloomsbury Publishing.

Dhar, R. L. (2015). Service quality and the training of employees: The mediating role of organizational commitment. *Tourism management, 46*, 419–430.

Drennan, L. T., McConnell, A., & Stark, A. (2014). *Risk and crisis management in the public sector*. Routledge.

Drucker, P. F. (1998). Management's new paradigms. *Forbes magazine, 10*(2), 98–99.

Easterby-Smith, P., Thorpe, R., & Lowe, A. (2002). *Management research: An introduction* (2nd ed.). Sage.

Epstein, M. J., & Buhovac, A. R. (2014). *Making sustainability work: Best practices in managing and measuring corporate social, environmental, and economic impacts*. Berrett-Koehler Publishers.

Fayol, H. (1949). *General and industrial management*. Pitman.
Fondas, N., & Stewart, R. (1994). Enactment in managerial jobs: A role analysis. *Journal of Management Studies, 31*(1), 83–103.
Ford, J. D., Ford, L. W., & D'Amelio, A. (2008). Resistance to change: The rest of the story. *Academy of management Review, 33*(2), 362–377.
Franco, S., Caroli, M. G., Cappa, F., & Del Chiappa, G. (2020). Are you good enough? CSR, quality management and corporate financial performance in the hospitality industry. *International Journal of Hospitality Management, 88*. https://doi.org/10.1016/j.ijhm.2019.102395
Furnham, A. (2002). Managers as change agents. *Journal of Change Management, 3*(1), 21–29.
Gephart Jr, R. P. (1996). Postmodernism and the future history of management: Comments on history as science. *Journal of Management History, 2*(3), 90–96.
Giousmpasoglou, C. (2014). Greek management and culture. *European Journal of Cross-Cultural Competence and Management, 3*(1), 51–67.
Giousmpasoglou, C., Marinakou, E., & Zopiatis, A. (2021). Hospitality managers in turbulent times: The COVID-19 crisis. *International Journal of Contemporary Hospitality Management, 33*(4), 1297–1318.
Griffith, S. B. (1963). *Sun Tzu: The art of war* (Vol. 39). Oxford University Press.
Hales, C. (1986). What do managers do? A critical review of the evidence. *Journal of Management Studies, 23*(1), 88–115.
Hales, C. (1999). Why do managers do what they do? Reconciling evidence and theory in accounts of managerial work. *British Journal of Management, 10*(4), 335–350.
Hales, C., & Nightingale, M. (1986). What are unit managers supposed to do? A contingent methodology for investigating managerial role requirements. *International Journal of Hospitality Management, 5*(1), 3–11.
Hansen, S. J., & Brown, J. W. (2020). *Sustainability management handbook*. CRC Press.
Hayes, J. (2022). *The theory and practice of change management*. Bloomsbury Publishing.
Hill, A. (2021). How management fashions can change the world. https://www.ft.com/content/ f14b3205-f140-4e74-8743-04b881b63134
Hirsh, W., & Bevan, S. (1988). *What makes a manager?* Report No.144, Brighton: Institute of Manpower Studies.
Iordanou, I. (2019). *Venice's secret service: Organising intelligence in the renaissance*. Oxford University Press.
Jensen, S. H. (2017). Frederick Winslow Taylor: The first change agent, from rule of thump to scientific management. In D. B. Szabla, W. A. Pasmore,

M. A. Barnes, & A. N. Gipson (Eds.), *The Palgrave handbook of organizational change thinkers* (pp. 1275–1290). Palgrave Macmillan.

Jeon, H., & Choi, B. (2012). The relationship between employee satisfaction and customer satisfaction. *Journal of Services Marketing, 26*(5), 332–341.

Kirton, G., & Greene, A. M. (2021). *The dynamics of managing diversity and inclusion: A critical approach*. Routledge.

Kotter, J. (1982). What effective general managers really do. *Harvard Business Review, 60*(6), 156–167.

Kotter, J. P., Kim, W. C., & Mauborgne, R. A. (2011). *HBR's 10 Must Reads on Change Management (including featured article "Leading Change," by John P. Kotter)*. Harvard Business Press.

Kraut, R. (2022). Aristotle's ethics. In E.N. Zalta & U. Nodelman (Eds.), *The stanford encyclopedia of philosophy* (Fall 2022 Edition). https://plato.stanford.edu/archives/fall2022/entries/aristotle-ethics/

Lai, I. K. W., & Wong, J. W. C. (2020). Comparing crisis management practices in the hotel industry between initial and pandemic stages of COVID-19. *International Journal of Contemporary Hospitality Management, 32*(10), 3135–3156.

Luthans, F., Rosenkrantz, S., & Hennessey, H. (1985). What do successful managers Really Do? An Observation Study of Managerial Activities. *The Journal of Applied Behavioural Science, 21*(3), 255–270.

Mark, J. (2022). Cuneiform. https://www.worldhistory.org/cuneiform/

Martin, N. (1956). Differential decisions in the management of industrial plant. *Journal of Business, 29*(4), 249–260.

Martinko, M. J., & Gardner, W. L. (1985). Beyond structured observation: Methodological issues and new directions. *Academy of Management Review, 10*(4), 676–695.

Menghwar, P. S., & Daood, A. (2021). Creating shared value: A systematic review, synthesis and integrative perspective. *International Journal of Management Reviews, 23*(4), 466–485.

Mintzberg, H. (1973). *The nature of managerial work*. Harper and Row.

Mintzberg, H. (1989). *Mintzberg on management: Inside our strange world of organizations*. Simon and Schuster.

Mintzberg, H. (1994). Rounding out the manager's job. *Sloan Management Review, 36*, 11–11.

Mullins, L. J., & McLean, J. E. (2019). *Organisational behaviour in the workplace*. Pearson.

Oakland, J. S., Oakland, R. J., & Turner, M. A. (2020). *Total quality management and operational excellence: Text with cases*. Routledge.

Oriade, A., Osinaike, A., Aduhene, K., & Wang, Y. (2021). Sustainability awareness, management practices and organisational culture in hotels: Evidence from developing countries. *International Journal of Hospitality Management, 92*. https://doi.org/10.1016/j.ijhm.2020.102699

Ortiz-de-Mandojana, N., & Bansal, P. (2016). The long-term benefits of organizational resilience through sustainable business practices. *Strategic Management Journal, 37*(8), 1615–1631.

Paauwe, J., & Boon, C. (2018). Strategic HRM: A critical review. In D. G. Collings, G. T. Wood, & L. T. Szamosi (Eds.), *Human resource management* (pp. 49–73). Routledge.

Paraskevas, A., & Quek, M. (2019). "When Gastro seized the Hilton": Risk and Crisis Management lessons from the past. *Tourism Management, 70*, 419–429.

Parasuraman, A., Berry, L. L., & Zeithaml, V. A. (1991). Perceived service quality as a customer-based performance measure: An empirical examination of organizational barriers using an extended service quality model. *Human Resource Management, 30*(3), 335–364.

Pindur, W., Rogers, S. E., & Suk Kim, P. (1995). The history of management: A global perspective. *Journal of Management History, 1*(1), 59–77.

Plato. (2003). *Plato: The Republic*. Penguin Books.

Ravazzani, S. (2016). Understanding approaches to managing diversity in the workplace: An empirical investigation in Italy. *Equality, Diversity and Inclusion: An International Journal, 35*(2), 154–168.

Reddington, M. (2008). Book Review: Sun Tzu, The Art of War. *Journal for the Certified Forensic Interviewer, 4*, 13–14.

Romani, L., Barmeyer, C., Primecz, H., & Pilhofer, K. (2018). Cross-cultural management studies: State of the field in the four research paradigms. *International Studies of Management & Organization, 48*(3), 247–263.

Ross, J. E. (2017). *Total quality management: Text, cases, and readings*. Routledge.

Rutgers, M. R. (1999). Be rational! But what does it mean? A history of the idea of rationality and its relation to management thought. *Journal of Management History, 5*(1), 17–35.

Sayles, L. R. (1964). *Managerial behaviour*. McGraw-Hill.

Schein, E. H. (2010). *Organizational culture and leadership* (4th ed.). Jon Wiley & Sons Inc.

Seppälä, E., & Cameron, K. (2015). Proof that positive work cultures are more productive. https://hbr.org/2015/12/proof-that-positive-work-cultures-are-more-productive

Seuring, S., & Gold, S. (2013). Sustainability management beyond corporate boundaries: From stakeholders to performance. *Journal of Cleaner Production, 56*, 1–6.

Sroufe, R., & Gopalakrishna-Remani, V. (2019). Management, social sustainability, reputation, and financial performance relationships: An empirical examination of US firms. *Organization & Environment, 32*(3), 331–362.

Steers, R. M., Mowday, R. T., & Shapiro, D. L. (2004). The future of work motivation theory. *Academy of Management review, 29*(3), 379–387.

Stewart, R. (1967). *Managers and their jobs*. Macmillan.

Stewart, R. (1976). *Contrast in management*. McGraw-Hill.

Stewart, R., Smith, P., Blake, J., & Wingate, P. (1980). *The district administrator in the national health service*. King Edward's Hospital Fund.

Storey, J., Ulrich, D., & Wright, P. M. (2019). *Strategic human resource management: A research overview*. Routledge Focus.

Talbot, P. A. (2003). Management organisational history–a military lesson? *Journal of European Industrial Training, 27*(7), 330–340.

Thomas, D. C., & Peterson, M. F. (2016). *Cross-cultural management: Essential concepts*. Sage.

Torrington, D., & Weightman, J. (1994). *Effective management: People and organisation*. Prentice Hall.

Wang, J., & Ritchie, B. W. (2010). A theoretical model for strategic crisis planning: Factors influencing crisis planning in the hotel industry. *International Journal of Tourism Policy: Special Issue on Crisis and Risks in Tourism, 3*(4), 297–317.

Watson, T., & Harris, P. (1999). *The emergent manager*. Sage.

Weber, M. (1930). *The protestant ethic and the spirit of capitalism* (T. Parsons, Trans.). Routledge.

Weber, M. (1968). *Economy and society: An outline of interpretive sociology* (Vol. 3). Bedminster Press.

Whitley, R. (1989). On the nature of managerial tasks and skills: Their distinguishing characteristics and organization. *Journal of Management Studies, 26*(3), 209–224.

Witzel, M. (2016). *A history of management thought* (2nd ed.). Routledge.

Zeithaml, V. A., Parasuraman, A., & Malhotra, A. (2002). Service quality delivery through web sites: A critical review of extant knowledge. *Journal of the Academy of Marketing Science, 30*(4), 362–375.

4

Managerial Skills and Competencies

Photo Credits: *Crew (Free to use under the Unsplash License).* (Source: https://unsplash.com/photos/photo-of-man-and-woman-mixing-beverages-szCvt1gP2d4)

Introduction

This chapter delves into the managerial work in hotels, exploring hotel managers' diverse roles. Our focus spans from the early 1980s to the present day. A critical review of the "unique" characteristics, such as hotel managers' personality traits and job functions, is conducted. Furthermore, we analyse the key managerial skills and competencies required to perform proficiently at both operational and strategic levels.

Managerial Work in Hotels

Empirical studies have highlighted the challenges faced by hotel managers since the hospitality industry's early stages of internationalisation in the 1950s (Hales & Tamangani, 1996). This research primarily centres around upscale establishments that demand careful consideration to maintain exceptional service quality and guest satisfaction, effective people management, and healthy financial performance. A set of precise objectives must be accomplished to guarantee the high standards of a perishable product or service consumed directly on the hotel premises (Parasuraman et al., 2002). To meet or exceed these high standards, hotel managers must proactively deal with the ever-changing external and internal factors affecting their sensitive and complex products (Giousmpasoglou et al., 2021).

There is an ongoing discussion about whether hotel managers differ from managers in other industries due to the specific nature of their work. To formally recognise hospitality managers as a profession, the Corpus of Management Excellence (assisted by the Hotel and Catering International Management Association) has taken action to develop a hierarchical managerial structure (HCIMA, 1994). This structure aimed to establish management standards in the industry. The Corpus identified three levels of management in the hospitality, leisure, and tourism industry: supervisory, operational, and senior management. According to the proposed structure, front-line managers are responsible for the daily operations of a department or a smaller unit (i.e., a restaurant, a kitchen section, the hotel's front office): they implement procedures, make short-term plans, and make daily business decisions. At the operational management level, individuals are accountable for making long-term decisions, planning, budget setting, and taking necessary actions. Senior management, on the other hand, is responsible for corporate or strategic planning and policymaking. Their primary role is to direct business policies and operations. In a hotel unit, supervisors may hold job titles such as Assistant Bar/Restaurant Manager, Chef de Partie, and Assistant Housekeeper (Fig. 4.1). At a higher level (Middle Management), one may find job titles like Front Office Manager, Restaurant Manager, and Sous Chef, all reporting to the perspective department manager. The senior management team includes General Manager (GM) and the department heads (Rooms Division Manager, F&B Manager, Executive Chef, and Executive Housekeeper).

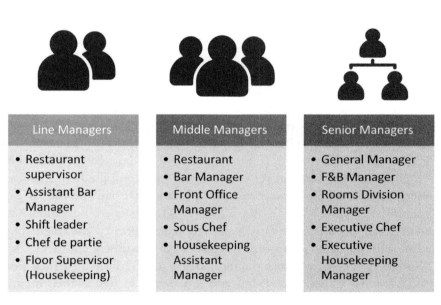

Fig. 4.1 Three levels of management in hotel units. (Source: Authors' creation)

According to Eder and Umbreit (1989), the role of the GMs is crucial as they implement the business strategy for the property and serve as a behavioural role model for the entire management team. Based on this argument, one could suggest that the GM plays a pivotal role in overseeing the hotel business unit. Jayawardena (2000, p. 67) provides a vivid description of the hotel GMs' responsibilities:

> *The general manager of a hotel can be compared to the captain of a ship or the conductor of an orchestra or the main performer of a stage show. Often in hotels, the general manager will be in the limelight while performing his (or her) normal duties. He/she depends on the support of 'front of the house' employees (similar to the musicians and dancers of a stage show) and the 'back of the house employees' (similar to the sound engineers, lighting specialists, choreographers, stage managers and set designers of a show) to enhance his/her performance. The hotel manager also uses the directions of the hotel owners and operating company (similar to the producers of a show) and the manuals/guidelines set for each hotel operation (similar to the theme, script and music score of a show). The hotel general manager has to ensure that most of the guests/customers of the hotel (similar to an audience at a show) are satisfied and the hotel employee teams are motivated.*

Research interest in the hospitality industry during the 1980s and 1990s focused on managers' roles and how they relate to managerial effectiveness and performance. Mintzberg's (1973) early work on managerial roles in the hospitality sector has been replicated or tested by several researchers (i.e., Hales & Tamangani, 1996; Kim, 1994; Nebel III & Ghei, 1993). His seminal yet controversial work proposed ten management roles, including interpersonal, informational, and decisional elements (see also Chap. 3). According to Mintzberg's observations, all managerial jobs share similarities in pace, variety, brevity, and fragmentation. His conceptual reasoning, elaborated in subsequent work (see Mintzberg, 1994), was that the individual's role is affected by their personal history, values, knowledge, and experience, as well as their mental models of interpreting the world; thus, he proposed a framework with three specific components, namely, purpose, perspective, and position. Mintzberg's work has been criticised for its small sample size (five CEOs), assuming CEOs represent typical managers, and not allowing testing of his assertions about function and level (Mount & Bartlett, 1999). Furthermore, the Managerial Roles model has been criticised by Fondas and Stewart (1994) for overlooking the influence of an individual's socio-cultural context, which various occurrences, such as crises and contingencies, can shape. Despite these criticisms, Mintzberg's ideas are still widely taught in business schools, although it is worth noting that simply describing "what managers do" is not necessarily linked to effectiveness.

In the 1990s, multiple studies conducted on managerial work in the hospitality industry mainly focused on two themes (Guerrier & Deery, 1998): how the hotel managers' work is impacted by industry context and whether they react or reflect in their approach. Are they solely responsible for addressing immediate operational concerns, or should they also contribute to strategic decision-making? To answer these questions, Nebel III and Ghei (1993) developed a conceptual framework for the GM's work roles in hotels (Table 4.1). They emphasised that a hotel GM's job can be better understood by examining the contextual variables that influence and shape it.

Hotel General Managers face various job demands and relationship issues that must be handled effectively to ensure successful performance. These contextual factors vary depending on the short-term, medium-term, or long-term timeframe. As a result, GMs carry out specific job functions through various work roles. In the short term, GMs act as operational controllers, performing the managerial tasks of monitoring and distributing internal information, managing unexpected issues, and prioritising their scarce time to address important operational matters. Effective communication within the hotel is crucial to this job function. In the medium term, GMs are responsible for cultivating their team's growth, developing, implementing, and monitoring service strategies, and staying up to date with market trends by engaging with external sources.

Table 4.1 An integrated framework for the GMs' work roles, demands, and relationships in hotels

Time frame	GM job function and roles	Key job demands	Key relationship issues
Short term	**Operational Controller:** • Monitor and Disseminator (internal information) • Disturbance Handler • Resource Allocator (own time) • Leader	Day-to-day operational control of service, costs, and revenues. Intense pressure to earn profits and render high-quality service.	Intense and frequent downward, internal verbal communication and interaction with hotel subordinates.
Intermediate term	**Organisational Developer:** • Liaison • Monitor and Disseminator (of both external and internal information) • Entrepreneur • Resource Allocator (own time, programs, and funds) • Leader	Train and develop subordinates. Fine-tune the hotel's service strategy to changing external environment. Develop and refine the organisation structure.	Downward internal communication. Lateral communication with the external environment. Upward communication with corporate superiors and staff specialists or owners.
Long term	**Business Maintainer:** • Liaison • Monitor and Disseminator (external and internal information) • Resource Allocator (of programs and funds) • Entrepreneur • Leader	Capital expenditure decisions in line with the hotel's strategic service vision. Develop and sustain organisational stability and vitality.	Downward internal communication to further stability and vitality. Lateral communication with the external environment. Intense upward communication with corporate office or owners.

Source: Adapted from Rutherford and O'Fallon (2007, pp. 94–97)

Additionally, hotel GMs must provide upward communication to ensure operational plans' collaboration and act as a liaison between the hotel and the outside world by monitoring internal and external information. GMs are also the key decision-makers in the hotel's capital expenditure decisions and are responsible for maintaining organisational stability to ensure its sustainability. All of these tasks are interconnected and require exceptional leadership skills. It is therefore argued that GMs play a crucial role in securing the enduring success of the business in the long term; this involves making capital expenditure decisions aligned with the hotel's strategic vision and fostering organisational stability.

Maintaining good relationships with corporate superiors, staff, owners, and local community members is also vital. The GM acts as a liaison between all parties, allocating capital funds and preserving stability. Hales and Tamangani (1996) conducted a study on hotel unit GMs and came to similar conclusions. They found that the majority of operational problems in hotels revolve around service-related issues, so hotel managers must primarily focus on managing service quality. Unlike retail unit managers, who follow a reactive customer service approach, hotel managers prioritise proactive service quality management. Additionally, most hotel business problems have short-time leads, often taking precedence over longer-term considerations such as staff development.

Recent studies have identified new responsibilities and roles for hotel GMs during the twenty-first century (Giousmpasoglou et al., 2021). These roles are influenced by each hotel unit's specific context and setting, including the operational, managerial, leadership, and interpersonal requirements. Also, GMs are expected to possess expertise in information technology, financial management, and marketing. Other studies mention the need for GMs to be adept at strategy and HRM, work-life balance (Deery & Jago, 2015), customer handling, and networking (Giousmpasoglou, 2012). Based on the existing studies, it is argued that managerial roles in hospitality vary, and managers must adapt their work roles to their circumstances. Echoing this sentiment, Jones and Comfort (2020) recently suggested that managers should be able to design and implement strategies beyond traditional business models, to ensure operational transition and sustainability. Furthermore, strategic HRM requires GMs to demonstrate sophisticated and integrated talent management practices, including a multicultural perspective, a focus on people management, technological proficiency, and leadership skills (Marinakou & Giousmpasoglou, 2019).

Significant occurrences in the twenty-first century, like terrorist attacks, natural disasters, political unrest, and the COVID-19 pandemic, have led to numerous research studies centred around managerial resilience and crisis management. According to Wang and Ritchie (2012), hotel managers must undertake various roles to mitigate the effects of crises, minimise negative consequences, and guide the organisation through the pre- and post-crisis stages. Chen et al. (2019) suggest that hotel managers must have the foresight to anticipate and prepare for potential crises by identifying threats, risks, and vulnerabilities and training their teams to prevent and minimise damage. Pappas (2018) notes that this complex process involves decision-making on various fronts, including operations, marketing, and pricing policies. Building resilience and managing crises require applying managerial expertise across all areas, but most importantly, it requires managers' willingness and determination to deal with the crisis head-on (Giousmpasoglou et al., 2021). Filimonau et al. (2020) suggest that proactive attitudes in dealing with crises and managing staff are more likely to be observed if managers feel secure in their jobs. Sigala (2020) argues that hotel managers must establish strong collaborations with external systems; to achieve this, they should take collaborative action and practice social bricolage.

Based on the above discussion, it is clear that hotel managers are required to fulfil multiple roles within a dynamic and unpredictable environment. To effectively manage these responsibilities, specific personality traits are essential. We will explore these traits in detail in the following section.

Box 4.1 A day in the life of a luxury hotel GM

My name is Michael Clitheroe, and I am writing this on the week of my eighth anniversary of being the general manager (GM) at Balmer Lawn Hotel in the New Forest (U.K.). I consider myself lucky to have followed in the footsteps of some incredible leaders and managers in the Hospitality industry. I have learned just as much from the great as I have from the not-so-great mentors, and this is a daily driver for my standards. One of the most important things I have learned over my 25-year career is that we are nothing without our customers and staff. These two factors drive the 'routine' in my day.

It is important to realise that I always knew I had a routine at work; however, after so many years, I never knew the importance of what crafted it and what an anchor it would be to my professional life and many others. Typically, there is an order of precedence with work being carried out. Firstly, I check the rota for the expectations of the business—the functions, room presentations, meeting preparations, and timings for the day. It is a 5 to 10-minute exercise, but it is vital as a general manager never to lose touch with the guests or our operations. I then check staffing; who is on the floor, on the stoves, kitchen porters, housekeeping, and sales; literally every staff member is checked. I genuinely make a point to walk around and meet all the team at the start of the shift or, where possible, through the day. With the ultimate responsibility of standards and culture setting on my shoulders, I take time to check that we have procured the skill sets and resources appropriately to exceed customers' expectations and deliver the standards I expect of our staff. With enough resources, enough personnel, and enough materials to let them have a great day at work, delivering their career goals.

From this point onwards, my time is spent on '*reactives*', meaning whatever the main pinch points are for the business at the time; these include emails, maintenance updates, recruitment campaigns, and resolving customer-related issues. Once the house operation is in order, it is typically the time to step back and deal with the strategic aspects of the job. Preparation for meetings, revenue updates, viewing historic data and forecasting, and then engaging with project work I am either leading or involved with. These activities range from team, product, or business development to working on industry or regional matters.

The pride and hard work I have put into my career extends beyond the hotel and the team I manage. I am lucky to have been nominated twice by the Boutique Hotelier Magazine for *General Manager of the Year* in 2019 and 2022 and have won multiple personal and professional accolades. I am incredibly proud to be a chartered Manager, Mentor, Springboard Ambassador, Fellow of the Institute of Hospitality, and Chair of the New Forest Hotels Association.

No two days at work are the same. Most hoteliers are eternal optimists, yet expect the unexpected daily. Thus, I cannot leave any working day without a walk around the front of the house; typically, I will spot something out of place or a regular guest and, of course, will have to say hi. Before you know it, a long but rewarding day ends—time to do it all over again tomorrow!

Michael Clitheroe
General Manager
Balmer Lawn Hotel & Spa
Source: M. Clitheroe, personal communication, 5 July 2023.

Personality Traits for Hotel Managers

Several studies on hotel managerial work have focused on whether particular personality traits (Fig. 4.2) set hotel managers apart from other professions (i.e., Ladkin, 1999; Mullins & Davies, 1991; Wilson, 1998). The work of hotel GMs has been described as highly individualistic, and thus a particular type of personality seems to be attracted to this job (Wood, 1994). This fact can be justified due to work-related factors such as stress, working long hours, and dealing with uncertainty, complexity, and high demands, which are part of the GMs' daily routine. In his study, Stone (1988; cited in Mullins & Davies, 1991) argues that hotel managers are more assertive, stubborn, cheerful, competitive, active, independent, cynical, calm, socially bold and spontaneous, hard to fool, and more concerned with self than other non-hotel managers. In the same tune, Worsfold (1989) defined the abilities and characteristics that a person must have to become a successful hotel general manager; he has discriminated these requirements into people handling, spirituality and physical stamina, self-motivation, personality characteristics such as personal style, natural talent, tolerance, willingness to undertake risks, and

Fig. 4.2 Hotel managers' traits and personal characteristics. (Source: Authors' creation)

the need for sentimental stability and intelligence where common sense and strong memory are included. Similarly, Brownell (1994) found that personal attributes such as hard work, positive attitude, and strong communication skills are essential ingredients for those who aspire to top management positions in hotels; personal sacrifice and having the right personality (i.e., being likeable, having physical attractiveness, and being charismatic) received high rankings, as well. Later studies (i.e., Kay & Moncarz, 2004) challenge the value of the above findings by arguing that hospitality managers have much in common with managers from other sectors, especially at higher hierarchical levels. The reason behind this convergence is that the work of hotel GMs has evolved from operational to strategic level, at least in corporate and multinational hotel chains (Bharwani & Talib, 2017; Gannon et al., 2015).

Since the early 1990s, the rapid growth of international hotel chains and its effects on managerial work have also drawn the attention of researchers (i.e., Gilbert & Guerrier, 1997; Jones et al., 1998; Nebel et al., 1995). The personality characteristics required of international hotel managers include people and interpersonal skills, adaptability, flexibility and tolerance, cultural sensitivity, and intercultural competence, followed by emotional maturity, industry experience, and self-confidence (i.e., Bharwani & Talib, 2017; Feng & Pearson, 1999; Wang & Ritchie, 2012). Additionally, the above studies identify skills like managing limited resources, understanding international etiquette, and understanding international business matters as necessary for international hotel managers. In contrast, functional and technical skills were rated as the lowest priority for managers. Research also indicates that building managers' cross-cultural skills in an international hospitality organisation may be complex but more important than developing their functional and technical skills (Kriegl, 2000). This can be justified by the high level of interpersonal and relational skills required where the host country's culture and the needs of a diverse customer base must be understood and handled. The knowledge and competencies of GMs are wide-ranging and include the enabling capabilities essential for survival within the international hotel industry and the supplemental and core capabilities specific to companies' market positions and strategies and competitive advantage (Giousmpasoglou et al., 2021).

Box 4.2 International Hotel Managers' development—Ned's story

I started my career with Marriott International in 1997 with The Ritz-Carlton brand in my home city of Sydney, Australia. Over the last quarter of a century, I have thoroughly enjoyed being a hotelier. In 2000, with the support of my remarkable leaders and mentors, I was encouraged to travel abroad with Marriott International and have not looked back!

I have had the privilege of working in ten hotels, opening an additional five as a trainer, and participating in an opening task force in three more hotels. These experiences have resulted in me living and working in ten countries (Australia, the United States of America, the United Arab Emirates, Qatar, Russia, Singapore, Bahrain, Egypt, Israel, and Spain), all unique in their way and an enormous learning and development opportunity. I genuinely feel that travel is an education that has allowed me to develop as a human and a career professional. In addition, management and leadership development courses such as the Elevate programme, the Jack Canfield Success Principles, and the Legendary Service Program Ambassador have also boosted my career potential.

Some of the most important traits in a successful and happy career include having a positive attitude, the willingness to learn and improve, and enjoying the moment in each position as you come across it. Devote yourself wholeheartedly, as it is a phenomenal industry filled with new opportunities and adventures. Push the boundaries and make a difference, improving the lives of others, including your colleagues, your guest, your stakeholders, your loyal members, and the local community.

Be passionate, be genuine, and love what you do, as this will bring you success naturally. The satisfaction and fulfilment you will feel are gratifying, and it is actually beyond words! Enjoy the journey of discovery, be willing to listen, have an open mind, and take on new challenges.

Certain principles I live by and feel are fundamental include integrity, work ethic, honesty, and respect. Remember that your reputation will precede you, and emotions are fact. In a leadership capacity, being a role model, walking the talk, and ensuring you build the strongest team around you is crucial. Develop your team to be stronger collectively, be united, and enjoy celebrating the growth and promotion of your colleagues.

Ultimately what remains in our dynamic hospitality industry is meeting the most incredible individuals and creating unique memories. Reflecting on my journey, I truly feel grateful and fortunate for what our sector represents, and I look forward to what is ahead!

Ned Capeleris
Multi-property General Manager
Marriott International
Source: N. Capeleris, personal communication, 27 June 2023

International hospitality managers are seen as change agents who help corporations to cope with the fast-changing environment. In addition, global hotel chains such as Marriott, Hilton, IHG, and Accor invest in developing a cohort of international managers using staff from the host and parent countries they operate (Nickson, 2013). The recruitment and selection process of this management "cadre" is conducted in assessment centres and requires a variety of aspects, such as a mix of competencies, technical skills, strong personality, cultural sensitivity, and adaptability (D'Annunzio-Green, 1997; Gannon, 2003). Furthermore, Kriegl (2000) argues that successful international hospitality operations depend mainly on qualified managers who can translate their operational standards and maintain service consistency across borders. Therefore, identifying the required competencies to become and flourish as an international hotel unit GM is important, and it seems to influence national managerial contexts as well when companies use host country's nationals (HCNs) in senior management positions. The various efforts to identify and develop managerial competencies that will lead hotel GMs to high or superior performance are discussed in the following section.

Managerial Competencies

Research into managerial competencies and developing consequent competency frameworks gained momentum during the 1970s. The rapid technological change, combined with growth in service and knowledge-based industries (Neef, 1998), has led to the need for ongoing competence development for competitive success (Porter, 1990). As a result, the demand for managerial competencies has increased interest in how organisations select, train, and develop managers; to accomplish this, they must understand what constitutes human competence at work. Without such an understanding, competence development cannot be managed effectively (Sandberg, 2000), and therefore, managerial effectiveness in organisations cannot be achieved.

Early approaches to managerial competence focused on the relationship between person and work. Mintzberg (1973) claimed that a manager's work is central to all management aspects but that research in this area had been limited and inconsistent and had not built upon prior knowledge. Consequently, his study utilised both primary research and an integration of the relevant findings of previous research (Mintzberg, 1975). Several management competencies emerged from Mintzberg's (1975) work, which considered them essential for effective management. These were developing relationships, resolving conflicts, motivating subordinates, establishing information networks, disseminating information, and allocating resources. Katz (1974) attempted to address the concerns that Mintzberg raised and investigated management competencies as an extension to the previous work that had predominantly examined management functions. Katz claimed that managers at all levels require technical, human, and conceptual skills, and the emphasis on particular types of skills will depend on the individual's management level. For example, technical skills have a greater focus at lower levels of management, while well-developed conceptual skills are crucial to senior management. It is also significant to clarify the relationship between the desired performance, required job activities, and underlying competencies since many organisations may lose sight of their true concern: what a person can accomplish by concentrating on specific traits or qualities. The different approach that Katz (1974) used to evaluate what makes an effective manager has profoundly impacted management development and signalled the possibility that practising management competencies can achieve effective management. Research and scholars have extensively used Katz's management competency framework, developing it further or creating new frameworks based on it (Peterson & Van Fleet, 2004). For example, Sandwith (1993) expanded Katz's model by splitting competencies into interpersonal, leadership, and administrative.

Despite the popularity of various competency-based approaches, what they are and what they do in the managerial work context remain unclear. Boyatzis (1982, pp. 20–21) defined job competency as "an underlying characteristic of a person which results in effective and/or superior performance in a job." The term "competency" in the workplace has various meanings, which can sometimes be confusing (Antonacopoulou & FitzGerald, 1996), that is, it is very common to confuse competencies with skills (Fig. 4.3). However, it generally includes an individual's personal traits, knowledge, and motivation towards their job. According to Boyatzis (2015), competence (or competency) can be defined in various

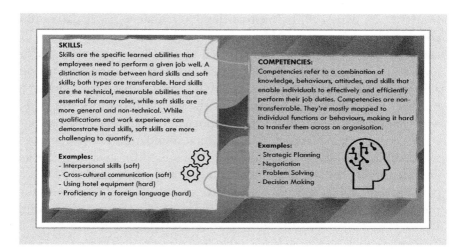

Fig. 4.3 Differences between skills and competencies. (Source: Adapted from McNeill (n.d.))

HRM, occupational, and organisational contexts. Furthermore, Suhairom et al. (2019) suggest that competencies are measurable patterns of knowledge, skills, abilities, behaviours, and other traits that distinguish high performers from those who perform at an average level. Boyatzis (1998) categorised competencies in *threshold* and *differentiating*. Threshold competencies are those clusters of minimum behaviours (skills) people need to do the job. In contrast, differentiating competencies are the distinct characteristics (i.e., behaviours, traits, and skills) determining high from average performers. In any case, Sandwith (1993) argued that organisations should adapt any competency model to their specific organisational needs or adopt those relevant to the particular business.

Two distinct approaches have been used for defining and studying managerial competencies in the US and the UK, respectively (Giousmpasoglou, 2012). On the one hand, Boyatzis (1982) proposed the behavioural approach, which has preoccupied academics in the US (i.e., Schroder, 1989; Spencer & Spencer, 1993). In this approach, managerial competencies are defined in terms of underlying personal characteristics like traits, knowledge, skills, and motives of the individual holding the job, which have been causally related to superior performance

(Stuart & Lindsay, 1997). This tradition has remained particularly influential in North America, with competency defined in terms of underlying characteristics of people causally related to effective or superior performance in a job, generalising across situations, and enduring for a reasonably long time (Spencer & Spencer, 1993). This approach has dominated managerial competencies literature for the past four decades and is also widely appreciated by industry practitioners (Giousmpasoglou, 2012).

In contrast, the National Occupational Standards (NOS) approach appeared in the UK in the mid-1980s; it focused on analysing the job and identifying the minimum requirements and standards for people to perform relevant tasks (www.ukstandards.org.uk). Other countries using the NOS approach include Australia, Singapore, South Africa, and South Korea (Lee & Jacobs, 2021). There are several ways to use NOS in developing skills and knowledge, including direct transfer into vocational programmes, development of training frameworks, measurement of workplace competence, and influencing job descriptions (NOS, n.d.). This approach focuses on the job rather than the individual holding the position (the basis of the behavioural approach). Competencies studies in the UK are dominated by the NOS approach, contributing to 85% of workforce training and development (Cheetham & Chivers, 1996; Lester, 2014). The NOS approach has been heavily criticised (i.e., Keep & Mayhew, 1999; Lee & Jacobs, 2021) mainly due to its focus on minimum standards; consequently, many UK firms have preferred to use behaviour-based competence models (Matthewman, 1999).

Managerial Competencies in the Hospitality Industry

The competencies movement in hotels appeared in the early 1990s when a growing number of Hospitality Management programmes aimed to meet the demands of a volatile and changing world (Umbreit, 1993); these programmes took up the challenge of preparing students by developing and enhancing the management competencies and skills needed to operate successfully. This movement was supported by the industry's growing demand for adequately qualified managerial staff. Research conducted to identify the right mix of competencies has used frameworks like Katz's (1974)

4 Managerial Skills and Competencies 81

Table 4.2 Functions performed by hospitality managers

Functional areas	Sub-areas
Managing operations	• Day-to-day operation • Specialist/technical areas • Managing a crisis
Managing the business	• Managing business performance • Managing products • Managing strategic decisions • Managing legal complexity
Managing people	• Managing individuals • Managing teams • Managing external contacts • Managing personnel administration
Personal management skills	• Making presentations • Interpersonal skills • Using computers in management • Self-development

Source: Adapted from Lockwood (1993)

hierarchical competency model and Sandwith's (1993) competency-domain model (which builds on Katz's model) and groups competencies into five areas: Conceptual-Creative, Leadership, Interpersonal, Administrative, and Technical. In addition, efforts were made to establish generic competencies frameworks for hotel managers, as reflected in the report on European Management Skills in the Hospitality Industry (Lockwood, 1993). This report identifies four broad functional areas: managing operations, managing the business, managing people, and personal management skills. These areas are broken into 15 sub-areas, as in Table 4.2. The report also takes this forward by outlining 78 indicative activities for the competencies of hospitality managers.

Okeiyi et al. (1994) investigated the importance of food and beverage companies' expectations of hospitality management graduates from the perspectives of hospitality practitioners, educators, and students. This study reported that human relations and managerial skills are rated most important, whereas technical skills are less critical. Similarly, Tas et al.'s (1996) study examined property management competencies prospective employers require. Their findings shaped a theoretical model based on Sandwith's (1993) competency domain model. They suggested (ibid.) that although technical and administrative domains are more numerous, the competencies are not rated as important as those of the conceptual/creative, interpersonal, and leadership domains.

Also receiving some attention in the literature has been the research that has specifically attempted to identify the importance of managers possessing a balanced range of skills and competencies (Ladkin & Riley, 1996). Guerrier and Lockwood (1989) questioned the validity of the traditional approach to developing hospitality managers, leading to an operational perspective on skill requirements being developed. At the time of their study, there was little evidence of any focus on "the development of human relations skills for managers and indeed little acceptance for this sort of development" (Guerrier & Lockwood, 1989, p. 85). Carper (1993) disputes the changing balance between operational and management skills; he indicates that there is still support for operational skills training, but hotel managers acknowledge the growing importance of managerial skills in enhancing the hotel's performance.

Studies conducted in the US show a broader perspective of hospitality managerial competencies, which escapes the predominant "human skills" approach. Perdue et al. (2000) investigated competencies required for Country Club Managers in the US; they found that they identified a need for expertise in accountancy and finance, human and professional resourcing, and food and beverage management. Kay and Russette (2000) studied the hospitality management competencies at entry and middle managerial levels within the front desk, food and beverage, and sales functional areas. They identified 18 essential core competencies, which lie in all of Sandwith's (1993) domains apart from the administrative, and discovered that "working knowledge of product-service" and "adapting creatively to change" are essential for all the managers studied. It is also reported that middle-level front desk and sales managers need more competencies than same-level food and beverage managers. Chung-Herrera et al. (2003) identified a link between leadership competencies and "future hospitality leaders." They argued that developing a competency model will help senior managers select, develop, and coach future leaders, map career paths, and plan management succession. Their study looked into eight factors—communication, critical thinking, implementation, industry knowledge, interpersonal skills, leadership, self-management, and strategic positioning. They identified 28 dimensions under these factors and 99 specific behavioural competencies that future leaders must possess.

Furthermore, a study by Kay and Moncarz (2004) suggests that, besides human skills, competencies in information technology, financial management, and marketing play a significant role in hospitality managers' success. Based on these findings, they argue (ibid.) that educational institutions and training providers should cover these areas to equip future managers with the required knowledge and skills. A recent conceptual study by Bharwani and Talib (2017) synthesised data from previous studies and proposed a competency framework for hotel GMs, divided into four broad categories: cognitive competencies (knowledge), functional competencies (skills), social competencies (attitudes and behaviours), and meta-competencies (motives and traits).

Until recently, only a handful of empirical studies were conducted outside the Anglo-American context. While some of these studies suffered from the same methodological weaknesses as those in the UK and the US, they arrived at some interesting findings and conclusions. Christou and Eaton (2000) replicated the studies of Tas (1988) and Baum (1991) to identify the competencies needed for hospitality graduate trainees in Greece. All three studies concluded that hotel GMs identified so-called soft skills as essential. Soft skills are personal attributes that enhance an individual's interactions, job performance, and career prospects; unlike hard skills, which tend to be specific to a particular task or activity, soft skills are broadly applicable. Agut et al. (2003) studied the competency needs and training demands among managers from Spanish hotels and restaurants. Their findings suggested that Spanish hotel and restaurant managers must mainly improve their knowledge and skills in competencies involving computing, languages, health and risk prevention, marketing, work organisation, human resources management, and customer profiles and behaviours. Brophy and Kiely (2002) developed a competency framework for middle managers in three-star hotels in Ireland. They clustered competencies by mapping these to the key results areas of customer care, quality and standards, managing staff, achieving profitability, and growing the business. Giousmpasoglou (2019) explored the mediating factors affecting GMs' work in Greek small and medium luxury hotels. Five critical areas shaping and informing the GMs' required competencies were identified: career development and mobility; contact intensity; owner-GM relations; dealing with corruption; and networking and reputation. Marneros et al. (2020) surveyed hotel professionals in Cyprus regarding the competencies needed for the job. They found that the industry prefers hiring employees with "soft" people management skills and a strong practical professional background.

Apart from Europe and North America, interest in developing competency frameworks has also sparked in Australasia. Dimmock et al. (2003) surveyed the existing competencies of hospitality and tourism management students in Australia. They based their study on the work of Quinn et al. (1990) and their Competing Values Framework (CVF), which builds on Di Padova's (1996) Self-Assessment of Managerial Skills (SAMS) instrument. The study found that students perceive most CVF competencies as significant (19 out of 24), many of which are meta-competences. These meta-competences address higher order skills and tasks an individual undertakes in their management role. Students in this study identified a lack of competencies in other management areas, such as those associated with designing work and managing across functions.

On the other hand, many studies focus on the link between industry requirements and competencies for hospitality graduates. Jauhari's (2006) study investigated the link between industry competency requirements and the current provisions for hospitality management education in India. In his findings, a gap exists in ensuring that the workforce's ongoing skills development meets the industry's needs. In addition, he notes that "hotel management in India has been seen more as a trade than as a business organisation" (ibid., p. 130). This notion indicates the source of the problems faced by the Indian hospitality industry. A similar study in Hong Kong by Cheung et al. (2010) found that hotel managers perceived leadership as the most important competency, followed by industry knowledge and communication skills. Hospitality graduate students, in contrast, believed that graduate programs enhance their communication, industry knowledge, and interpersonal skills. Their findings imply that hospitality management programmes should focus more on developing leadership skills, which hotel managers consider the most important competency. Shariff and Abidin (2015) researched the skills that Malaysian graduates in the hospitality industry needed to possess and created a competency index with 40 skills organised into eight key domains. The graduate competencies industry professionals considered most crucial included interpersonal, business, and communication skills. Similarly, Spowart (2011) emphasised the importance of soft skills for hospitality graduates in South Africa.

Jeou-Shyan et al. (2011) investigated how hotel GMs in Taiwan evaluated their competency needs. There were general and technical components to the competencies identified as essential for managerial work. According to the study, senior managers in Taiwan emphasised general, practice-oriented skills more than technical ones; they found that leadership, crisis management, and problem-solving were the highest priority competency domains. Tavitiyaman et al. (2014) explored the managerial competencies required of GMs in Thai hotels; teamwork, ethics, leadership, and communication skills came out on top. Flexibility and strategic orientation, on the other hand, were their least valued competencies.

Competency Frameworks in Hospitality Industry

The existing competencies frameworks/models in hospitality fall mainly in the behavioural approach, which assumes those models can be universally applicable regardless of the manager's background. This is unsurprising as hospitality is considered a "results-oriented" industry, and superior performance is believed to be the key to achieving organisational goals. Iversen (2000, p. 12) argues that "it is reasonable to conclude that there are some managerial competencies that are causally related to effective and/or superior performance in a job." Based on the above discussion on hospitality managerial competencies, some conclusions can be made from comparing seven hospitality management competency frameworks with Dulewicz's (1998) model (Table 4.3).

Table 4.3 A comparison of managerial competency frameworks in the hospitality industry

Competency areas (Dulewicz, 1998)	Tas (1988), Baum (1991), Christou and Eaton (2000)	Lockwood (1993)	Kay and Russette (2000)	Brophy and Kiely (2002)	Chung-Herrera et al. (2003)	Giousmpasoglou (2012)	Bharwani and Talib (2017)	Marneros et al. (2021)
Intellectual	Operational Awareness	Managing Operations and Business	Conceptual—Creative; Technical	Planning and Organising, Problem Solving	Industry Knowledge; Critical Thinking	Intellectual	Cognitive competencies (knowledge)	Leadership and Critical Thinking
Personal	Ethics; Professionalism; Legal Responsibility	Personal Management Skills	X	Enthusiasm	Self-Management	Personal	Functional competencies (skills)	Professional Image Operational Knowledge
Communication	Communication	X	Administrative	Effective Communication	Communication	Communication	Social competencies (attitudes and behaviours)	Human Relations—Communication
Interpersonal	Customer Problems Handling	X	Interpersonal	Teamwork	Interpersonal	Interpersonal	Social competencies	Interpersonal Communication—Cultural Diversity
Leadership	Employee Relations; Leadership; Motivation	Managing People	Leadership	X	Leadership	Leadership	Meta-competencies (motives and traits)	Leadership and Critical Thinking; Human Resources Management
Results—Orientation	Development and Control of Productivity; Customer Relations	X	X	Leading for results, Customer Service Focus; Financial Awareness; Strategic Thinking	Implementation; Strategic Positioning	Results—Orientation	Meta-competencies	Information Technology and Financial Analysis
Number of Competencies	36	78	18	36	99	45	43	40

Source: Authors' creation

Dulewicz's (ibid.) competencies framework was selected as a benchmark for being one of the most tested and validated models in the behavioural approach (Giousmpasoglou, 2012). It must be noted that it was impossible to present all the competencies that each framework includes; thus, only the broad competency areas are compared. Despite the diversity of these models, there are common areas or overlaps among them. Most of these frameworks cover five of six competency areas (intellectual, personal, communication, interpersonal, and leadership). Surprisingly the "results orientation" area is not covered by Lockwood (1993), possibly because their focus was on various managerial levels (Kay & Russette, 2000). The above discussion indicates that using a generic competency framework to assess hotel managers would be possible. On the other hand, it is argued that using a single managerial competencies model is insufficient to provide a credible account of managerial competencies in hotels, as contextual factors such as the national culture and the characteristics of the group studied must also be acknowledged (Giousmpasoglou, 2019).

Chapter Summary

This chapter critically investigated the managerial skills and competencies in the hotel industry context. According to literature published across four decades, managerial work in hotels differs to some extent from other sectors and industries. This results in a unique personality and competency profile made even more complicated and multifaceted in different cultural settings. The traits of effective hotel managers are a contentious topic in the literature on hospitality management. Despite the plethora of studies on this topic, there is no consensus on what is required to be a successful hotel manager. According to the available research, hotel general managers must possess and demonstrate a combination of personal qualities, experience in leadership and management, business acumen, and technical know-how.

In conclusion, practitioners and management scholars recognise the need to create a framework that assesses and develops competencies matching the hotel sector's needs. The existing literature proves that hotel managers are vested in creating generic managerial competency frameworks. On the other hand, contextual factors such as the national and organisational culture cannot be ignored in designing these frameworks, especially when hotel managers operate in a global environment. Further research is required to overcome the existing studies' limitations and arrive at a widely acceptable competencies framework for hotel managers.

References

Agut, S., Grau, R., & Peiro, J. M. (2003). Competency needs among managers from Spanish hotels and restaurants and their training demands. *Hospitality Management, 22*, 281–295.

Antonacopoulou, E. P., & FitzGerald, L. (1996). Reframing competency in management development. *Human Resource Management Journal, 6*(1), 27–48.

Baum, T. (1991). Comparing expectations of management trainees. *The Cornell Hotel and Restaurant Administration Quarterly, 32*(2), 79–84.

Bharwani, S., & Talib, P. (2017). Competencies of hotel general managers: A conceptual framework. *International Journal of Contemporary Hospitality Management, 29*(1), 393–418.

Boyatzis, R. (1982). *The competent manager: A model for effective performance*. John Willey and Sons.

Boyatzis, R. (1998). *Transforming qualitative information: Thematic analysis and code development*. SAGE.

Boyatzis, R. (2015). *Competency. Wiley Encyclopedia of Management* (pp. 1–2). John Wiley & Sons.

Brophy, M., & Kiely, T. (2002). Competencies: A new sector. *Journal of European Industrial Training, 26*(2–4), 165–176.

Brownell, J. (1994). Personality and career development: A study of gender differences. *Cornell Hotel and Restaurant Administration Quarterly, 35*(2), 36–43.

Carper, J. (1993, March). The painful truth: Operations is no longer king. *Hotels*, 50

Cheetham, G., & Chivers, G. (1996). Towards a holistic model of professional competence. *Journal of European Industrial Training, 20*(5), 20–30.

Chen, X., Li, D., Nian, S., Wu, K., Yang, L., Zhang, H., Zhang, J., & Zhang, J. (2019). Two sides of a coin: A crisis response perspective on tourist community participation in a post-disaster environment. *International Journal of Environmental Research and Public Health, 16*(12), 1–19.

Cheung, C., Law, R., & He, K. (2010). Essential hotel managerial competencies for graduate students. *Journal of Hospitality & Tourism Education, 22*(4), 25–32.

Christou, E., & Eaton, J. (2000). Management competencies for graduate trainees. *Annals of Tourism Research, 24*(4), 1058–1061.

Chung-Herrera, B., Enz, C., & Lankau, M. (2003). Grooming future hospitality leaders: A competencies model. *The Cornell Hotel and Restaurant Administration Quarterly, 44*(3), 17–25.

D'Annunzio-Green, N. (1997). Developing international managers in the hospitality industry. *International Journal of Contemporary Hospitality Management, 9*(5/6), 199–208.

Deery, M., & Jago, L. (2015). Revisiting talent management, work-life balance and retention strategies. *International Journal of Contemporary Hospitality Management, 27*(3), 453–472.

Di Padova, L. (1996). *Instructional guide to accompany becoming a master manager: A competency framework* (2nd ed.). John Willey & Sons.

Dimmock, K., Breen, H., & Walo, M. (2003). Management competencies: An Australian assessment of tourism and hospitality students. *Journal of the Australian and New Zealand Academy of Management, 9*(1), 12–26.

Dulewicz, V. (1998). *Personal competency framework manual*. ASE/NFER—Nelson.

Eder, R. W., & Umbreit, W. T. (1989). Measures of managerial effectiveness in the hotel industry. *Hospitality Education and Research Journal, 13*(3), 333–341.

Feng, F., & Pearson, T. E. (1999). Hotel expatriate managers in China: Selection criteria, important skills and knowledge, repatriation concerns, and causes of failure. *International Journal of Hospitality Management, 18*(3), 309–321.

Filimonau, V., Derqui, B., & Matute, J. (2020). The COVID-19 pandemic and organizational commitment of senior hotel managers. *International Journal of Hospitality Management, 91*, 1–13.

Fondas, N., & Stewart, R. (1994). Enactment in managerial jobs: A role analysis. *Journal of Management Studies, 31*(1), 83–103.

Gannon, J. M. (2003). International hospitality managers: Past, present and future. In B. Brotherton (Ed.), *International hospitality industry* (pp. 195–212). Butterworth-Heinemann.

Gannon, J. M., Roper, A., & Doherty, L. (2015). Strategic human resource management: Insights from the international hotel industry. *International Journal of Hospitality Management, 47*, 65–75.

Gilbert, D., & Guerrier, Y. (1997). UK hospitality managers: Past and present. *Service Industries Journal, 17*(1), 115–132.

Giousmpasoglou, C. (2012). *A contextual approach to understanding managerial roles and competencies: The case of luxury hotels in Greece*. Unpublished Ph.D. thesis,. University of Strathclyde.

Giousmpasoglou, C. (2019). Factors affecting and shaping the general managers' work in small-and medium-sized luxury hotels: The case of Greece. *Hospitality & Society, 9*(3), 397–422.

Giousmpasoglou, C., Marinakou, E., & Zopiatis, A. (2021). Hospitality managers in turbulent times: The COVID-19 crisis. *International Journal of Contemporary Hospitality Management, 33*(4), 1297–1318.

Guerrier, Y., & Deery, M. (1998). Research in hospitality human resource management and organizational behaviour. *International Journal of Hospitality Management, 17*(2), 145–160.

Guerrier, Y., & Lockwood, A. (1989). Developing hotel managers—a reappraisal. *International Journal of Hospitality Management, 8*(2), 82–89.

Hales, C., & Tamangani, Z. (1996). An investigation of the relationship between organizational structure, managerial role expectations and managers' work activities. *Journal of Management Studies, 33*(6), 731–756.

HCIMA. (1994). *European management skills in the hospitality industry*. HCIMA Publications.

Iversen, O. (2000). *Managing people towards a Multicultural workforce: Part A— Managerial competencies*. NIPA.

Jauhari, V. (2006). Competencies for a career in the hospitality industry: An Indian perspective. *International Journal of Contemporary Hospitality Management, 18*(2), 123–134.

Jayawardena, C. (2000). International hotel manager. *International Journal of Contemporary Hospitality Management, 12*(1), 67–70.

Jeou-Shyan, H., Hsuan, H., Lin, L., Chih-Hsing, L., & Chang-Yen, T. (2011). Competency analysis of top managers in the Taiwanese hotel industry. *International Journal of Hospitality Management, 30*(4), 1044–1054.

Jones, C., Thompson, P., & Nickson, D. (1998). Not part of the family? The limits to managing the corporate way in international hotel chains. *International Journal of Human Resource Management, 9*(6), 1048–1063.

Jones, P., & Comfort, D. (2020). The COVID-19 crisis and sustainability in the hospitality industry. *International Journal of Contemporary Hospitality Management, 32*(10), 3037–3050.

Katz, R. L. (1974). Skills of an effective administrator. *Harvard Business Review, 52*, 90–102.

Kay, C., & Moncarz, E. (2004). Knowledge, skills, and abilities for lodging management. *Cornell Hotel and Restaurant Administration Quarterly, 45*(3), 285–298.

Kay, C., & Russette, J. (2000). Hospitality management competencies. *The Cornell Hotel and Restaurant Administration Quarterly, 41*(4), 52–63.

Keep, M., & Mayhew, K. (1999). The assessment: Knowledge, skills, and competitiveness. *Oxford Review of Economic Policy, 15*(1), 1–15.

Kim, S. M. (1994). Tourist hotel general managers in Korea: A profile. *International Journal of Hospitality Management, 13*(1), 7–17.

Kriegl, U. (2000). International hospitality management: Identifying important skills and effective raining. *Cornell Hotel and Restaurant Administration Quarterly, 41*(2), 64–71.

Ladkin, A. (1999). Hotel general managers: A review of prominent research themes. *International Journal of Tourism Research, 1*(3), 167–193.

Ladkin, A., & Riley, M. (1996). Mobility and Structure in the career paths of UK hotel general managers: A labour market hybrid of the bureaucratic model? *Tourism Management, 17*(6), 443–452.

Lee, A. S., & Jacobs, R. L. (2021). A review of national occupational standards and the role of human resource development in their implementation. *Human Resource Development Review, 20*(1), 46–67.

Lester, S. (2014). Professional competence standards and frameworks in the United Kingdom. *Assessment & Evaluation in Higher Education, 39*(1), 38–52.

Lockwood, A. (1993). *European management skills in the hospitality industry: Based on the final report of the HCIMA's European research 1992–4.* Hotel & Catering International Management Association.

Marinakou, E., & Giousmpasoglou, C. (2019). Talent management and retention strategies in luxury hotels: Evidence from four countries. *International Journal of Contemporary Hospitality Management, 31*(10), 3855–3878.

Marneros, S., Papageorgiou, G., & Efstathiades, A. (2020). Identifying key success competencies for the hospitality industry: The perspectives of professionals. *Journal of Teaching in Travel & Tourism, 20*(4), 237–261.

Marneros, S., Papageorgiou, G., & Efstathiades, A. (2021). Examining the core competencies for success in the hotel industry: The case of Cyprus. *Journal of Hospitality, Leisure, Sport & Tourism Education, 28.* https://doi.org/10.1016/j.jhlste.2021.100303

Matthewman, J. (1999). The sixth HR-BC/IRS annual competency survey. *Competency: The annual benchmarking survey, 1998*(99), 2–11.

McNeill, J. (n.d.). Skills vs competencies—What's the difference and why should you care? https://social.hays.com/2019/10/04/skills-competencies-whats-the-difference/

Mintzberg, H. (1973). *The nature of managerial work*. Harper & Row.

Mintzberg, H. (1975). The manager's job: Folklore and fact. *Harvard Business Review, 53*(4), 49–61.

Mintzberg, H. (1994). Rounding out the manager's job. *Sloan Management Review, 36*, 11–11.

Mount, D. J., & Bartlett, A. L. (1999). The managerial role assessment survey: Design and test of an Instrument measuring Mintzberg's roles among hotel managers. *Journal of Hospitality & Tourism Research, 23*(2), 160–175.

Mullins, L., & Davies, I. (1991). What makes for an effective hotel manager? *International Journal of Contemporary Hospitality Management, 3*(1), 22–25.

Nebel, E. C., Lee, J., & Vidakovic, B. (1995). Hotel general manager career paths in the United States. *International Journal of Hospitality Management, 14*(3/4), 245–260.

Nebel, E. C., III, & Ghei, A. (1993). A conceptual framework of the hotel general manager's job. *Hospitality Research Journal, 16*(3), 27–38.

Neef, D. (1998). *The knowledge economy*. Butterworth-Heinemann.

Nickson, D. (2013). *Human resource management for hospitality, tourism and events*. Routledge.

NOS. (n.d.). About national occupational standards. https://www.ukstandards.org.uk/en/about-nos

Okeiyi, E., Finley, D., & Postel, R. (1994). Food and Beverage management competencies: Educator, industry and student perspectives. *Hospitality and Tourism Educator, 6*(4), 37–40.

Pappas, N. (2018). Hotel decision-making during multiple crises: A chaordic perspective. *Tourism Management, 68*, 450–464.

Parasuraman, A., Berry, L., & Zeithaml, V. (2002). Refinement and reassessment of the SERVQUAL scale. *Journal of Retailing, 67*(4), 114.

Perdue, J., Ninemeier, J., & Woods, R. (2000). Competencies required for club managers. *Cornell Hotel & Restaurant Administration Quarterly, 41*(2), 79–85.

Peterson, T. O., & Van Fleet, D. D. (2004). The ongoing legacy of R.L. Katz: An updated typology of management skills. *Management Decision, 42*(10), 1297–1308.

Porter, M. E. (1990). *The competitive advantage of nations*. Macmillan.

Quinn, R., Faerman, S., Thompson, M., & McGrath, M. (1990). *Becoming a master manager: A competency framework*. John Wiley and Sons.

Rutherford, D. G., & O'Fallon, M. J. (2007). *Hotel management and operations*. John Wiley & Sons.

Sandberg, J. (2000). Understanding human competence at work: An interpretative approach. *Academy of Management Journal, 43*(1), 9–25.

Sandwith, P. (1993). A hierarchy of management training requirements: The competency domain model. *Public Personnel Management, 22*(1), 43–62.

Schroder, H. M. (1989). *Managerial competence: The key to excellence*. Kendal/Hunt.

Shariff, N. M., & Abidin, A. Z. (2015). Developing an index of the Malaysian tourism and hospitality graduates competencies. *International Journal of Business and Society, 16*(3), 422–435.

Sigala, M. (2020). Tourism and COVID-19: Impacts and implications for advancing and resetting industry and research. *Journal of Business Research, 117*, 312–321.

Spencer, L., & Spencer, S. (1993). *Competence at work: Models for superior performance*. John Wiley & Sons.

Spowart, J. (2011). Hospitality students' competencies: Are they work ready? *Journal of Human Resources in Hospitality & Tourism, 10*(2), 169–181.

Stuart, R., & Lindsay, P. (1997). Beyond the frame of management competenc(i)es: Towards a contextually embedded framework of managerial competence in organizations. *Journal of European Industrial Training, 21*(1), 26–34.

Suhairom, N., Musta'amal, A. H., Amin, N. F. M., Kamin, Y., & Wahid, N. H. A. (2019). Quality culinary workforce competencies for sustainable career development among culinary professionals. *International Journal of Hospitality Management, 81*, 205–220.

Tas, R. (1988). Teaching future managers. *The Cornell Hotel and Restaurant Administration Quarterly, 29*(2), 41–43.

Tas, R., Labrecque, S., & Clayton, H. (1996). Property-management competencies for management trainees. *Cornell Hotel & Restaurant Administration Quarterly, 37*(3), 90–96.

Tavitiyaman, P., Weerakit, N., & Ryan, B. (2014). Leadership competencies for hotel general managers: The differences in age, education, and hotel characteristics. *International Journal of Hospitality & Tourism Administration, 15*(2), 191–216.

Umbreit, T. (1993). Essential Skills: What graduates need to succeed. *Hosteur, 3*, 10–12.

Wang, J., & Ritchie, B. W. (2012). Understanding accommodation managers' crisis planning intention: An application of the theory of planned behaviour. *Tourism Management, 33*(5), 1057–1067.

Wilson, M. E. (1998). Gendered career paths. *Personnel Review, 27*(5), 396–411.

Wood, R. C. (1994). *Organisational behaviour for hospitality management.* Butterworth-Heinemann Ltd.

Worsfold, P. (1989). A personality profile of the hotel manager. *International Journal of Hospitality Management, 8*(1), 51–62.

5

Leadership

Photo Credits: *Andrea Piacquadio* (*Free to use under the Pexels License*). (Source: https://www.pexels.com/photo/positive-businesswoman-doing-paperwork-in-office-3756678/)

Introduction

The study of leadership spans across cultures, eras, and theoretical beliefs. This chapter focuses on leadership as a concept and leadership issues and challenges in hospitality management. The purpose is to provide an understanding and a critical review of the various implications for contemporary hospitality organisations and the future leadership skills and competencies development for successful hospitality managers.

Although leadership has been a well-researched area in hospitality management, there is no definitive definition. There are different approaches to defining leadership, which are discussed in this chapter. According to Guchait et al. (2023), leadership has a favourable effect on organisational and employee performance, commitment, satisfaction, and motivation. A leader's ability to understand and manage an organisation's culture will help the organisation achieve its goals and follow its strategic direction, according to Marinakou (2012). The leadership style "has a consistent influence on the organisation's productivity and profitability," according to Youssef (1998, p. 275).

The hospitality industry faces a plethora of challenges that highlight how difficult it is to manage and lead people in this particular and ever-changing environment, including a hierarchical organisational structure, temporary and part-time employment, cultural diversity, customer interaction, and demanding working conditions (Marinakou, 2012; Huertas-Valdivia et al., 2022). Customer satisfaction is at the core of hospitality, so certain employee behaviours are essential in managing people and customer expectations in such bureaucratic and centralized decision-making organisations (Yu et al., 2020). The hospitality industry has been facing an economic downturn since COVID-19 (Elkhwesky et al., 2022), with challenges in the labour market such as high staff turnover, low employee satisfaction, recruitment issues and ongoing staff shortages, as well as the Great Resignation (Giousmpasoglou et al., 2021). In addition, hospitality employees are challenged with increasing customer demands that require a commitment to service quality and creativity in the service provision (Hoang et al., 2021). They are also facing high job uncertainty causing occupational stress, overload, low pay, and often unsupportive cultures leading to high staff turnover and absenteeism (Huertas-Valdivia et al., 2022). Contemporary hospitality organisations can support their employees with autonomy and encouragement to participate in decision-making, to create solutions and find meaning in their work, all of which demand an effective leadership style to achieve business success in a turbulent and highly competitive environment.

Moreover, Shum et al. (2020) found that hospitality employees' wellbeing is jeopardised due to abusive and/or destructive leadership behaviour, pushing them to their limits and suffering damaging treatment from colleagues, supervisors, and even customers. Huertas-Valdivia (2022, p. 2401) suggests that a more participative leadership style is required to replace traditional leadership styles that fail to maximise employees' resources. Despite the increased number of studies on leadership and leadership styles, there is a need to study leadership in the hospitality and tourism industry with empirical studies to propose the most effective leadership style for hotel managers.

Defining Leadership

Although leadership is considered a modern concept, the word "leader" was discussed in the Oxford English Dictionary in 1300 AD. Later, the concept was included in writings for political influence, but its current form only appeared recently (Marinakou, 2012). Interestingly there have been more than 350 definitions of leadership hence defining leadership is a challenge. There are many debates on whether leadership is an art or discipline, whether it is based on traits or style; however, all studies conclude that leadership is significantly important for managing hospitality and tourism organisations. For example, leadership boosts hospitality employees' performance (Wu et al., 2020), impacts employee and customer satisfaction and employee retention (Gill et al., 2011), and strengthens organisational commitment (Huertas-Valdivia et al., 2022). Giousmpasoglou et al. (2021) in their study during the COVID-19 pandemic found that leadership is one of the critical qualities hospitality managers should demonstrate to motivate and encourage hotel employees to stay in this industry. Nevertheless, not all leadership styles are found to be effective in hospitality management or in making employees feel respected and valued (Huertas-Valdivia et al., 2022). Hence, there is a need to identify and determine the most effective leadership style in managing today's hospitality organisations, as new traits, behaviours, and leadership styles must be explored to address the challenges in hospitality management.

Bass (1990, p. 19) defined leadership as "an interaction between two or more members of a group that often involves a structuring or restructuring of the situation and the perceptions and expectations of the members." Barker (2001) identified two main errors in Bass' studies, and he claimed that Bass' views suggest that the leader has this role continuously and that the leader's role and behaviour will bring the expected outcome. In general, leadership refers to the interaction between group members; it is a process in which the leader behaves in certain ways to meet the organisation's goals and influences the followers to perform effectively. Regardless of which approach to leadership is adopted, the common idea is directing a group towards a common goal.

The Distinction Between Leadership and Management

Leadership, as discussed above, is getting things done through people. Some studies propose that managers are, by definition, leaders who perform specific tasks with the support of their teams, which in turn must be inspired or persuaded to follow them. Leadership is similar to management in terms of people influence, working with people, and accomplishing a goal (Northouse, 2022). Both terms are used interchangeably, with an overlap between the work that leaders and managers do. Nevertheless, leadership differs from management, as summarised in Fig. 5.1.

The differences between management and leadership are clearly illustrated in the above figure. Evidently, the role of management is to achieve organisational objectives; in contrast, leadership is the ability of an individual to influence, motivate, and empower others to contribute to the organisational success. According to Gavin (2019), they also differ in

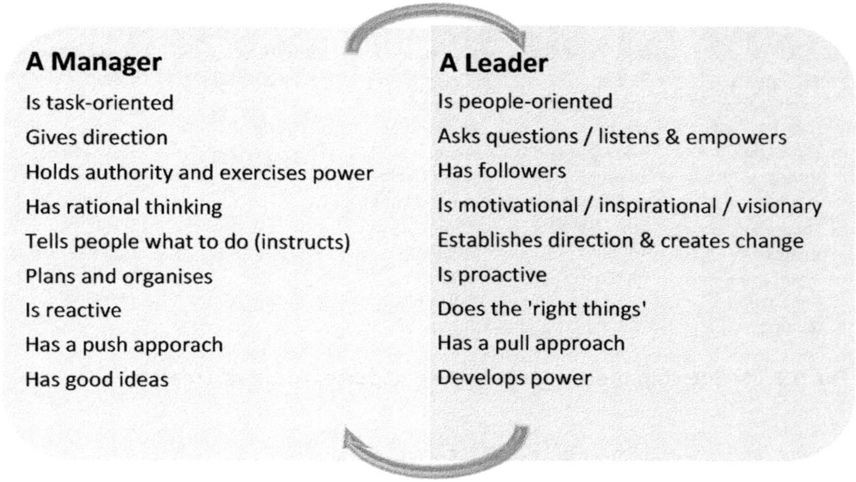

A Manager	A Leader
Is task-oriented	Is people-oriented
Gives direction	Asks questions / listens & empowers
Holds authority and exercises power	Has followers
Has rational thinking	Is motivational / inspirational / visionary
Tells people what to do (instructs)	Establishes direction & creates change
Plans and organises	Is proactive
Is reactive	Does the 'right things'
Has a push apporach	Has a pull approach
Has good ideas	Develops power

Fig. 5.1 Management vs Leadership. (Source: Authors' creation)

critical areas such as process versus vision, organising versus aligning, and position versus quality; he also proposes that:

- the manager administers, the leader innovates;
- the manager maintains, the leader develops;
- the manager focuses on systems and structures, and the leader focuses on people.

Leadership Theories

Leadership has been conceptualised in multiple ways; Northouse (2022, p. 34), however, proposes that the following components are central to leadership: (a) *leadership is a process*, (b) *leadership involves influence*, (c) *leadership occurs in groups*, and (d) *leadership involves common goals*. Leadership is viewed as an interactive process between the leader and his/her followers. This process relates to how the leader influences the followers and their communication (Ruben & Gigliotti, 2017). Leadership

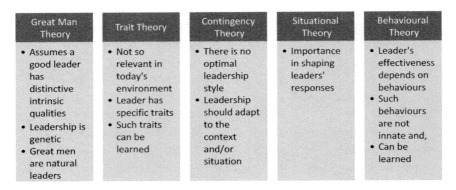

Fig. 5.2 Leadership theories summarised. (Source: Authors' creation)

involves a *group* of individuals who share a common purpose and *common goals*. Several studies on leadership in the hospitality industry focus on different areas, contexts, and cultures; most of these studies identify leadership as a trait or a process. A summary of the key leadership theories is provided in Fig. 5.2.

Leadership Styles

Leadership styles are another approach to defining leadership. The distinction between leadership theory and leadership style was established in the 1960s, as the leader's style varies according to the work situation (Northouse, 2022). The three leadership styles identified at the time were authoritarian (or autocratic), democratic, and laissez-faire. The style approach reminds leaders that their actions impact others and that they can change their style if they wish (Marinakou, 2014). Other styles were developed through the years to reflect the work situations in each context. Leaders should be able to adapt to changes in the environment, to business competitiveness, to crises, to information availability, and to transform organisations. Therefore, different mindsets and skill sets are required for today's hospitality leaders, who operate in a fast-changing business environment (Marinakou, 2012; Giousmpasoglou et al., 2021).

Transformational and Transactional Leadership

Transformational leadership is the most studied leadership style in hospitality and tourism. It refers to a theory originally developed by Burns (1978) for political studies and extended by Bass (1985) to organisational studies. This leadership style focuses on the tasks and employee motivation to consider the organisation's interest and benefit instead of their own. Burns (1978, p. 425) defined *transformational leadership* as "the reciprocal process of mobilizing, by persons with certain motives and values, various economic, political and other resources, in a context of competition and conflict, in order to realize goals independently or mutually held by both leaders and followers." Transformational leaders transform and motivate followers by generating greater awareness of the importance of the purpose of the organisation and task outcomes. Bass and Avolio (1994) clearly understood transformational and transactional leadership; they proposed that *transformational leadership* has four basic components which enable leaders to transform their organisations:

- *Idealised influence* involves the leader's charisma and the followers' respect and admiration by showing them they can accomplish more than they thought.
- *Inspirational motivation* describes the leader's behaviour, which provides meaning and challenge to the followers' work, motivates people, and generates enthusiasm to make followers committed to the organisation and part of the vision.
- *Intellectual stimulation* refers to leaders who solicit new and novel approaches for the performance of work and creative problem solutions from followers.
- *Individualised consideration* refers to leaders who listen and give particular concern to followers' growth and developmental needs and those who delegate, coach, and give constructive feedback.

Transformational leadership is considered the new force in leadership research and has dominated the debate on contemporary leadership approaches. Studies suggest that this leadership style increases positive emotions (Lee et al., 2011), organisational commitment, employee engagement and job satisfaction, employee self-efficacy and creativity (Wang et al., 2014), positive perception of organisational climate and branding, and internal service quality. Furthermore, it can decrease emotional exhaustion, depersonalisation, and employee stress at work (Marinakou, 2012, 2014; Gui et al., 2020). More importantly, transformational leadership is effective in hospitality as it influences employees' attitudinal and behavioural outcomes (Gui et al., 2020) based on an exchange process to achieve specific predetermined performance standards (Avolio et al., 2004) (Fig. 5.3).

Bass (1996) created the Multifactor Leadership Questionnaire (MLQ) in the mid-1990s to measure transformational leadership. Several hospitality studies using the MLQ have highlighted the benefits of transformational leadership on employees, organisational commitment, and work performance. Most of these studies imply that this leadership style is best suited for the hospitality sector (Marinakou, 2012; Gui et al., 2020). On

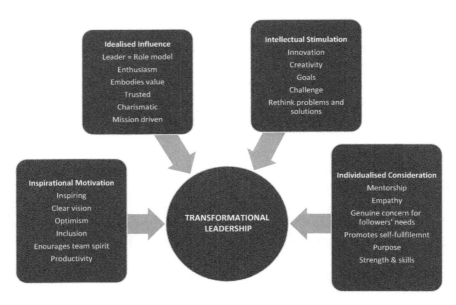

Fig. 5.3 Transformational leadership components. (Source: Author's creation)

the other hand, Antonakis et al. (2014) criticised the MLQ and claimed that the effects of transformational leadership measured by MLQ are overstated.

Burns (1978) and Bass (1985) defined *transactional leadership* as this in which the leaders exchange with their followers and pursue a cost-benefit economic exchange with them. They propose that the transactional leadership style has three components:

- *The contingent reward:* such rewards are used by leaders to explain performance expectations to followers.
- *The management-by-exception (active)*: the leader continually looks at each subordinate's performance and makes changes to the subordinate's work to make corrections throughout the process.
- *The management-by-exception (passive):* leaders wait for issues to arise before fixing the problem.

Based on the definition provided by Bass (1985), transactional leaders monitor employee performance in line with the organisational goals and take actions (penalty—reward). Within this style, the leader uses threats to make employees meet the standards set. The advantages and disadvantages of this leadership style are illustrated in Fig. 5.4.

The laissez-faire (or non-transactional) leadership style is part of the transformational and transactional model. Guchait et al. (2023) claim that this is the worst leadership style in hospitality; this style negatively impacts organisational performance, generating low satisfaction, high stress, and low commitment to followers (Erkutlu & Chafra, 2006). In addition, the leader takes no responsibility, lacks communication skills, and does not support the subordinates. Sobaih et al. (2022) suggest that transactional leadership leads to moderate outcomes, while transformational leadership leads to high efficiency and engagement. Overall, transformational leadership is recognised as the most *effective leadership style in hospitality* (Marinakou, 2012).

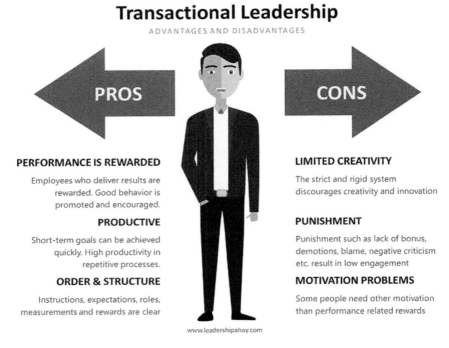

Fig. 5.4 Advantages and disadvantages of transactional leadership. (Source: https://www.leadershipahoy.com/transactional-leadership-what-is-it-pros-cons-examples/)

Servant Leadership

Servant leadership is another leadership style compatible with the hotel sector (Brownell, 2010). The hotel sector is based on human interaction and customer service, aiming to provide genuine care for guests and employees (Bavik, 2020). When describing this leadership style, Greenleaf (1977) emphasised the support for employees, their development, and their comfort. Servant leaders are "empathetic listeners strongly committed to the growth of their teams. Such leaders manage with humility, compassion and justice" (Murari & Gupta, 2012, p. 29). Huertas-Valdivia et al. (2022) propose that servant leadership in hospitality promotes service culture and elevates engagement. Ye et al. (2019) add that it boosts passion for work and it generates higher job, career, and life satisfaction showing trust and commitment to the organisation (Ling et al., 2017).

Greenleaf (1977) first studied and identified servant leaders' traits. Qiu and Dooley (2019) state that these traits were unorganised. Others provided traits such as listening, empathy, persuasion (Spears, 1995), or two categories which include functional attributes or accompanying attributes (Russell & Stone, 2002). Bavik (2020) proposes ten dimensions of servant leadership: listening, empathy, healing, conceptualisation, awareness, stewardship, persuasion, foresight, building communities, and commitment to the growth of the people. Furthermore, Qiu et al. (2020) found that servant leadership and service quality are influenced by self-efficacy; when service quality was improved, both servant leadership and self-efficacy were perceived to be higher.

Empirical studies in hospitality have proposed that servant leadership positively impacts job satisfaction, work engagement, and creativity (Gui et al., 2021). They also suggest that servant leadership mediates the positive effect on employees' behaviour in hospitality. Servant leadership demonstrates positive values such as trust, honesty, and fair treatment and envisions ethical behaviour (Chon & Zoltan, 2019). For example, servant leadership has been adopted in Starbuck's organisational culture, which thrives on empowerment and is supported by the relationship-driven approach of the company (Chon & Zoltan, 2019, p. 3373). Similarly, the Ritz Carlton Hotel Company L.L.C. established the motto "*We are Ladies and Gentlemen serving Ladies and Gentlemen*" (The Ritz-Carlton Gold Standards, 2017), demonstrating their approach to servant leadership. It is, therefore, evident that servant leadership empowers and develops followers through coaching, mentoring, and relevant training. This leadership style provides direction and humility as leaders are altruistic and set practices along with service orientation, trust, and empowerment (Marinakou, 2012).

Empowering Leadership

Empowering leadership is another style compatible with hospitality organisations (Lin et al., 2019; Hoang et al., 2021). It refers to "a process of sharing power and allocating autonomy and responsibilities to followers, teams or collectives through a specific set of leader behaviours for employees to enhance internal motivation and achieve work success" (Cheong et al., 2019, p. 36). Sharma and Kirkman (2015) define empowering leadership as leader behaviours aimed at people or entire teams that include granting authority to staff members, encouraging their autonomy and self-direction in decision-making, providing coaching, disseminating knowledge, and soliciting feedback.

Autonomy and independence are key components of empowering leadership, which are suitable for the hotel sector as it has flattened and decentralised structures with high levels of complexity (Hoang et al., 2021). Empowering leadership is positively linked to employee service-oriented behaviours (Lin et al., 2019), innovative behaviour, creativity, knowledge exchange, and service performance (Guchait et al., 2023). Huertas-Valdivia et al. (2022) propose that empowering leadership impacts employee engagement, satisfaction, and retention. As the hospitality industry is service-oriented, this leadership style is effective in cases of customer incivility, as it may reduce employees' stress, rumination, and withdrawal intentions (Boukis et al., 2020). Baum et al. (2020) highlight the need for agility and innovation among hotel employees since the negative impact of the COVID-19 pandemic. Hotel managers exhibiting empowering leadership styles were found to be customer-driven and demonstrated high organisational commitment (Guchait et al., 2023); they also shared power with their team members allowing them to participate in decision-making and showing confidence in their capabilities (Huertas-Valdivia et al., 2022).

The measurement of empowering leadership can be conducted with nine different measures; however, two are the most represented in the hospitality and tourism field. Arnold et al. (2000) empirically validated a scale with 15 items or five factors of empowering leadership behaviour (leading by example, participative decision-making, coaching, informing, and showing concern). The other scale was developed by Ahearne et al. (2005) with 12 items and four factors (enhancing the meaningfulness of the work, fostering participation in decision-making, expressing confidence in high performance, and providing autonomy from bureaucratic constraints).

Team and organisational culture, climate, and the leader's characteristics are antecedents to empowering leadership (Hoang et al., 2021). Lim and Gon (2021) found a positive association between empowering leadership and products, processes, and innovation in European and American hospitality organisations. Examples of empowering leadership implementation are found in several large hospitality corporations, such as the Ritz Carlton or the Four Seasons, where empowering leadership style development is encouraged as employees tend to depart from regular duties and creatively satisfy customers (Hoang et al., 2021).

Authentic Leadership

Authentic leadership consists of four components during the interaction between the leader and the followers: "greater self-awareness, an internalised moral perspective, balanced processing of information and relational transparency" (Walumbwa et al., 2008, p. 94). It is argued that there are currently only a few studies on authentic leadership in the hospitality industry, although many contend that this may be because this leadership style is relatively new (Gatling et al., 2020). Huertas-Valdivia et al. (2022, p. 2411) suggest that research in "authentic leadership in hospitality will rise in the coming years." Authentic leaders are found to act transparently and morally and positively affect emotional labour (Wang & Xie, 2020). This leadership style is found to positively relate to creating a trust climate (Ling et al., 2017), follower learning and vitality (Chang et al., 2020) and service innovation behaviour, employee work engagement, career satisfaction, and reduced employee turnover (Ribeiro et al., 2020). Job insecurity is reduced as authentic leaders create perceptions of justice in the workplace. Such leaders evaluate all available information and are open to criticism of their views (Wang & Xie, 2020). They continue (ibid.) that authentic leaders act consistently based on their values and are truthful in their relationships, whereas leaders lacking authenticity can increase their followers' work stress. Cole et al. (2012, p. 460) argue that authentic leaders "make subordinates' menial or tedious tasks exciting and enjoyable, leading to job engagement and good performance." Authentic leaders motivate their front-line employees in hospitality to provide service excellence with empowerment and support through incentives such as bonuses, promotion, or recognition; hence employees' emotional regulation is improved, and their work stress is decreased (Walumbwa et al., 2008).

Ethical Leadership

The hospitality industry faces several ethical issues, such as overcharging, overbooking, mistreatment of individuals, theft, and sexual harassment (Schwepker & Dimitriou, 2021). These ethical issues profoundly impact customers and employees in hospitality organisations. *Ethical leadership* is proposed as a leadership style for enhancing the ethical behaviour of employees as it is positively associated with ethical behaviour, job performance, organisational commitment, and job satisfaction (Bedi et al., 2016). Although there is limited research on ethical leadership in hospitality (Hoang et al., 2021; Schwepker & Dimitriou, 2021), hospitality managers may influence the ethical decision-making of employees by primarily exhibiting ethical behaviours. Ethical leadership is defined by Brown et al. (2005, p. 120) as the "demonstration of normatively appropriate conduct through personal actions and interpersonal relationships, and the promotion of such conduct to followers through two-way communication, reinforcement, and decision-making." Ethical leaders are free of bias or prejudice, do not compromise their ethics, and put others' needs first. They also communicate ethical behaviour to their teams and reinforce organisational ethical policies and practices through rewards and punishment (Schwepker & Dimitriou, 2021). Employees may trust such leaders as they serve as role models embodying ethical values and principles. Ethical leaders make organisational ethical expectations clear to followers.

Research on ethical leadership in hospitality is relatively new (Guchait et al., 2023); however, a few studies explore its value in hospitality. For example, Kim and Brymer (2011) found that hotel middle managers' job satisfaction was related to their executives' ethical leadership. Tang et al. (2015) found a connection between ethical leadership, collectivism, and intention to leave. In addition, Schwepker and Dimitriou (2021) proposed that customer orientation and service quality are compatible with ethical leadership. They also propose that employees demonstrate reduced job stress, lower ethical ambiguity, and higher performance when they perceive their managers to act ethically. Tang et al. (2015) claim that the leader-follower value congruence mediates ethical leadership and intention to leave. Finally, job autonomy moderated the relationship between ethical leadership and service innovative behaviour in hospitality employees (Dhar, 2016). Measurement of ethical leadership can be conducted with the use of Reidenbach et al.'s (1991) multidimensional assessment scale. This tool provides a measurement scale of the individual's moral judgement.

If hospitality organisations wish to practice ethical leadership, they should ensure that respective principles and practices are in place. They should recruit based on screening candidates' ethical values, especially when hiring or promoting managers. A training programme for new employees could cover the organisation's ethical principles, values, and code of practice. Employees should be trained in handling ethical issues at work and reporting cases of unethical behaviour. Managers should be trained in communicating and modelling ethical practices and leadership to subordinates. Dimitriou (2020) contends that ethical behaviour should be instilled and emphasised through the hospitality curriculum, which should provide knowledge of multicultural behaviours, excellence in leadership and communication skills, business ethics, and professionalism. Hospitality students should be trained in real-life examples of developing ethical decision-making skills.

Charismatic Leadership

The theory of *charismatic leadership* developed by House (1976) was based on Weber's view of charismatic leaders who viewed them as extremely highly esteemed, gifted people with exemplary qualities (Bass, 1990). Elbaz and Haddoud (2017) propose that charismatic leadership influences wisdom leadership and creates positive job satisfaction in Egyptian hotels. This leadership style has not received much attention in the hospitality industry since charisma has been examined as a component of transformational leadership (Tuan, 2020). Nevertheless, Petrou et al. (2012) suggested that charisma drives followers to adapt to their tasks proactively. Esteves and Lopes (2017) propose that it is related to collective efforts and higher team performance, where employees demonstrate extra-role behaviours and a climate of active learning is developed by such charismatic leaders.

There is neither a specific definition nor a conceptualisation of charisma in organisational studies (Van Knippenberg & Sitkin, 2013). Weber (1947 cited in Northouse, 2001, p. 133) defined charisma as "a special personality characteristic that gives a person superhuman or exceptional powers and is reserved for a few, is of divine origin, and results in the person being treated as a leader." Antonakis et al. (2016) examined the definitions of charismatic leadership provided in six decades of studies (1954–2014) to clearly define this leadership style. By overcoming tautological problems and significant overlap with transformational leadership, their definition captures the common denominator while maintaining construct integrity (Banks et al., 2017). Therefore, Antonakis et al. (2016, p. 304) define charismatic leadership as "values-based, symbolic, and emotion-laden leader signaling," and they further stated that "there is a sore need for a well-done meta-analysis using correct measures of charisma, and this in models that are properly and causally specified" (ibid., p. 311).

Charismatic leadership emphasises emotions and values (Yukl, 1999), with behaviour out of the ordinary and with environmental sensitivity (Armandi et al., 2003), linking followers' self-concepts to the collective identity of the organisation (Tuan, 2020). Hence, charismatic leaders inspire their teams to achieve higher goals (Banks et al., 2017) as they act as role models and are viewed as saviours in crises and may transform the groups or organisations (Bass, 1990). Weber (in Tuan, 2020) provided five components of charismatic leadership:

- a personality with extraordinary abilities (leader),
- social crisis resolution success,
- ability to produce radical solutions in crisis,
- to gain followers' appreciation, and
- to have extraordinary abilities.

Charismatic leadership demonstrates a factor structure comprising six behavioural dimensions: strategic vision and articulation, sensitivity to the environment, sensitivity to follower needs, challenging the status quo, unconventional behaviour, and personal risk (Tuan, 2020, p. 246). A way to measure charismatic leadership is the 20-item scale developed by Conger et al. (2009); this scale has been validated by other studies (i.e., Antonakis et al., 2016; Banks et al., 2017; Conger et al., 2009).

Charismatic leaders are dedicated to their vision and instil faith in a better future (Tuan, 2020). Hence, managers should promote charismatic behaviour in articulating the vision and building trust and confidence in team members. For example, managers may set up regular meetings focusing on goals and discussion of teams' performance, with systematic reflection on performance. In such meetings, charismatic leaders articulate the goals, challenge the team members, and nurture collective identity by building team norms.

Leader-Member Exchange Theory (LMX)

The *Leader-Member Exchange theory* (LMX) has been studied in terms of the relationship developed between the leader and each follower and the quality of such relationships. Chang et al. (2020) argue that there is a lack of research on LMX in hospitality and tourism. Studies conceptualise LMX as a process based on the interaction between leaders and followers (Northouse, 2022); this interaction is a dyadic relationship. Chang et al.

(2020, p. 2155) suggest that "using LMX is likely to depict the specific influence of leadership than using an average leadership perspective." Two types of relationships are identified based on the role theory, in-group and out-group relationships. In-group relationships refer to mutual trust and respect between the leader and the follower, whereas out-group relationships are based on employment contracts. Northouse (2022) suggests that the out-group approach fails to articulate how followers can form relationships with their leaders. Studies on LMX suggest that it positively correlates with employee performance and citizenship behaviours (Chang et al., 2020). However, studies suggest that many outcomes are overlooked, for example, Martin et al. (2016) found trust, empowerment, and job satisfaction to mediate LMX and employee performance. Kim and Koo (2017) propose that in hotels, LMX positively influences job engagement and innovative behaviour, as well as employee voice and job satisfaction.

Leader-Member Exchange leadership is commonly measured with two scales in hospitality and tourism. Firstly, the LMX-7 developed by Graen and Uhl-Bien (1995); secondly, the LMX-MDM (LMX as a multidimensional measure) developed by Liden and Maslyn (1993) with 12 items reflecting four LMX dimensions including contribution, loyalty, affect, and professional respect. Chang et al. (2020) propose that LMX-7 is a simple measurement and more appropriate in the hospitality industry. Leadership in hospitality should be seen and developed at an organisational level due to the communication between leaders and followers. In addition, attention to training on leadership is vital; hence various leadership skills should be part of the training programmes to improve the quality of LMX and help hospitality organisations maintain a good image among employees (Chang et al., 2020).

Other Leadership Theories and Styles

Various leadership styles are proposed to be effective in hospitality and tourism management. Such styles vary depending on the culture, place and context studied. For example, *spiritual leadership* focuses on values and a sense of membership to motivate followers (Guchait et al., 2023).

Communication practices negotiated between the leader and the team form *discursive leadership* (Aritz et al., 2017), whereas leaders' humility forms *humble leadership* (Owens & Hekman, 2016). On the contrary, *abusive leadership* is identified as bad leadership in hospitality. Tepper (2000, p. 178) defined abusive supervision as "subordinates' perceptions of the extent to which supervisors engage in a sustained display of hostile verbal and nonverbal behaviours, excluding physical contact." Such leadership style negatively affects employees' customer service performance and leads to job dissatisfaction and lack of work engagement (Lyu et al., 2016). A similar style is proposed by Wu et al. (2021), titled *exploitative leadership*. Such leadership depends on the followers' perceptions of leaders, and it may not have a hostile component, as exploitative leaders may act in a friendly manner to ensure their interests are satisfied (Wu et al., 2021). Schmid et al. (2019) (cited in Wu et al., 2021, p. 2) proposed five different dimensions of exploitative leadership:

- Demonstrating genuine egoistic behaviours, which reflects a leader's willingness to pursue his or her own goals over followers' needs;
- Exerting pressure, which indicates the pressure put on followers to reach a leader's goals;
- Taking credit, which refers to when a leader represents followers' achievements as his or her own;
- Under challenging followers, which leaves followers with little opportunity to grow; and
- Manipulating followers refers to manipulating or deceiving followers for personal gain.

Finally, *inclusive leadership* focuses on diversity and creating a feeling of belongingness in the team (Shore et al., 2018). Gender is found to moderate and/or mediate the leadership style exhibited by hotel employees. For example, Kara et al. (2018) found that gender plays a role in the way followers perceive their leaders, and Wang et al. (2017, p. 156) suggest that "the relationship between leaders' behavioural integrity and follower trust was stronger for women than for men." *Gender and leadership* are well-researched in hospitality and tourism, but it has been one of the most debated areas with contradicting findings. There are different views on whether gender influences a manager's leadership style and effectiveness. For example, some studies propose that there are *no differences* or interdependence between hotel leadership style and the gender of managers (Raguz, 2007).

Conversely, some argue that there *are differences*—sometimes minor—but in general, they claim that female leaders are more democratic and participative compared to their male counterparts who are more autocratic (Eagly & Johnson, 1990) or that male managers adopt a more transactional leadership style, whereas female managers are more transformational (Eagly & Carli, 2003; Rosener, 1995). Finally, Marinakou (2012), in her study of Greek hotel managers, found that both male and female managers adopt the same/similar leadership style (transformational leadership style), which was more effective for the services industry. Further discussion on gender is provided in Chap. 8.

Since the outbreak of COVID-19, new leadership styles have been introduced. Hospitality and tourism businesses are vulnerable to crisis and safety incidents challenging them with their survival. Nevertheless, a new leadership style, *resilient leadership*, has been introduced by Zhang et al. (2023). Lombardi et al. (2021, p. 1) define resilient leadership as the style that "reveals how leaders lead their teams to 'dance with crises' adapt to multiple adversities and promote business growth." Resilience derives from the managers' and leaders' response to crisis; resilient leadership may include collective leadership, learning, performance orientation, adaptation/change orientation, emotional intelligence, and strategic thinking (Dartey-Baah, 2015). Resilience is found to be a quality of hospitality leaders who deal with challenges and crises and facilitate the recovery of their businesses (Giousmpasoglou et al., 2021). In addition, a fast response to a crisis positively impacts employee job performance (Zhang et al., 2023). It is argued that due to the multidimensional nature of this style, further empirical research is required to rigorously develop the constructs and components of resilient leadership in the hospitality context. There are several instances of businesses that demonstrated resilience during the pandemic. For example, *Ctrip* developed the "BOSS live streaming," including a series of self-rescue measures that helped the business recover (Xie et al., 2022). Leaders with resilient characteristics can help hospitality organisations maintain their dynamic adaptability in crisis. In this case, resilient leaders should be familiar with threats and warning practices and develop contingency plans. Such leaders should be empowered with autonomy and resources to deal with emergencies and crises.

Other approaches are linked to sustainability and the environment; for example, *environmentally-specific servant leadership* is studied by Aboramadan et al. (2021), green inclusive leadership by Bhutto et al. (2021), and environmental transformational leadership by Gurmani et al. (2021) all cited in Hoang et al. (2021). Such leadership styles could be effective for green companies implementing green human resources practices.

Leadership in Contemporary Hotel Management

The predominance of theories borrowed from psychology and sociology is evident in research on leadership in hospitality (Hoang et al., 2021). Some theories or trends may not be applicable to hospitality research; hence research on leadership should address the distinctive conditions in hotel management. Various leadership styles are identified in hospitality management, some of which are effective in the services industries, such as transformational leadership (Marinakou, 2012). Employee expectations from the leader have changed in contemporary hospitality organisations. The leaders' attitudes and behaviours play an important role in the followers' integration with the organisation, their organisational commitment, job satisfaction, and intention to stay in business. Leaders who do not communicate effectively with their teams, are disrespectful, and do not create a culture of trust cause low employee morale, reduced performance, and increased staff turnover (Rose, 2016). Therefore, leadership styles such as transactional or authoritative are found to be dysfunctional in today's hospitality and tourism industry. Such leadership approaches are outdated and counterproductive, and hotel managers should reject them as they undermine collaboration, inspiration, and employees' wellbeing.

Empirical studies have shown that employees prefer to be empowered during a crisis, especially when they work from home (i.e., during COVID-19) (Stoker et al., 2021); hence empowering leadership may contribute to employees' wellbeing, resilience, and job performance. Regardless of the style hospitality managers adopt, an effective leadership style is needed to engage and retain employees in the hotel sector. High turnover, deviant behaviours, and low productivity create high costs and threaten the hotel sector. As a result, hotel managers should be aware of the elements and traits that make up each leadership style and choose the one they feel will work best for their teams. For example, servant and authentic leadership are relationship-oriented and focused on developing good connections. Transformational leadership is leader-organisation centred and is effective in luxury hospitality (Marinakou, 2012). Effective leadership requires characteristics associated with women and men, such as emotional intelligence, risk-taking, empathy, and integrity (Marinakou, 2014). Both women and men demonstrate the same degree of commitment to their jobs; as a result, they can both be effective hotel leaders.

On the other hand, a more feminine transformational leadership style is effective for hotel management and outperforming organisations (McKinsey, 2020). Although reports indicate the lack of women in leadership positions, many propose that women may be better leaders in hotels and are found to be rated by others as more effective than male managers. Contemporary hotels face many challenges in managing human resources, motivating employees, and encouraging them to make decisions, think outside the box, solve problems, and adapt their behaviour to provide efficient service. In such a competitive environment, hotel leaders should develop and use the most effective leadership style, which we argue is transformational leadership; this promotes all the required employee skills (mentioned above) and encompasses ethical, authentic, servant, and inclusive leadership styles. Therefore, we can easily assume that an effective leadership style is the catalyst to achieve performance towards success and cohesion.

Box 5.1 Women in Leadership—The Carlyle Example

Making History at The Carlyle: Marlene Poynder is the First Woman to Lead the Iconic NYC Hotel

Australian Marlene Poynder is in a place everyone wants to be, leading a bastion of New York City's style and glamour, The Carlyle Hotel, a Rosewood Hotel. An Upper East Side institution since it opened in 1930, The Carlyle, a Rosewood Hotel has become synonymous with luxury, status, and sophistication. The Carlyle, a Rosewood Hotel was home base for the Duke and Duchess of Sussex on their visit to New York, where a video of them at the famed Bemelmans bar surfaced on the 'net. And now the iconic property is making history once again by choosing a woman to continue to uphold its impressive legacy. Heavy lies the crown. She responded to some questions:

What qualities make for an effective leader? Stamina, Empathy, and Emotional Intelligence. A willingness to admit when you are wrong.

You're the first woman to lead The Carlyle, a Rosewood Hotel in the 90+ year history of the property. Congrats! Do you think there was a barrier for women to lead iconic hotels that has been broken now? If so, why? You know I have been hoping for the past 30 years that the barrier would break. I do truly believe we are at a turning point now for women in hospitality. There are enough women leaders in place and men in power now that see the value a woman can bring to the leadership roles in hospitality. Caring and nurturing are within our DNA. Both skills are required in our industry.

What are your biggest challenges in taking over this beloved NYC institution? An almost one-hundred-year-old building. Being the steward to manage the legacy of The Carlyle whilst introducing the iconic lady to a new generation.

Source: Goldfischer (2022); www.hertelier.com

Moreover, globalisation has transformed how hotels are structured, becoming less hierarchical. Such flat organisations require a transformational leadership style based on collaborative, caring, and nurturing characteristics (Giousmpasoglou et al., 2021; Marinakou, 2014; Sobaih et al., 2022). With its constant evolution and globalisation, the dynamic work environment in the hospitality industry requires transformational leaders. To sum up, transformational leaders are associated with a "feminine style" in which they are caring, encourage followers, and directly and positively impact the employees, the organisation, and the industry.

Leaders have different roles in different cultures and types of businesses; hence what works in one case may not apply in another (Hoang et al., 2021). Based on this argument, research and empirical data should be provided from cross-cultural studies on leadership, comparing leadership styles, or study leadership in underexplored countries to enrich the findings on theories on leadership in hotel management. Moreover, younger generations (i.e., Generation Z) seek inspiration, feedback on their performance, collaboration, prioritize roles, and are interested in career development and growth opportunities, but most importantly, they are passionate and pursue value-driven work (Giousmpasoglou et al., 2021). Hotel managers should allocate resources to address their needs and develop future leaders, as such, employees prefer companies that offer balanced approaches to work and life, have wellbeing practices, and provide opportunities to grow (Goh & Okumus, 2020).

In today's hospitality and tourism industry, demand for quality services is erratic; hence, human capital should be managed effectively to fit each business' budget and revenue targets. All studies discussed above provide evidence that hospitality organisations should focus on recruiting leaders who will inspire their teams and will contribute to retaining staff. In this case, leadership training and advancement programmes for managers should be provided to demonstrate the recognition of the importance of leadership and practicing the necessary skills to empower subordinates and lead teams successfully. Figure 5.5 summarizes the key issues, challenges, and findings discussed in this chapter in an effort to illustrate what it takes for effective leadership development and practice in hospitality management.

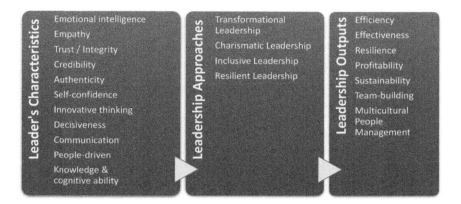

Fig. 5.5 Effective leadership in contemporary hotel management. (Source: Authors' creation)

Chapter Summary

Leadership is a concept widely researched in management and organisational studies; however, there is still a need to define leadership in hospitality management and explore the most effective style in hotel management to improve guest services and maintain high performance. Hotels operating in a fiercely competitive sector challenged by a diversified workforce and a talent shortage may see leadership as a way to acquire a competitive edge. Such organisations should utilize human resources effectively to increase performance, deal with competition, adapt to changes, and show resilience (Giousmpasoglou et al., 2021). Most hospitality leadership studies argue that no leadership style can be used in every circumstance and that leaders have different approaches to managing their teams and organisations. Nevertheless, we argue that traditional approaches to leadership in the hotel sector are less effective in engaging and empowering employees, considering the growing complexity of today's hospitality and tourism context. Transformational leadership may be the most effective leadership style, including hiring, training, and empowering employees in creating a competitive organisation.

References

Ahearne, M., Mathieu, J., & Rapp, A. (2005). To empower or not to empower your sales force? An empirical examination of the influence of leadership empowerment behavior on customer satisfaction and performance. *Journal of Applied Psychology, 90*(5), 945–955.

Antonakis, J., Bastardoz, N., Jacquart, P., & Shamir, B. (2016). Charisma: An ill-defined and ill-measured gift. *Annual Review of Organizational Psychology and Organizational Behavior, 3*(1), 293–319.

Antonakis, J., Bastardoz, N., Liu, Y., & Schriesheim, C. A. (2014). What makes articles highly cited? *The Leadership Quarterly, 25*(1), 152–179.

Aritz, J., Walker, R., Cardon, P., & Li, Z. (2017). Discourse of leadership: The power of questions in organizational decision making. *International Journal of Business Communication, 54*(2), 161–181.

Armandi, B., Oppedisano, J., & Sherman, H. (2003). Leadership theory and practice: A case in point. *Management Decision, 41*(10), 1076–1088.

Arnold, J. A., Arad, S., Rhoades, J. A., & Drasgow, F. (2000). The empowering leadership questionnaire: The construction and validation of a new scale for measuring leader behaviors. *Journal of Organizational Behavior, 21*(3), 249–269.

Avolio, B. J., Zhu, W., Koh, W., & Bhatia, A. (2004). Transformational leadership and organizational commitment: Mediating role of psychological empowerment and moderating role of structural distance. *Journal of Occupational and Organizational Psychology, 25*, 951–968.

Banks, G. C., Engemann, K. N., Williams, C. E., Gooty, J., McCauley, K. D., & Medaugh, M. R. (2017). A meta-analytic review and future research agenda of charismatic leadership. *The Leadership Quarterly, 28*, 508–529.

Barker, R. A. (2001). The nature of leadership. *Human Relations, 54*(4), 469–494.

Bass, B. M. (1985). *Leadership and performance beyond expectations*. The Free Press.

Bass, B. M. (1990). *Bass and Stogdill's handbook of leadership, theory, research and managerial implications* (3rd ed.). The Free Press.

Bass, B. M., & Avolio, B. J. (Eds.). (1994). *Improving organizational effectiveness through transformational leadership*. Sage Publications, Inc.

Baum, T., Mooney, S. K., Robinson, R. N., & Solnet, D. (2020). COVID-19's impact on the hospitality workforce–new crisis or amplification of the norm? *International Journal of Contemporary Hospitality Management, 32*(9), 2813–2829.

Bavik, A. (2020). A systematic review of the servant leadership literature in management and hospitality. *International Journal of Contemporary Hospitality Management, 32*(1), 347–382.

Bedi, A., Alpaslan, C. M., & Green, G. (2016). A meta-analytic review of ethical leadership outcomes and moderators. *Journal of Business Ethics, 139*(3), 517–536.

Boukis, A., Koritos, C., Daunt, K. L., & Papastathopoulos, A. (2020). Effects of customer incivility on frontline employees and the moderating role of supervisor leadership style. *Tourism Management, 77*, 103997.

Brown, M. E., Trevino, L. K., & Harrison, D. A. (2005). Ethical leadership: A social learning perspective for construct development and testing. *Organizational Behavior Human Decision Process, 97*(2), 117–134.

Brownell, J. (2010). Leadership in the service of hospitality. *Cornell Hospitality Quarterly, 51*(3), 363–378.

Burns, J. M. (1978). *Leadership*. Harper and Row.

Chang, W., Liu, A., Wang, X., & Yi, B. (2020). Meta-analysis of outcomes of leader–member exchange in hospitality and tourism: What does the past say about the future? *International Journal of Contemporary Hospitality Management, 32*(6), 2155–2173.

Cheong, M., Yammarino, F. J., Dionne, S. D., Spain, S. M., & Tsai, C. Y. (2019). A review of the effectiveness of empowering leadership. *The Leadership Quarterly, 30*(1), 34–58.

Chon, K. K., & Zoltan, J. (2019). Role of servant leadership in contemporary hospitality. *International Journal of Contemporary Hospitality Management, 31*(8), 3371–3394.

Cole, M. S., Bruch, H., & Vogel, B. (2012). Energy at work: A measurement validation and linkage to unit effectiveness. *Journal of Organizational Behavior, 33*(4), 445–467.

Conger, J. A., Kanungo, R. N., & Menon, S. T. (2009). Measuring Charisma: Dimensionality and validity of the Conger-Kanungo Scale of Charismatic Leadership. *Canadian Journal of Administrative Sciences, 14*(3), 290–301.

Dartey-Baah, K. (2015). Resilient leadership: A transformational-transactional leadership mix. *Journal of Global Responsibility, 6*(1), 99–112.

Dhar, R. L. (2016). Ethical leadership and its impact on service innovative behavior: The role of LMX and job autonomy. *Tourism Management, 57*(12), 139–148.

Dimitriou, C. K. (2020). Adjusting our teaching strategies, material, and techniques to the new standards. In *The Tourism Education Futures Initiatives*

(TEFI) 11-What's tourism got to do with it? York St. John University. York, United Kingdom (Virtual Conference).

Eagly, A. H., & Carli, L. L. (2003). The female leadership advantage: An evaluation of the evidence. *The Leadership Quarterly, 14*(6), 807–834.

Eagly, A. H., & Johnson, B. T. (1990). Gender and leadership style: A meta-analysis. *Psychological Bulletin, 108*(2), 233–256.

Elbaz, A. M., & Haddoud, M. Y. (2017). The role of wisdom leadership in increasing job performance: Evidence from the Egyptian tourism sector. *Tourism Management, 63*, 66–76.

Elkhwesky, Z., Salem, I. E., Ramkissoon, H., & Castaneda-Garcia, J. A. (2022). A systematic and critical review of leadership styles in contemporary hospitality: A roadmap and a call for future research. *International Journal of Contemporary Hospitality Management, 34*(5), 1925–1958.

Erkutlu, H. V., & Chafra, J. (2006). Relationship between leadership power bases and job stress of subordinates: Example from boutique hotels. *Management Research News, 29*(5), 285–297.

Esteves, T., & Lopes, M. P. (2017). Leading to crafting: The relation between leadership perception and nurses' job crafting. *Western Journal of Nursing Research, 39*(6), 763–783.

Gatling, A., Molintas, D. H. R., Self, T. T., & Shum, C. (2020). Leadership and behavioral integrity in the restaurant industry: The moderating roles of gender. *Journal of Human Resources in Hospitality and Tourism, 19*(1), 62–81.

Gavin, M. (2019). *Leadership vs management: What's the difference?* Business Insights. https://online.hbs.edu/blog/post/leadership-vs-management

Gill, A., Mathur, N., Sharma, S. P., & Bhutani, S. (2011). The effects of empowerment and transformational leadership on employee intentions to quit: A study of restaurant workers in India. *International Journal of Management, 28*(1), 217.

Giousmpasoglou, C., Marinakou, E., & Zopiatis, A. (2021). Hospitality managers in turbulent times: The COVID-19 crisis. *International Journal of Contemporary Hospitality Management, 33*(4), 1297–1318.

Goh, E., & Okumus, F. (2020). Avoiding the hospitality workforce bubble: Strategies to attract and retain generation Z talent in the hospitality workforce. *Tourism Management Perspectives, 33*, 100603.

Goldfischer, E. (2022). *Making history at the Carlyle: Marlene Poynder is the first women to lead the iconic NYC hotel.* https://www.hertelier.com/post/the-carlyle-marlene-poynder

Graen, George B., & Uhl-Bien, M. (1995). *Relationship-Based Approach to Leadership: Development of Leader-Member Exchange (LMX) Theory of Leadership over 25 Years: Applying a Multi-Level Multi-Domain Perspective.* Management Department Faculty Publications. 57. https://digitalcommons.unl.edu/managementfacpub/57

Greenleaf, R. K. (1977). *Servant leadership: A journey into the nature of legitimate power and greatness.* Paulist Press.

Guchait, P., Peyton, T., Madera, J.M., Gip, H., & Molina-Collado, A. (2023). 21st century leadership research in hospitality management: A state-of-the-art systematic literature review. *International Journal of Contemporary Hospitality Management*, Vol. ahead-of-print No. ahead-of-print. https://doi.org/10.1108/IJCHM-05-2022-0620

Gui, C., Luo, A., Zhang, P., & Deng, A. (2020). A meta-analysis of transformational leadership in hospitality research. *International Journal of Contemporary Hospitality Management, 32*(6), 2137–2154.

Gui, C., Zhang, P., Zou, R., & Ouyang, X. (2021). Servant leadership in hospitality: A meta-analytic review. *Journal of Hospitality Marketing & Management, 30*(4), 438–458.

Hoang, G., Wilson-Evered, E., Lockstone-Binney, L., & Luu, T. T. (2021). Empowering leadership in hospitality and tourism management: A systematic literature review. *International Journal of Contemporary Hospitality Management, 33*(12), 4182–4214.

Huertas-Valdivia, I., Gonzalez-Torres, T., & Najera-Sanchez, J. (2022). Contemporary leadership in hospitality: A review and research agenda. *International Journal of Contemporary Hospitality Management, 34*(6), 2399–2422.

Kara, D., Kim, H. L., Lee, G., & Uysal, M. (2018). The moderating effects of gender and income between leadership and quality of work life (QWL). *International Journal of Contemporary Hospitality Management, 30*(3), 1419–1435.

Kim, M. S., & Koo, D. W. (2017). Linking LMX, engagement, innovative behavior, and job performance in hotel employees. *International Journal of Contemporary Hospitality Management, 29*(12), 3044–3062.

Kim, W. G., & Brymer, R. A. (2011). The effects of ethical leadership on manager job satisfaction, commitment, behavioral outcomes, and firm performance. *International Journal of Hospitality Management, 30*(4), 1020–1026.

Lee, Y. K., Kim, Y., Son, M. H., & Lee, D. J. (2011). Do emotions play a mediating role in the relationship between owner leadership styles and manager customer orientation, and performance in service environment? *International Journal of Hospitality Management, 30*(4), 942–952.

Liden, R. C., & Maslyn, J. (1993). Multidimensionafity of Leader-Member Exchange: An empirical assessment through Scale development. *Journal of Management, 24*(1), 43–72.

Lim, S., & Gon, E. (2021). Fostering absorptive capacity and facilitating innovation in hospitality organizations through empowering leadership. *International Journal of Hospitality Management, 94*, 102780.

Lin, M., Ling, Q., Luo, Z., & Wu, X. (2019). Why does empowering leadership occur and matter? A multilevel study of Chinese hotels. *Tourism Management Perspectives, 32*, 1–11.

Ling, Q., Liu, F., & Wu, X. (2017). Servant versus authentic leadership: Assessing effectiveness in China's hospitality industry. *Cornell Hospitality Quarterly, 58*(1), 53–68.

Lombardi, S., Cunha, P., & Giustiniano, L. (2021). Improvising resilience: The unfolding of resilient leadership in covid-19 times. *International Journal of Hospitality Management, 95*, 1–13.

Lyu, Y., Zhu, H., Zhong, H. J., & Hu, L. (2016). Abusive supervision and customer-oriented organizational citizenship behavior: The roles of hostile attribution bias and work engagement. *International Journal of Hospitality Management, 53*, 69–80.

Marinakou, E. (2012). *An investigation of gender influences on transformational leadership style in the Greek hospitality industry*. PhD Thesis, Business School, University of Strathclyde.

Marinakou, E. (2014). Women in hotel management and leadership: Diamond or Glass? *Journal of Tourism and Hospitality Management, 2*(1), 18–25.

Martin, R., Guillaume, Y., Thomas, G., Lee, A., & Epitropaki, O. (2016). Leader–member exchange (LMX) and performance: a meta-analytic review. *Personnel Psychology, 69*(1), 67–121.

McKinsey & Company. (2020). *Diversity wins. How inclusion matters.* https://www.mckinsey.com/~/media/mckinsey/featured%20insights/diversity%20and%20inclusion/diversity%20wins%20how%20inclusion%20matters/diversity-wins-how-inclusion-matters-vf.pdf

Murari, K., & Gupta, K. S. (2012). Impact of servant leadership on employee empowerment. *Journal of Strategic Human Resource Management, 1*(1), 28.

Northouse, P. G. (2001). *Leadership theory and practice* (2nd ed.). Sage Publications.

Northouse, P. G. (2022). *Leadership, theory and practice* (9th ed.). SAGE.

Owens, B. P., & Hekman, D. R. (2016). How does leader humility influence team performance? Exploring the mechanisms of contagion and collective promotion focus. *The Academy of Management Journal, 59*(3), 1088–1111.

Petrou, P., Demerouti, E., Peeters, M. C., Schaufeli, W. B., & Hetland, J. (2012). Crafting a job on a daily basis: Contextual correlates and the link to work engagement. *Journal of Organizational Behavior, 33*(8), 1120–1141.

Qiu, S., & Dooley, L. M. (2019). Servant leadership development and validation of a multidimensional measure in the Chinese hospitality industry. *Leadership & Organization Development Journal, 40*(2), 193–212.

Qiu, S., Dooley, L. M., & Xie, L. (2020). How servant leadership and self-efficacy interact to affect service quality in the hospitality industry: A polynomial regression with response surface analysis. *Tourism Management, 78*, 104051.

Raguz, I. V. (2007). The interdependence between characteristics and leadership style of Managers in the hospitality industry in Dubrovnik-Neratva country. *Empirical Research Management, 12*(2), 57–68.

Reidenbach, R. E., Robin, D. P., & Dawson, L. (1991). An application and extension of a multidimensional ethics scale to selected marketing practices. *Journal of Academic Marketing Science, 19*(2), 83–92.

Ribeiro, N., Duarte, P., & Fidalgo, J. (2020). Authentic leadership's effect on customer orientation and turnover intention among Portuguese hospitality employees: The mediating role of affective commitment. *International Journal of Contemporary Hospitality Management, 32*(6), 2097–2116.

Rose, A. (2016). *6 Reasons hospitality employees leave and contribute to high turnover.* https://www.hcareers.com/article/employer-articles/6-reasons-hospitality-employees-leave-and-contribute-to-high-turnover

Rosener, J. B. (1995). Ways women lead. *Harvard Business Review, 68*, 119–125.

Ruben, B. D., & Gigliotti, R. A. (2017). Communication: Sine qua non of organizational leadership theory and practice. *International Journal of Business Communication, 54*(1), 12–30.

Russell, R. F., & Stone, A. G. (2002). A review of servant leadership attributes: Developing a practical model. *Leadership and Organization Development Journal, 23*(3), 145–157.

Schwepker, C. H., & Dimitriou, C. K. (2021). Using ethical leadership to reduce job stress and improve performance quality in the hospitality industry. *International Journal of Hospitality Management, 94*, 102860.

Sharma, P., & Kirkman, B. (2015). Leveraging leaders: A literature review and future lines of inquiry for empowering leadership research. *Group and Organization Management, 40*(2), 193–237.

Shore, L. M., Cleveland, J. N., & Sanchez, D. (2018). Inclusive workplaces: A review and model. *Human Resource Management Review, 28*(2), 176–189.

Shum, C., Gatling, A., & Tu, M. H. (2020). When do abusive leaders experience guilt? *International Journal of Contemporary Hospitality Management, 32*(6), 2239–2256.

Sobaih, A. E. E., Hasanein, A. M., Aliedan, M. M., & Abdallah, H. S. (2022). The impact of transactional leadership on employee intention to stay in deluxe hotels: Mediating role of organisational commitment. *Tourism and Hospitality Research, 22*(3), 257–270.

Spears, L. C. (1995). *Reflections on leadership: How Robert K. Greenleaf's Theory of Servant Leadership Influenced Today's Top Management Thinkers*. John Wiley.

Stoker, J. I., Garretsen, H., & Lammers, J. (2021). Leading and working from home in times of COVID-19: On the perceived changes in leadership behaviors. *Journal of Leadership Organizational Studies*, 1–11.

Tang, G., Cai, Z., Liu, Z., Zhu, H., Yang, X., & Li, J. (2015). The importance of ethical leadership in employees' value congruence and turnover. *Cornell Hospitality Quarterly, 56*(4), 397–410.

Tepper, B. J. (2000). Consequences of abusive supervision. *Academy of Management Journal, 43*(2), 178–190.

The Ritz Carlton Gold standards. (2017). *Motto*. https://www.ritzcarlton.com/en/about/goldstandards/

Tuan, L. T. (2020). Crafting the sales job collectively in the tourism industry: The roles of charismatic leadership and collective person-group fit. *Journal of Hospitality and Tourism Management, 45*, 245–255.

Van Knippenberg, D., & Sitkin, S. B. (2013). A critical assessment of charismatic—Transformational leaders research: Back to the drawing board? *The Academy of Management Annals, 7*(1), 1–60.

Walumbwa, F., Avolio, B., Gardner, W., Wernsing, T., & Peterson, S. (2008). Authentic leadership: Development and validation of a theory-based measure. *Journal of Management, 34*(1), 89–126.

Wang, C. J., Tsai, H. T., & Tsai, M. T. (2014). Linking transformational leadership and employee creativity in the hospitality industry: The influences of creative role identity, creative self-efficacy and job complexity. *Tourism Management, 40*, 79–89.

Wang, L., Jiang, W., Liu, Z., & Ma, X. (2017). Shared leadership and team effectiveness: The examination of LMX differentiation and servant leadership on the emergence and consequences of shared leadership. *Human Performance, 30*(4), 155–168.

Wang, Z., & Xie, Y. (2020). Authentic leadership and employees' emotional labour in the hospitality industry. *International Journal of Contemporary Hospitality Management, 32*(2), 797–814.

Wu, L. Z., Sun, Z., Ye, Y., Kwan, H. K., & Yang, M. (2021). The impact of exploitative leadership on frontline hospitality employees' service performance: A social exchange perspective. *International Journal of Hospitality Management, 96*, 102954.

Wu, L. Z., Ye, Y., Cheng, X. M., Kwan, H. K., & Lyu, Y. (2020). Fuel the service fire. *International Journal of Contemporary Hospitality Management, 32*(5), 1755–1773.

Xie, C., Zhang, J., Morrison, A. M., & Chen, Y. (2022). Hotel employee perceived crisis shocks: Conceptual and scale development. *Journal of Hospitality and Tourism Management, 51*, 361–374.

Ye, Y., Lyu, Y., & He, Y. (2019). Servant leadership and proactive customer service performance. *International Journal of Contemporary Hospitality Management, 31*(3), 1330–1347.

Youssef, D. A. (1998). Correlates of perceived leadership style in a culturally mixed environment. *Leadership and Organization Development Journal, 19*(5), 275–284.

Yu, Y., Xu, S., Li, G., & Kong, H. (2020). A systematic review of research on abusive supervision in hospitality and tourism. *International Journal of Contemporary Hospitality Management, 32*(7), 2473–2496.

Yukl, G. (1999). An evaluation of conceptual weaknesses in transformational and charismatic leadership theories. *The Leadership Quarterly, 10*(2), 285–305.

Zhang, J., Xie, C., & Huang, S. (2023). Resilient leadership in hospitality and tourism enterprises: Conceptualization and scale development. *International Journal of Contemporary Hospitality Management*. https://www.emerald.com/insight/0959-6119.htm

6

Human Resources Management in Hotels

Photo Credits: *Tima Miroshnichenko* (*Free to use under the Pexels License*). (Source: https://www.pexels.com/photo/coworkers-in-a-conference-room-having-a-meeting-5439486/)

Introduction

The hotel sector is fast-growing and contributes significantly to the global economy; it is also the biggest employer in the global hospitality and tourism industry. The sector peaked at 1.52 trillion US dollars in 2019, estimated to reach 1.21 trillion US dollars in 2023 after the drop between 2020 and 2022 due to COVID-19 (Statista, 2023). McCain (2023) reports that there are at least 187,000 hotels worldwide, making the hospitality industry worth over 4.6 trillion US dollars in 2022 and the hotel market worth over 1.5 trillion US dollars in 2019. According to Thoreson (2023), reporting on the AHLA survey, 47% of the hotels in the research were severely understaffed in 2021, making it impossible to fill the available vacancies. Managing people in the hotel sector is challenging, particularly in terms of recruitment, training, and talent management.

This chapter investigates the hospitality industry's Human Resources Management (HRM) function, focusing on hotels. More specifically, the application of the core HRM functions (namely, Planning, Recruitment and Selection, Training and Development, Performance and Reward, and Employee Relations) as fundamental components of global Hospitality Management are critically discussed. This chapter includes examples of best practices from the industry as well as contemporary research findings. There are also recommendations on how employers should manage HRM challenges.

HRM in the Hotel Management Context

The hospitality industry is challenged by environmental changes, increased competition, radical technological changes, crises, and other social events that impact employment. Rising labour costs, shortage of skills, changing employees' attitudes, labour law, and legislation are among the many aspects that impact managing people in the hospitality industry. Successful hospitality organisations should be able to react, adapt, and change to the challenges in the context in which they operate. The most recent example is the hotel sector's response to the COVID-19 pandemic, which caused numerous problems. Many hotels had to close, some did not reopen, and hotel managers had to be resilient and adaptive in managing their businesses and employees (Giousmpasoglou et al., 2021). Furthermore, the exponential growth of multinational hotel chains such as Marriott, Hilton, and Accor and the rapid development of franchising and management contracts and businesses in the sharing economy, such as Airbnb, intensified the competition in attracting qualified hospitality workers. The hotel sector is not only heterogeneous in structure and ownership but also labour-intensive, with great diversity among people working there (Baum et al., 2020).

The unfavourable working conditions in the hotel sector have always been a barrier to attracting qualified employees. People are discouraged from seeking hotel employment due to the long hours, low pay, and low status, all of which exacerbate many of the sector's resourcing challenges (Baum, 2015). Other factors that impact perceptions about employment in the hotel sector include the characteristics of the hospitality workforce, such as age, gender, transient and migrant workers, labour turnover posing skills shortages, and recruitment issues; all these factors have implications for managing people effectively in hotels (Boella & Goss-Turner, 2020).

Within this context, hospitality organisations should employ people capable of managing employees and human resources. Until the 1960s, personnel management was a hotel specialist function, emphasising the administrative and transactional aspects of managing employees (Boella & Goss-Turner, 2020). Personnel management focuses on routine tasks such as hiring, payroll, compliance with labour laws, and managing employee benefits. Personnel management is often seen as reactive, primarily ensuring legal compliance and maintaining a stable workforce. Today, almost all hotels employ Human Resource (HR) specialists; medium- and large-sized hotels have an HR department with various titles for managers, such as *Director of People* and *Talent Acquisition Manager* among others (Baum, 2015). The HRM perspective places a greater emphasis on the strategic role of employees within an organisation. HRM is viewed as a more comprehensive and integrated approach that aligns human resource practices with the hotel's overall strategic objectives. This approach emphasises employee development, performance management, talent acquisition, employee engagement, and creating a positive work culture. The main difference is the scope and orientation of the two management practices: personnel management is limited to managing staff's day-to-day tasks; on the other hand, HRM has a broader scope in managing people effectively and responsibly to enhance the hotel's performance.

Defining HRM

The Human Resources Management (HRM) debate revolves around the various interpretations and perspectives on what constitutes HRM and how it differs from traditional personnel management. This debate has been ongoing since the emergence of the field in the mid-twentieth century (Heery & Noon, 2008). Storey (2007, p. 6) defined HRM as:

> *the distinctive approach to employment management, which seeks to achieve competitive advantage through the strategic deployment of highly committed and capable workforce, using an integrated array of cultural, structural and personnel techniques.*

According to Stone (1998), HRM is the productive use of people to attain an organisation's strategic business objectives and fulfil individual employee needs. Furthermore, Armstrong and Taylor (2020) defined HRM as all those activities associated with managing employment relationships in the firm. Today, HRM is seen as a strategic approach to managing people integrated with corporate strategy, organisational culture, and the goals of high staff commitment and organisational performance (Boella & Goss-Turner, 2020). HRM plays an active role in strategic planning in hotels in terms of managing human capital. According to Ashton (2018), HRM's primary objectives are to improve employee satisfaction, increase employee commitment, and address labour and skill shortages issues.

There are two approaches to human resources management proposed: hard and soft. *Hard HRM* refers to people management strategies driven by an organisational strategy to gain competitive advantage while simultaneously maximising control with the lowest possible labour cost. This approach emphasises the resource management aspects of HRM. *Soft HRM*, on the other hand, is a people management approach that is more humanistic, aims to foster reciprocal commitment, and focuses on the human aspects of HRM (Nickson, 2013). According to Worsfold (1999) the soft HRM version is preferred in luxury hotels, while the hard version is preferred in budget hotels.

The Human Resources Management Functions

As already discussed, managing human resources is vital for hospitality organisations. The right people in the right position are necessary to attain organisational goals based on the organisation's strategy and quality standards to deliver services. Therefore, we argue that HRM contributes to the failure or success of hotels. There is no doubt that people are the most valuable resource in hotels. The HR department's responsibilities and functions include how hotel employees and managers are hired and managed (Armstrong & Taylor, 2020). The basic HRM processes and practices are usually the same in any organisation, including hotels. The HRM key functions and the HRM cycle in hotels are clearly illustrated in Fig. 6.1.

Human Resources Planning

Human Resources (HR) Planning is the foundation of all HRM activities as it is the stage where decisions are made based on analysis of staff requirements in the hotel. HRM practices emphasise strategic (long-term) planning of the workforce (Armstrong, 2017); decisions linked to the overall performance of the hotel should be based on relevant and appropriate data (Madera et al., 2017). Furthermore, labour costs are associated with growth and development in HR plans to ensure future competitiveness and profitability (Baum et al., 2020). Hence, successful HRM in hotels requires understanding the organisation, its culture, objectives, management style, and operating environment. HR planning is defined by Boella and Goss-Turner (2020, p. 96) as:

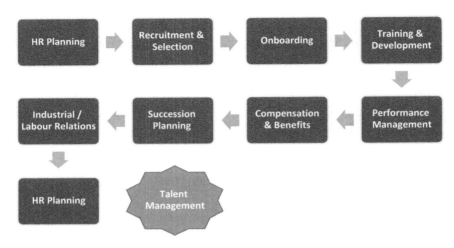

Fig. 6.1 The HRM cycle in hotels. (Source: Authors' creation)

the process of interpreting the employment environment, predicting its effects on the organisation, evaluating these effects and planning and controlling appropriate recruitment measures in order that the company possesses an effective and efficient human resource; basically the right people in the right place at the right time.

The HR Planning may be divided into the *Strategic* and *Operational* functions. *Strategic HR Planning* is concerned with aligning HR practices with the overall goals and objectives of the hotel, ensuring that the right people with the right skills are in place to deliver exceptional guest experiences and meet business objectives. Strategic planning includes functions and practices such as talent acquisition and retention, training and development, succession planning, and diversity management. On the other hand, *Operational HR Planning* focuses on the day-to-day activities of the HR department and the execution of strategies formulated at the strategic level. Operational HR planning activities include scheduling, performance management, employee relations, compensation and benefits, and compliance (Storey, 2007).

Recruitment and Selection

Recruitment and Selection are crucial HR functions in the hotel industry to ensure that the right candidates are hired for various positions, from front-line staff to managerial roles. The hotel industry is highly customer-oriented, so having a skilled and motivated team is essential for providing exceptional service and maintaining the hotel's reputation. *Recruitment and Selection (R&S)* refers to the process of finding, recruiting, and selecting people to fill new or existing positions, and it is considered an important process for organisational success. Heery and Noon (2008, p. 381) defined Recruitment as "the process of generating a pool of candidates from which to select the appropriate person to fill a job vacancy." It is a dynamic process as organisations seek the best candidate but at the same time try "to portray a positive image to potential applicants" (Nickson, 2013, p. 92). Consequently, hotels with excellent brand reputations attract 50% more qualified applicants (Liu-Lastres et al., 2023).

For Recruitment, a range of tools is available for HR managers, such as job analysis, job description, and person specification to determine potential employees' knowledge, skills, attributes, and competencies. Recruitment is an activity where line managers also participate as they contribute to the decision on Selection; hence, anyone involved in this process should be equipped with the appropriate knowledge and skills (CIPD, 2023a).

The first step in R&S refers to *internal recruitment methods*, that is, promoting or transferring existing employees. Looking internally to fill vacancies is considered a good management practice that positively impacts staff morale, loyalty, and commitment to the organisation. Information on such jobs may be announced internally at information boards, meetings, the employees' intranet, or through an application process. *External recruitment methods* are often used when the vacancy is not covered internally. The cost of R&S, the best method to attract suitable candidates, and the time needed for the process are key factors to consider (Boella & Goss-Turner, 2020). Recruitment campaigns are often expensive; for example, the Chartered Institute of Personnel and Development (CIPD) in 2017 estimated an average cost of £6000 for recruiting a senior manager and £2000 for other posts.

The R&S process is found to be challenging for smaller hotels as they lack systematic procedures and resources (Nickson, 2013). Furthermore, poor R&S practices negatively affect hotels, resulting in high labour turnover, absenteeism, and low morale (Baum, 2015). Finding and selecting the best candidates requires proper HR planning, effective R&S strategy and practices, and acknowledgement that this process should be done cost-effectively. For example, good knowledge of the local market could decrease the impact of a lack of practices for small hotels (Lockyer & Scholarios, 2004). The notion of "fit" between the candidate and the organisation should be considered.

A variety of recruitment methods are available nowadays. Internet-based methods have replaced traditional job advertisements. Independent operators and hotel chains use their websites to attract candidates under sections usually titled "Careers" or "Working with Us" with details on job vacancies, job descriptions, and instructions on applying online. Other professional networks are used for recruitment advertising, that is, LinkedIn, Hospitality Associations, or even Twitter (CIPD, 2017). Hotels' websites and other online recruitment forms ensure that the recruitment process is transparent and fair. Nevertheless, there are concerns as recruiters often delve into candidates' social media instead of looking at their professional online profiles. Hawes (2018) warns candidates, especially young people, to ensure their profiles have appropriate privacy settings and to check on platforms like "Glassdoor" the company's profile and comments from other people.

R&S for hotels is an important HR function, requiring various strategies and approaches in tackling the challenges of skills shortage and the poor industry image. HR managers should use various methods to attract new candidates and talent, such as participating in career fairs, supporting apprenticeships, and developing graduate training schemes. Regardless of the approach used, country-specific employment legislation relating to recruitment practices should be considered. Compliance with such laws significantly impacts managers' decisions on the entire R&S process.

Induction and Onboarding

Induction and *Onboarding* in hotels are critical processes that involve introducing new employees to the organisation, its culture, policies, procedures, and their specific roles and responsibilities within the hotel setting. Effective Induction and Onboarding help new employees feel welcome, informed, and prepared to contribute to the hotel's success.

Employee Induction has been a regular HRM activity in hotels. Hotels rely heavily on temporary staff and external labour supply, causing high turnover rates (Boella & Goss-Turner, 2020). For this purpose, induction events are organised regularly by HR to introduce new employees to the company, as well as to provide training relevant to their job. *Employee Onboarding* is a practice similar to induction, but it is better planned and organised with a long-term focus. This process ensures that new employees feel part of the team, blend in, and quickly familiarise themselves with the organisational culture (Ghani et al., 2022).

For such events, HR managers prepare a detailed programme incorporating various activities, that is, they may distribute staff handbooks to provide information about the company, its culture, values, goals, and regulations, and also include some ice-breaking games and exercises to welcome newcomers. Moreover, new and existing employees should be aware of their responsibilities and resources, which may also be provided with some training during induction. It is often the case to assign a mentor or "buddy" to new employees; this person is an experienced member of staff who can guide them, answer questions, and provide additional support during the initial weeks. Effective induction and Onboarding set the tone for a positive employee experience and can ultimately impact guest satisfaction and the hotel's overall reputation. Customising the process to match the hotel's and employees' specific needs and the unique nature of the hospitality industry is essential for any successful Induction or Onboarding programme.

Training and Development

Training and *Development (T&D)* in hotels refer to processes that enhance employees' skills, knowledge, and overall performance but have distinct focuses and goals. Both processes ensure that people are equipped to cope with job requirements. Training primarily focuses on improving specific job-related skills and competencies essential for an employee to perform their current role effectively. It is a more immediate and practical process aimed at getting employees up to speed and ensuring they can perform their tasks proficiently. Training activities cover the entire spectrum of hospitality operations, from short courses on customer service to longer-term training (i.e., specialised software on sales and reservations and property management systems). Development, on the other hand, has a broader and longer-term focus. It aims to enhance employees' overall personal and professional growth, preparing them for future organisational roles and responsibilities. Development goes beyond immediate job skills and focuses on building leadership qualities, strategic thinking, and adaptability (Table 6.1).

T&D should be seen as a strategic process to formulate learning and development aligned with the hotel's core strategy (Nickson, 2013). Hotel and HR managers are challenged with the diverse characteristics of the workforce, high staff turnover, and lack of skills. The global hotel sector is competitive, and skills and competencies are crucial for success, creating the need for generic skills like problem-solving and customer-handling training. Therefore, training is an investment for the hotels' long-term efficiency, productivity, and effectiveness. Nevertheless, managers often overlook training, particularly in smaller organisations, due to a lack of time, knowledge of the benefits of training, or lack of financial resources; as a result, they conduct training themselves. Nickson (2013) suggests that the employees' different learning styles, awareness of all available training methods, and feelings towards training should be carefully considered when training is planned. In order to decide on the content of the training programme, a *training needs analysis* must be conducted. This is required to identify problems and opportunities with the employee and organisational performance, to use training to tackle such issues, and to reinforce the organisation's service culture.

Table 6.1 Differences between training and development

	Training	Development
Target group	Is a learning process mainly for new employees in which they acquire or improve the key skills required for the job.	Is a process for life-long learning and growth, targeting mainly managers (all levels).
Duration	Is a short-term process, that is, one to six months	Is a continuous, long-term process.
Focus	A reactive process that enhances the knowledge or skills for a particular role or job (present orientation).	A proactive process that focuses on career building and progression (future orientation).
Scope	Has a limited scope; it is specific job oriented.	It is career oriented and hence its scope is comparatively wider than training.
Instruction	The trainees are assigned a trainer who delivers the training programme.	The manager self-directs him/herself; an experienced mentor can provide guidance and feedback when required.

Source: Authors' creation

There are different types and settings to consider when designing T&D programmes in hotels. *On-the-job training* is widely used in hotels so that employees obtain a "hands-on" experience in a "real-world" working environment. On the other hand, *off-the-job training* is used for other purposes, such as briefings and knowledge exchange. *Digital and online training* are utilised to enhance the learning experience and the effectiveness of training programmes. Nowadays, many hotels use *synchronous* (in real-time) and *asynchronous* (not synchronous) online training, games, and simulations, which are engaging, and people may participate from different locations at different times. In international hotels, *cross-cultural training* is also important to train local employees and expatriates on organisational and national culture to avoid service failure.

Performance Management

Performance management in hotels is another vital HRM function involving monitoring, evaluating, and improving the performance of individual employees and overall hotel operations. Effective performance management helps hotels achieve their goals, maintain service standards, and enhance guest and employee satisfaction. It is imperative that hotel employees and managers meet the required performance standards and handle the stress and pressure that comes with their jobs, fulfil their job objectives, and become effective assets on their teams (Ghani et al., 2022). Performance management concentrates on the annual employee performance appraisal and embraces a range of activities across the complex nature of hotels (Nickson, 2013). *Performance appraisal* helps employees develop future-ready skills and competencies; therefore, it should not be viewed as a "once-a-year" activity. In addition, this process should allow all participants to engage in a dialogue about their performance and development (Hayes & Ninemeier, 2009). Such appraisals are used to both assess recent performance and focus on future objectives and opportunities and identify resources needed (CIPD, 2023b). As a strategic HRM process, performance management should include other formal or informal processes for analysing and monitoring employees' performance. Some propose that such approaches to performance management may positively impact employees' perception of careers in hotels and develop committed and loyal employees (Cascio, 2014).

There is a variety of methods for performance appraisals, such as *absolute methods* (assess based on absolute standards), *comparative methods* (rank and compare people's performance), *critical incident techniques* (based on positive and negative employee behaviour), and *results-oriented methods* (based on results and achieving targets) (Boella & Goss-Turner, 2020, pp. 174–175). The "360-degree feedback" has been adopted by many organisations. The evaluation of employees' performance is based on feedback from different levels in the hierarchy, including superiors, subordinates, peers, customers (in some cases), and the employees themselves (Armstrong, 2017). A meeting between the employee and the line manager takes place to discuss the appraisal findings and mutually agree on future goals. Performance management is an ongoing process. It requires consistent effort, adaptability, and a commitment to continuous improvement to ensure successful hotel operations and maintain high levels of guest satisfaction.

Compensation and Benefits

In hotels, employee *Reward Systems* (also known as *pay, compensation,* or *remuneration systems*) play a key role in motivating and retaining staff while enhancing overall job satisfaction. These systems are designed to recognise and reward employees for their contributions and achievements. Compensation and benefits are central to attracting suitable candidates. Compensation is a complex process, as hotels employ various reward systems (Nickson, 2013); for example, rewards may be calculated on hourly or session rates. Such schemes are developed due to the variability of demand and seasonality in hotels (Baum, 2015). The system can be more complicated because rewards can often include more than monetary benefits.

Furthermore, a reward system may include relational and psychological outcomes. For example, it may include meals, childcare arrangements, sick pay, savings schemes, or time off for charitable works. Regardless of the approach, rewards should consider the organisation's culture, strategies, and values to produce reciprocal benefits for the organisation and the individual. Reward systems and benefits may vary by country and culture

(Liu-Lastres et al., 2023). For example, in the US, health insurance (private) is often part of a job offer. However, this is not as common in countries such as the UK, where a public health system provides free healthcare.

Labour costs are high operating expenses in the hotel sector, posing challenges to pay and rewards systems. A balanced approach is required to avoid discrepancies in pay differences and to reduce exploitation practices and modern slavery (French, 2018). Although the reward system should aim at achieving the owner's overall business objective, it should also encourage long-term service and career development among employees. Reward systems are critical in attracting, recruiting, and retaining hotel employees in a volatile business environment. With Brexit, for example, the UK hospitality industry faces a shortage of workers since most migrant European workers have returned to their countries (Liu-Lastres et al., 2023; Baum et al., 2020). Furthermore, the COVID-19 pandemic forced hotel businesses to revise their reward systems and create new packages attractive to UK workers. *Incentives* are also introduced to affect and influence employee behaviour and align the employees' focus with the hotel's objectives (Ghani et al., 2022).

In conclusion, effective employee reward systems in hotels should align with the hotel's values, encourage desired behaviors, and create a sense of loyalty and motivation among the staff. Regular evaluation and adjustment of these systems based on employee feedback and changing circumstances are also essential for the systems' viability and successful implementation.

Employee Relations

The *Employee* (or *Industrial*) *Relations* function is critical for efficient HRM implementation in hotels. It describes the relationship between management and the workforce, usually through their representatives in the collective sense. Lucas (1995, p. 81) defined employee relations in hotels and catering as:

> *the management of employment and work relationships between managers and workers, and, sometimes, customers; it also covers contemporary employment and work practices.*

The collective term *"industrial relations"* is still applied, where employees are organised and represented within a strong union. Unionisation is still prevalent in the hotel sector in some countries like the US, as conditions of employment are determined by negotiation, and there is evidence of national agreements resulting in higher participation of hotel employees at unions. A union's collective power varies by country and culture, with evidence of sporadic and low participation in the hotel sector (Storey, 2007). Contemporary HRM practices move away from the large-scale conflict between managers and employees; as a result, the need for unionisation has decreased. On the other hand, employee relations are highly valued in contemporary organisations; employees engage with the organisation, the decision-making process, leadership, and open communication. Joint consultation and negotiation are conducted between employees and employers, reducing the cases of conflict even at large organisation and hotel chains. A contented workforce and a healthy organisational climate are at the core of HRM in hotels, forcing HR managers to understand and empathise with employees.

Succession Planning

Succession planning in hotels refers to the HRM process of identifying and developing employees within an organisation to prepare them for key leadership roles and positions that may become vacant due to promotions, retirements, or other reasons. It is a strategic approach to ensuring a smooth transition of leadership and maintaining the continuity of operations within the hotel industry.

This process requires adequate plans and resources to ensure that positions are covered promptly and organised. Such planning is aligned with long-term strategic HRM and decisions to be made about the sources of future management. "Succession planning is a process used by human resources managers to help ensure that they will continue to have the key professional and other staff needed to support their planned growth" (Hayes & Ninemeier, 2009, p. 425). A succession plan compares future management requirements with the currently available management. Specific time frameworks are used, as well as information about specific positions. By implementing a robust succession planning strategy, hotels can ensure a steady pipeline of capable leaders who are ready to step into key roles when the need arises, ultimately contributing to the long-term success and sustainability of the business.

Process Evaluation

The HRM key functions' *evaluation* process is a continuous cycle, with insights and feedback from one performance period informing the goal setting and development plans for the next (Storey, 2007). Monitoring and control are required at every stage of each function to ensure that practices are effective and appropriate to contribute to the organisation's goals and objectives. Organisational and employee performance should be checked, verified, and compared to the HRM plan. If the actual performance deviates from the plan, measures and relevant actions should be taken (Hayes & Ninemeier, 2009). Hotels must invest in training managers to conduct effective evaluations and provide meaningful employee feedback, contributing to employee engagement, development, and overall organisational success (Baum, 2015).

Talent Management

Talent Management (TM) in hotels refers to the strategic process of recruiting, developing, retaining, and optimising employees' skills and abilities to meet the hospitality industry's needs. It involves identifying and nurturing individuals who have the potential to contribute significantly to the success of the hotel business (Marinakou & Giousmpasoglou, 2019). A debate has been ongoing regarding the nature of TM and whether it should be treated as a distinct function within HRM or as a separate management function (Morley et al., 2015). In this book, we treat TM as an overarching HRM function that encompasses all HRM activities. HRM covers a wide range of functions, such as HR administration, compliance, and day-to-day employee support. TM, on the other hand, is a strategic approach that concentrates on identifying and nurturing top-performing employees to drive organisational success in the long run (Shet, 2020). Both HRM and TM play essential roles in managing an organisation's workforce effectively.

As a concept, TM appeared in management studies in the early 2000s. The *"war for talent"* was proposed by Michaels et al. (2001); they included people's abilities, skills, and knowledge acquiring the potential for development. Talent is perceived as a strategic resource for organisations to gain and maintain their competitive advantage (Gallardo-Gallardo et al., 2013). Baum (2015) proposed that talent in hospitality may have a different meaning from other sectors, as he proposed that the definition of talent should focus on inclusiveness and that HRM efforts and strategies should focus on retaining talent. Marinakou and Giousmpasoglou (2019, p. 3870) defined talent in the hotel context as:

the employee who thinks outside the box and can make decisions, has knowledge and expertise in his/her area, is willing to learn and progress in his/her career, is adaptable to various circumstances with a customer-driven personality, and may fit the organisational culture.

A profound need for talented employees is exponentially growing in the hospitality sector. Nevertheless, Gallardo-Gallardo and Thunnissen (2016) argue that only a few empirical studies conceptualise TM in hospitality. CIPD (2006, p. 1) proposed that talent management is "concerned with […] identification, development, engagement/retention, and deployment of 'talent' within a specific organisational context". Hughes and Rog (2008) defined talent management as a multifaceted concept that can help organisations achieve competitive advantage through effective people management.

Marinakou and Giousmpasoglou (2019) found that a hybrid approach was adopted in their study of TM in luxury hotels in four countries. They suggest (ibid.) that luxury hotels adopt an inclusive and exclusive approach with explicit practices in each case. In the *inclusive approach*, TM is seen as a continuous, systematic HRM process that provides opportunities for all employees to grow and progress. In the *exclusive approach*, hotels personalise the talent development process (Kaliannan et al., 2023). Instead of adopting a "one-size-fits-all" approach, they develop training and development programmes and retention strategies to allow talented individual employees to progress and develop. Figure 6.2 demonstrates the proposed model.

HRM Strategies for Talent Management

Although several HRM strategies have been proposed for *People Management* in the hospitality industry context, few studies have focused on the development and retention of talent in hotels. Deery and Jago (2015) argue that hotels should create a brand that promotes empowerment and develops knowledge to attract talent. Employees in such empowering working environments feel that their opinion matters, and their ideas are heard. Similarly, Scott and Revis (2008) proposed that hotel managers should ensure that talented employees remain loyal by creating an environment in which they feel like members of a family and so are committed. A good work-life balance contributes to talent retention, especially with younger employees. Marinakou and Giousmpasoglou (2019) proposed two categories of talent retention strategies (see Fig. 6.2). The first is titled *employee practices*, which include organisational practices such as flexible work, benefits (i.e., childcare), and brand management. Such practices "should strive to develop an organisational culture that incorporates a friendly open working environment with good internal communication" (Marinakou & Giousmpasoglou, 2019, p. 3871). Staff empowerment, achievement recognition, and monetary rewards were also included in this category. Training and Development are the other parts of employee practices that should be strategically and systematically designed with reference to practices such as annual performance, systematic feedback, and compensation among others. The second category is titled *employee relations* which focuses on engagement activities. Such activities allow participation in decision-making and taking initiatives. Succession planning, preparation for promotion, and/or professional development were also added.

Therefore, the main strategies to retain talent in hotels include the development of family-oriented, friendly organisational cultures that foster teamwork, mentoring, and leadership, key success factors for managing people in hospitality. For this purpose, recruitment and selection for talent should be done with a focus on values, but with a formal, structured, and strategically aligned approach to TM.

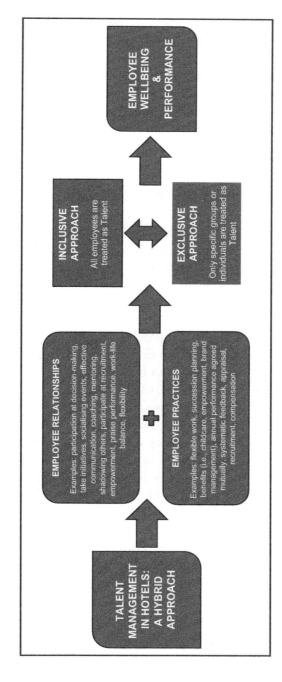

Fig. 6.2 Talent management in luxury hotels. (Source: Adapted from Marinakou and Giousmpasoglou [2019, p. 3870])

The hospitality industry and the hotel sector specifically depend on human resources and emphasise the role employees play in the organisation's performance and competitive advantage. After the COVID-19 pandemic, the hotel job market has changed leaving behind all those hotels that have not created workforce planning strategies. In this highly competitive environment, well-designed and executed talent management strategy may help reduce staff turnover and improve employee engagement and customer service quality.

Contemporary HRM Issues in Hotels

The hotel sector is characterised by a diverse and non-standard workforce, which requires an in-depth understanding of employee relationships and management. It is important to recognise such different demographic features especially when the wellbeing, job satisfaction, motivation, commitment, and loyalty of employees are priorities for the organisation. The importance of effective work teams makes HRM a critical component of rostering people from different backgrounds to work together on regular shifts. High-quality service is a key element in hotel operation, where group dynamics and social interaction become significant factors (Boella & Goss-Turner, 2020). Ashton (2018) characterised labour and skill shortage as a worldwide crisis. *Shortage of skills* and *high staff turnover* are further challenged by Brexit and the exchange rate impact it had which discouraged EU workers from coming to the UK for employment. The pool of potential employees shrunk, as working permits and visas have become an issue for many businesses including hotels (Boella & Goss-Turner, 2020). Since then, significant changes in the diversification of working patterns in the EU have been observed (Baum et al., 2020). On top of all these challenges, the "*Great Resignation*" has also hit the hospitality industry (Liu-Lastres et al., 2023). For example, the accommodation and food sectors in the US weathered a quit rate of 6% in January 2022 (US Bureau of Labor, 2022). This trend known as the *Big Quit* or the *Great Attrition* was first noticed in the spring of 2021 and grew further after the COVID-19 pandemic. This mass exodus is mainly associated with the pandemic that created job insecurity and employee burnout but also a desire for remote work and more stable professions (Box 6.1).

Box 6.1 Marriott uses a Careers Chatbot for Facebook Messenger

Marriott has always been at the forefront of innovation in People Management. Marriot International is a global hospitality industry leader with more than 6200 properties in 30 leading hotel brands spanning 125 countries and territories. Marriott receives an excessive number of applications for job vacancies and extends offers to a fraction of them! It is easily understood that the recruitment and selection process is a challenging part of the job of any HR Manager not only in Marriott but in any hospitality business, especially after the COVID-19 pandemic and the unprecedented staff shortages.

Back in 2017 Marriott Int. introduced AI-based cutting-edge technology to enhance the job applicants' experience with the launch of MC, a Marriott Careers Chatbot for Facebook Messenger. This algorithmic-based application creates a personalised experience for each applicant. In addition to conversing with job applicants like a human, MC helps them apply for open jobs based on discipline and location and educates them about the company's culture and values. Optionally, applicants can take a quick quiz during the conversation to learn which Marriott hotel brands best match their interests.

At Marriott International, Inc., we believe that the key to success in using AI in the workplace is for HR to develop deeper and tighter relationships with strategic consumer-focused departments. While AI is being currently used to source, screen, interview, and make offers to job candidates, this should just be the start of using AI in all key HRM functions in hotels. Obviously, IT and AI cannot replace HR specialists; on the contrary, we can dramatically improve how we (HR specialists) work while enhancing the overall experience of our employees.

Tammy Markley
Marriott Hotels (U.K.)
Cluster Director of HR—Southwest England & Wales
Source: T. Markley, personal communication, 11 September 2023.

A variety of factors, such as technology, demographic changes, and contemporary business formats, have contributed to the challenges in HRM. People who seek employment have access to information as digital *technology* gives them access to many hotels worldwide. HR managers should be alert to the use of technology and data in the strategic and operational HR planning process. Modern *Computerised Personnel Information Systems* (CPIS) and electronic HRM (eHRM) may support even smaller businesses in the recruitment, selection, and retention of staff. The Global Human Capital Trends report by Deloitte (2016) highlights that HRM is no longer a service provider but is seen as a group of talent and employee experience experts that foster innovative approaches on how to manage human resources and do business. Artificial Intelligence and robotic devices are incorporated into routine tasks such as room delivery, creating the need to develop or update skills for staff via training. Nevertheless, Khaliq et al. (2022) propose that such organisational changes bring a sense of employment uncertainty and higher turnover intentions among hotel employees.

A significant *demographic change* refers to young people who enter the labour market and are not keen on staying with the same employer for long, as they anticipate developing "portfolio careers" (Boella & Goss-Turner, 2020, p. 63). They are keen to have career progression, to be given opportunities to work in more than one country and receive feedback frequently (Self et al., 2019). Employees from different age groups have different values, experiences, lifestyles, and attitudes towards work, life, and the future. With a younger workforce, the hierarchy will shift, with younger employees holding managerial positions and older workers reporting to them (Mooney, 2016). Such age gaps can also be seen in communication, where misunderstandings can lead to frustration as older employees perceive younger supervisors to be inexperienced. Based on this fact, managers should understand and appreciate each generation's contribution to the business with their ideas. Goh and Okumus (2020) found that the Australian hospitality workforce is dominated by young talent, and they recommend specific talent retention strategies for this group. They propose a focus on job functional attitudes, on the fun part of work in hospitality through activities such as weekly sporting events between departments or different units. Marriott hotel group used social media and gamification to attract the younger generation such as "My Marriott Hotel" where they run their own department on Facebook (Freer, 2012). Visual career pathway is another proposition, where Goh and Okumus (2020) propose that career counselling by HRM should be provided to younger employees to engage them with the company and retain them through career advancement programmes such as Graduate Management Traineeships. Travel opportunities are also valued, as the "future hospitality worker is a global employee expected to work across properties in different countries" (Goh & Okumus, 2020, p. 3). Younger employees see little distinction between work and leisure aspects, changing jobs can be a positive lifestyle choice and the freedom to travel during work can be seen as a lifestyle mobility (Cohen et al., 2015). Among other strategies, equal opportunities and a sustainable work environment are key retention practices. Large hotel chains such as Marriott, Hilton, and Wyndham recruit diverse groups to attract more talent and promote diversity (Goh & Okumus, 2020). Younger employees embrace green and sustainable practices, hence they prefer to work for hotels that have adopted sustainability (Goh et al., 2017).

Other demographic changes refer to changes in *social patterns* including single-parent families, female participation increase, diverse working time, and the role of the "gig economy" that contribute to the increase in the forms of employment. The ongoing changes in childcare and school systems during the pandemic have rendered it difficult to ensure the safety of employees' children (Shet, 2020), hence they moved to other jobs with more flexible working hours or part-time employment. The expansion of the gig economy has shaped the contemporary workforce, as it offers the freedom and the power to select projects based on individual interests. The hospitality industry should cultivate a "sustainable, positive and long-term relationship' with the gig economy workforce" (Liu-Lastres et al., 2023, p. 240).

New *diverse forms of employment* include part-time options, remote working (where possible), flexible time, agency staff, and outsourcing. Evidence suggests that such working patterns are associated with negative working conditions, fewer opportunities for training and development, and reduced productivity, forcing hotels to ensure their employees are properly inducted and trained into the business culture. Such changes require a planned reaction from different stakeholders. Sull et al. (2022) argue that businesses with a positive reputation and a healthy workplace experienced lower attrition during the Great Resignation. Associations like *UK Hospitality*, the *Institute of Hospitality*, and *People 1st* attempt to tackle the image of the hotel sector and recruitment challenges (Baum et al., 2020). In addition, the pandemic has had a positive effect on the labour shortage in hospitality. Most hotels after the crisis crafted a more secure environment for customers and employees which had a positive effect on perceptions about work in hotels (Giousmpasoglou et al., 2021).

Sustainable HRM

According to a survey by Statista (2023), 81% of travellers worldwide intended to stay at least once in an eco-friendly or green accommodation. Environmental pressures from the market and consumers, modern regulations, and legislation have created a relationship between sustainability in hotels and HRM. *Sustainable HRM* is a new perspective that requires further research and concept development. It is a complementary approach to HRM with various "levels of analysis (effects on individuals, process management, organisation and society), dimensions (economic, ecological, social and human) and different time perspectives (short and long term)" (Macke & Genari, 2019, p. 807). Emphasis is now placed on environmental hotel management strategies with the necessity of employees' involvement in green behaviour to maintain competitive advantage (Pham et al., 2019). The term *green human resource management* (GHRM) was proposed by Renwick et al. (2013) who define it as covering the HRM-related aspects of environmental management. In sustainable HRM, the role of HRM is to promote organisational sustainability with the assumption that such HRM processes are sustainable. An example of sustainability and HRM in hotels is provided in Box 6.2.

All HRM processes and practices such as training and development and planning are linked to HR sustainable management. Implementing sustainable management practices brings change in hotels and consequently to employee behaviours (Pham et al., 2019). Creating awareness and training employees on environmental sustainability strategies

Box 6.2   Green Key Training—Geraniotis Hotel and Resort

Green Key is an eco-certificate for hotels based on strict criteria for sustainability management (i.e., water, energy, waste, food waste, and guest information) as well as sustainability training for hotel employees. To acquire this certification, we went through a rigorous screening process including a very detailed application, with site audits and third-party verification. We received our accreditation in July 2021.

We already had a *Blue Flag* for our beach, hence we wanted to expand our sustainable strategy to more eco-friendly practices. The Green Key has already helped our hotel to reduce energy and water consumption. For example, we started using LED lighting throughout the business. The challenging part was to introduce the idea of environmental protection and reverse our employees' poor understanding of the concept of sustainability. As I was involved in the certification process from the very beginning, I performed the staff training. Based on my employee's skills analysis I realised that the best approach was to make them relate to the issue. So, I clearly explained the benefits of such green practices not only for the hotel but also for them in their personal life, as well as the society. I must admit that all new practices were very well accepted and implemented by everyone in the hotel. Recycling is now part of our family business culture and includes customers, management, and staff. We have gone plastic-free, which initially raised the operational costs for the business, but on the other hand, had a very positive environmental impact on the establishment. Our image is also enhanced, and more eco-friendly customers book our hotel which has given us a competitive advantage in the market. Finally, regular monitoring and support are provided to ensure the effective use of sustainable practices. Regular team meetings take place, we have a green ambassador among staff and of course, we have established incentives to reward the Green Key initiatives in practice.

Dimitrios Sikalias, GM
Geraniotis Hotel & Resort, Crete

Green Key

Source: D. Sikalias, personal communication, 25th August 2023.

enhance employees' green behaviour and their willingness to implement such strategies (Luu, 2018). As a result, hotels benefit from investing in GHRM practices by boosting pro-environmental behaviour, as well as their reputation and financial performance.

Chapter Summary

HRM plays a vital role in organisations' success in today's globalised business environment. Recruiting, developing, and retaining a diverse workforce contribute to the hotel's competitive advantage. Various external business environment factors and events such as the "Great Resignation" resulted in high employee turnover and skills shortages, putting the hotel sector's long-term growth and competitiveness at risk. HRM can help hotels foster an inclusive culture, embrace diversity values, and contribute to employee wellbeing and better employee and organisational performance. HRM practices may support hotels in building more attractive workplaces, which in return will create the willingness to commit and continue employment in the hotel. Fostering a good company image with a good quality workplace can provide a healthy and happy environment, enhance attitudes towards quality of service, demonstrate respect for employees' needs, and value their ideas. Hotel managers should eliminate poor working conditions and create an employee-centred organisational culture that provides not only more flexibility but also employment security. The success of today's hospitality and tourism organisations relies on the effective management and development of talent, which should be a strategic priority.

References

Armstrong, M. (2017). *A handbook of human resource management* (14th ed.). Kogan Page.

Armstrong, M., & Taylor, S. (2020). *Armstrong's handbook of human resource management practice*. Kogan Page Ltd.

Ashton, A. S. (2018). How human resources management best practice influence employee satisfaction and job retention in the Thai hotel industry. *Journal of Human Resources in Hospitality and Tourism, 117*(2), 175–199.

Baum, T. (2015). Human resources in tourism: Still waiting for change? *Tourism Management, 50*(4), 204–212.

Baum, T., Mooney, S. K., Robinson, R. N., & Solnet, D. (2020). COVID-19's impact on the hospitality workforce—New crisis or amplification of the norm? *International Journal of Contemporary Hospitality Management, 32*(9), 2813–2829.

Boella, M. J., & Goss-Turner, S. (2020). *Human resource management in the hospitality industry: A guide to best practice* (10th ed.). Routledge.

Cascio, W. F. (2014). Leveraging employer branding, performance management and human resource development to enhance employee retention. *Human Resource Development International, 17*(2), 121–128.

CIPD. (2006). *Reflections on Talent Management*. CIPD.

CIPD. (2017). *Resourcing and Talent Planning: Survey report 2017*. CIPD publications.

CIPD. (2023a). Recruitment: An Introduction. https://www.cipd.org/en/knowledge/factsheets/recruitment-factsheet/

CIPD. (2023b). Performance management: An introduction. https://www.cipd.org/en/knowledge/factsheets/performance-factsheet/#four

Cohen, S., Duncan, T., & Thulemark, M. (2015). Lifestyle mobilities: The crossroads of travel, leisure and migration. *Mobilities, 10*(1), 155–172.

Deery, M., & Jago, L. (2015). Revisiting talent management, work-life balance and retention strategies. *International Journal of Contemporary Hospitality Management, 27*(3), 453–472.

Deloitte. (2016). *Global human capital trends. The new organisation: Different by design.* https://www2.deloitte.com/content/dam/Deloitte/global/Documents/HumanCapital/gx-dup-global-human-capital-trends-2016.pdf

Freer, T. (2012). Social media gaming: A recipe for employer brand success. *Strategic HR Review, 11*(1), 13–17.

French, S. (2018). Between globalisation and Brexit: Migration, pay and the road to modern slavery in the UK hospitality industry. *Research in Hospitality Management, 8*(1), 23–31.

Gallardo-Gallardo, E., Dries, N., & Gonzalez-Cruz, T. (2013). What is the meaning of talent management in the world of work? *Human Resource Management Review, 23*(4), 290–300.

Gallardo-Gallardo, E., & Thunnissen, M. (2016). Standing on the shoulders of giants? A critical review of empirical talent management research. *Employee Relations, 38*(1), 31–56.

Ghani, B., Zada, M., Menon, K. R., Ulla, R., Khattak, A., Han, H., Ariza-Montes, A., & Araya-Castillo, L. (2022). Challenges and strategies for employee retention in the hospitality industry: A review. *Sustainability, 14*(5), 2885.

Giousmpasoglou, C., Marinakou, E., & Zopiatis, A. (2021). Hospitality managers in turbulent times: The COVID-19 crisis. *International Journal of Contemporary Hospitality Management, 33*(4), 1297–1318.

Goh, E., Muskat, B., & Tan, A. (2017). The nexus between sustainable practices in hotels and future gen Y hospitality students' career path decision. *Journal of Teaching in Travel and Tourism, 17*(4), 237–253.

Goh, E., & Okumus, F. (2020). Avoiding the hospitality workforce bubble: Strategies to attract and retain generation Z talent in the hospitality workforce. *Tourism Management Perspectives, 33*, 1006603. https://doi.org/10.1016/j.tmp.2019.100603

Hawes, D. (2018). *I'll tell you something: It's no surprise recruiters are prying into candidates' social media*. CIPD Publications.

Hayes, D. K., & Ninemeier, J. D. (2009). *Human resources management in the hospitality industry*. John Wiley & Sons.

Heery, E., & Noon, M. (2008). *A dictionary of human resource management* (2nd ed.). Oxford University Press.

Hughes, J. C., & Rog, E. (2008). Talent management: A strategy for improving employee recruitment, retention and engagement within hospitality organisations. *International Journal of Contemporary Hospitality Management, 20*(7), 743–757.

Kaliannan, M., Darmalinggam, D., Dorasamy, M., & Abraham, M. (2023). Inclusive talent development as a key talent management approach: A systematic literature review. *Human Resource Management Review, 33*(1), 100926.

Khaliq, A., Waqas, A., Nisar, Q. A., Haider, S., & Asghar, Z. (2022). Application of AI and robotics in hospitality sector: A resource gain and resource loss perspective. *Technology in Society, 68*, 101807.

Liu-Lastres, B., Wen, H., & Huang, W. (2023). A reflection on the great resignation in the hospitality and tourism industry. *International Journal of Contemporary Hospitality Management, 35*(1), 235–249.

Lockyer, C., & Scholarios, D. (2004). Selecting hotel staff: Why best practice does not always work. *International Journal of Contemporary Hospitality Management, 16*(2), 121–135.

Lucas, R. (1995). *Managing employee relations in the hotel and catering industry*. Cassell.

Luu, T. T. (2018). Employees' green recovery performance: The roles of green HR practices and serving culture. *Journal of Sustainable Tourism, 26*(8). https://doi.org/10.1080/09669582.2018.1443113

Macke, J., & Genari, D. (2019). Systematic literature review on sustainable human resource management. *Journal of Cleaner Production, 208*, 806–815.

Madera, J. M., Dawson, M., Guchait, P., & Belarmino, A. M. (2017). Strategic human resources management research in hospitality and tourism: A review of current literature and suggestions for the future. *International Journal of Contemporary Hospitality Management, 29*(1), 48–67.

Marinakou, E., & Giousmpasoglou, C. (2019). Talent management and retention strategies in luxury hotels: Evidence from four countries. *International Journal of Contemporary Hospitality Management, 31*(10), 3855–3878.

McCain, A. (2023). *25 hotel industry statistics*. https://www.zippia.com/advice/hotel-industry-statistics/

Michaels, E., Handfield-Jones, H., & Axelrod, B. (2001). *The War for talent*. Harvard Business School Press.

Mooney, S. (2016). Wastes youth in the hospitality industry: Older workers' perceptions and misconceptions about younger workers. *Hospitality and Society, 6*(1), 9–30.

Morley, M. J., Scullion, H., Collings, D. G., & Schuler, R. S. (2015). Talent management: A capital question. *European Journal of International Management, 9*(1), 1–8.

Nickson, D. (2013). *Human resources management for the hospitality and tourism industries*. Routledge.

Pham, N. T., Tuckova, Z., & Jabbour, C. J. C. (2019). Greening the hospitality industry: How do green human resource management practices influence organisational citizenship behaviour in hotels? A mixed-methods study. *Tourism Management, 72*, 386–399.

Renwick, D. W. S., Redman, T., & Maguire, S. (2013). Green human resources management: A review and research agenda. *International Journal of Management Reviews, 15*(1), 1–14.

Scott, B., & Revis, S. (2008). Talent management in hospitality: Graduate career success and strategies. *International Journal of Contemporary Hospitality Management, 20*(7), 781–791.

Self, T., Gordon, S., & Jolly, P. (2019). Talent management: A Delphi study of assessing and developing Gen Z hospitality leaders. *International Journal of Contemporary Hospitality Management., 31*(10), 4126–4149.

Shet, S. V. (2020). Strategic talent management—contemporary issues in international context. *Human Resource Development International, 23*(1), 98–102.

Statista. (2023). *Global tourism industry—Statistics and facts.* https://www.statista.com/topics/962/global-tourism/#topicOverview

Stone, R. J. (1998). *Human resource management.* John Wiley and Sons.

Storey, J. (2007). *Human resource management: A critical text* (3rd ed.). Thomson Learning.

Sull, D., Sull, C., & Zweig, B. (2022). *Toxic culture is driving the great resignation.* https://sloanreview.mit.edu/article/toxic-culture-is-driving-the-great-resignation/

Thoreson, B. (2023). *The 33 definitive hospitality industry statistics you need to know for 2023.* https://www.hotel-online.com/press_releases/release/the-33-definitive-hospitality-industry-statistics-you-need-to-know-for-2023/

U.S. Bureau of Labor. (2022). *Quit levels and rates by industry and region, seasonality adjusted.* www.bls.gov/

Worsfold, P. (1999). HRM, performance, commitment and service quality in the hotel industry. *International Journal of Contemporary Hospitality Management, 11*(7), 340–348.

7

Hospitality Management Education

Photo Credits: *Dylan Gillis* (*Free to use under the Unsplash License*). (Source: https://unsplash.com/photos/people-sitting-on-chair-in-front-of-table-while-holding-pens-during-daytime-KdeqA3aTnBY)

© The Author(s), under exclusive license to Springer Nature Switzerland AG 2024
C. Giousmpasoglou, E. Marinakou, *The Contemporary Hotel Industry*, Palgrave Advances in Managing and Marketing Tourism, Hospitality, and Events, https://doi.org/10.1007/978-3-031-52803-3_7

Introduction

The hotel managers responsible for meeting tomorrow's challenges are the hospitality management students of today. How well they are prepared to meet these challenges depends on the quality of the hospitality management curriculum and the educators who deliver it. The study of hospitality management has become an established part of higher education (HE), but the question of whether hospitality is a worthwhile area for study still lingers. This chapter investigates the role and contribution of *Hospitality Education* in hotel management. Specific areas like curriculum development, quality, internationalisation, and use of technology are discussed. In addition, the role of internships as an integral part of the hospitality curricula is also investigated.

The Birth of Hospitality Education

The world's first hotel schools appeared in Switzerland in the late nineteenth century. Switzerland was a popular destination for wealthy travellers at the time, and it was featured in the first package holidays across Europe, created by Thomas Cook in 1853 (Slater, 2013). The birth of the tourism industry created the need for trained employees alongside hospitality workers in luxury hotels. The world's first hotel school was founded in 1893 by Jacques Tschumi as *Ecole hôtelière de Lausanne (EHL)*. The school delivered the first classes in *Hôtel d' Angleterre* on the shores of Lake Leman in Lausanne (EHL, n.d.). The first cohort consisted of 27 students who studied arithmetic, accounting, geography, and languages and developed their understanding of hospitality through practice: they directly applied their newly acquired knowledge as trainees at the *Hôtel d' Angleterre* (Fig. 7.1). At that time, the typical hotel school curriculum focused on operations management, that is, teaching students how to manage the restaurant, reception, accommodation, and guest services, with some "book-keeping." Another famous hotel school, the École Hôtelière de Genève (EHG), was founded in Neuchâtel in 1914 by GastroSuisse, an employers' association of the hospitality industry containing at the time 21,000 members. The above two schools are examples

Fig. 7.1 Student life at *Ecole hôtelière de Lausanne*. (Source: photos courtesy of EHL Archives [© 2023 EHL. All rights reserved])

of a long line of Swiss hospitality education institutions that attract students from all over the world until today; many appear at the top of table leagues on this subject (Table 7.1). Reputable hotel schools based on the Swiss model were also established in European countries, such as *Hotelschool The Hague* in 1929 (the Netherlands) and *The Scottish Hotel School* in 1944 (UK).

A key milestone in hospitality education was establishing the *Cornell School of Hotel Administration* in the US in 1922 at the request of leading hotel magnates and the American Hotel Association. The world's first undergraduate hospitality management degree programme was launched with 21 students under the direction of a single professor, Howard B. Meek (hospitalitynet.org, 2012). This degree was created to meet the industry's demand for better service quality and the introduction of standards in the fast-growing hospitality industry. The emergence of an *American approach* (as opposed to the *Swiss approach*) has created two distinctive directions in hospitality education. The American approach typically adopts a broader curriculum, offering a wide range of subjects such as business management, marketing, accounting, and entrepreneurship alongside hospitality-specific courses. On the other hand, the Swiss

Table 7.1 Top 20 hospitality programmes globally in 2023

Ranking	University	Ranking	University
1	**EHL Hospitality Business School** Lausanne, Switzerland	11	**Vatel, Hotel & Tourism Business School** Lyon, France
2	**University of Nevada** Las Vegas, United States	12	**The Hong Kong Polytechnic University** Hong Kong SAR, Hong Kong SAR
3	**SHMS—Swiss Hotel Management School** Caux, Switzerland	13	**The Emirates Academy of Hospitality Management (EAHM)** Dubai, United Arab Emirates
4	**Les Roches Global Hospitality Management Education** Crans-Montana, Switzerland	14	**EUHT StPOL Barcelona— Escuela Universitaria de Hotelería y Turismo de Sant Pol de Mar** Sant Pol de Mar, Spain
5	**Glion Institute of Higher Education** Glion-sur-Montreux, Switzerland	15	**University of Surrey** Guildford, United Kingdom
6	**Cesar Ritz Colleges Switzerland** Le Bouveret, Switzerland	16	**University of Central Florida** Orlando, United States
7	**Hotel Institute Montreux** Montreux, Switzerland	17	**Taylor's University** Subang Jaya, Malaysia
8	**Culinary Arts Academy Switzerland** Le Bouveret, Switzerland	18	**HTMi Hotel and Tourism Management Institute Switzerland** Sörenberg, Switzerland
9	**Hotelschool The Hague** The Hague, the Netherlands	19	**Bournemouth University** Poole, United Kingdom
10	**Macao Institute for Tourism Studies (IFTM)** Macao, Macau SAR	20	**Cornell University** Ithaca, United States

Source: Adapted from QS World Universities Rankings 2023 (https://www.topuniversities.com/university-rankings/university-subject-rankings/2023/hospitality-leisure-management?&page=0)
QS Quacquarelli Symonds (www.topuniversities.com), Copyright © 2004–2022 QS Quacquarelli Symonds Ltd

approach often focuses more on specialised training in hospitality operations, including food and beverage management, hotel operations, and event planning. The cultural context also plays a significant role in shaping hospitality education (Giousmpasoglou, 2012). The American approach often emphasises customer service, guest satisfaction, and the diverse needs of a multicultural society. The Swiss approach often strongly emphasises precision, attention to detail, and traditional service values, reflecting the country's reputation for high-quality hospitality.

The years after the Second World War saw an explosion of Hospitality Management programmes offered mainly in the US and Europe due to the internationalisation of the industry (Ricci, 2022). The fast-growing global hospitality and tourism industry created the need for graduates with distinctive competencies and attributes to do the job. Nevertheless, hospitality management programmes on both sides of the Atlantic had a vocational orientation until the late 1970s (Hsu et al., 2017). It was not until 1981 that Hospitality education received academic attention for the first time after the Annals of Tourism Research publication under the theme "Tourism Education" (Ayikoru et al., 2009). According to the *International Council on Hotel, Restaurant and Institutional Education* (ICHRIE, 2021), hundreds of degree programs are available today with a wide variety in content and multiple specialisations (i.e., leadership, finance, marketing, HRM, and sustainability). These include two-year (diploma), four-year (bachelor), graduate (Master of Science or MBA or comparable) degrees, and professional certificates of every sort.

The Debate on Hospitality Education

The educational structure in hospitality management and related fields has highlighted the operational aspects of the industry for more than a century. Until the early 1980s, only hands-on vocational programmes were offered in hospitality and tourism. The curricula were based on skills-oriented training, and students received a narrow education (Fidgeon, 2010). During the 1990s, there was a strengthening international movement driven by hospitality academics towards the "liberation" of hospitality management in HE from its vocational base and to explore the inclusion in the curriculum of a broader and more reflective orientation (Morrison & O'Mahony, 2003). Baum and Nickson (1998) suggest that hospitality students were uncritical perpetrators of the status quo at that time rather than effective and thinking would-be managers ready to improve things. In the post-2000s, hospitality education moved towards a mature state where educators and researchers embraced the mainstream social science trends and shared the same concerns with colleagues from other disciplines, such as conducting quality research and facilitating effective teaching (Hsu et al., 2017).

In the past 40 years, hospitality studies have been plagued with uncertainties and controversies. Unsurprisingly, a long-standing debate about the knowledge hospitality courses should offer emerged during the 1980s; for many years, this topic area was not classified as an academic discipline (Airey, 2015). Research suggests (i.e., Baum, 2019; Marinakou & Giousmpasoglou, 2019) that a critical aspect in the development of hospitality educational programmes is the relevance of the curriculum to student's expectations and the needs of the hospitality industry. Hewitt (2006) argues that it is also important to consider the nature of the learner and practical social needs. If hospitality education aims to provide a starting point for developing a skilled workforce, then dialogue with the industry and future students is imperative (Ladkin, 2005). Riley et al. (2002) propose that hospitality education has to balance three imperatives: promoting individual development, advancing knowledge, and being practical and relevant to the industry.

At the same time, Casado (2003) proposes that hospitality curricula should be scrutinised by educators, graduates, students, and industry professionals. Tribe (2014) proposes that curriculum design in hospitality education is a complex construct of influences of all stakeholders, such as students, employers, and governmental bodies. Velo and Mittaz (2006) add that stakeholders' views should be continuously consulted to keep the hospitality and tourism curriculum abreast of the industry changes and norms. Furthermore, the curriculum content should balance varied stakeholders' demands (Felisitas et al., 2012). On the one hand, the hospitality curriculum in HE should not be narrowed to vocationalism, as this "undermines genuine occupational preparation and also impoverishes the intellectual and civic roles that higher education can play"

(Grubb & Lazerson, 2005: 16). On the other hand, it should not be too theoretical, as technical skills should also be developed (Chipkin, 2004). Tribe (2014) states that the lack of empirical research to base hospitality curriculum planning has been mainly addressed in general and in reference to the industry's needs. Some also claim that most programmes were designed by educators with little or no industry experience (McKercher, 2002). Moreover, students' motivation to pursue hospitality studies relies on their perception of the degree programme (Hearns et al., 2007). Thus, the hospitality and tourism education should not only rely on what the industry needs but also on the demands of other stakeholders.

The Hospitality Educator's Profile

The controversial subject of faculty staff qualifications and tenure has raised considerations about the quality of the available hospitality management programmes in HE. During the 1980s and the 1990s, assistant and associate professors with industry experience and a master's degree staffed many hospitality programs. The research requirements to achieve tenure were minimal. A terminal degree became a requisite for getting a tenure track in the late eighties and early nineties. Schmidgall and Woods (1994) determined that the three most important attributes for gaining tenure were a PhD, a track record of publications, and a track record of good teaching. Rutherford and Samenfink (1992) also argued that the frequency and quality of publications are vital considerations when discussing tenure and promotion.

Today, most hospitality programmes in the Western world require faculty staff to have a terminal degree (PhD); this way, they can provide graduates with research skills. On the other hand, the focus on research and the lack of professional background has distanced the younger generations of researchers and educators from the hospitality industry (Hsu et al., 2017). The absence of industry relationships weakens the curriculum design and course delivery, which is detrimental to student qualifications upon graduation (McKercher, 2002). In addition, as most universities focus on research, the pressure for academic staff to publish is increasing (Larson et al., 2019). Bowen (2005) asserts that the department, college, or school occasionally adopts a relatively objective strategy concerning the research criteria for tenure. It is not uncommon for faculty members to be expected to produce 12–16 peer-reviewed articles to fulfil the research requirements for tenure. This quantitative requirement has the unintended consequence of encouraging faculty staff to publish only to achieve tenure or promotion. Additionally, they publish in various fields according to the chances available at the time, either inside or outside their university. Furthermore, they look for low-quality publications that will allow them to publish with the least resistance; these journals are not widely read or indexed. As a result, faculty staff chasing quantity to meet tenure requirements are often not known as experts in any area, and few people have read their work.

It appears that the public perceives faculty members only to teach, while little is known about their work in research, industry engagement, and administration (Deale & Lee, 2019). Evidence suggests that job stress (Devonport et al., 2008) and work-life balance issues (Small et al., 2011) profoundly impact faculty staff performance, motivation, and wellbeing. A recent international survey (Deale & Lee, 2019) revealed that faculty members in hospitality programmes work long hours that vary by rank and age. Faculty members also spend considerable time on activities that might not traditionally be considered a significant part of their job (such as e-mailing); their typical workload includes teaching, research, and administration responsibilities, regardless of rank (Ladkin & Weber, 2009). A distinction between full-time and non-tenure-track faculty members of staff is made, with the latter assigned full teaching loads and almost no time for research (Haviland et al., 2017). A further problem arises from the fact that HE establishments with teaching or research focus differ in what hospitality educators are expected to do due to their direction. The authors argue that with the demise of Hotel Schools / Departments since the early 2010s (Ricci, 2022) and the inclusion of Hospitality Management programmes in Business Schools, we move towards homogenising faculty staff requirements regarding teaching, research, professional practice, qualifications, and attributes.

The Internationalisation of Hospitality Education

Hospitality education in many countries is highly international in terms of both student and faculty populations. However, this internationalism has not often been well developed to facilitate wider cultural dimensions to the study (Jayawardena, 2001) or to provide wider mobilities (Airey & Tribe, 2007). The developments under the Bologna initiative in the European Union countries provided an opportunity to increase student mobility and internationalisation in this part of the world (Powell & Finger, 2013). The significant number of international students, particularly from China, India, and South East Asia, suggests that there is scope for a much more adventurous approach to internationalism (Airey, 2015). In part, this is about ensuring that the development of hospitality management knowledge, the delivery of programmes, and the production of resources do not pursue an exclusively "Western" orientation (Dredge et al., 2014). In addition, it is equally important providing mobility opportunities for staff and students.

It is also argued that an international industry invariably attracts international students and employees, making the question of whether or not learning might be influenced by culture increasingly pertinent (Barron, 2014). Grey (2002: 165) suggests that "it is no longer appropriate to restrict one's frame of reference to one culture." It is imperative, therefore, that educators and trainers, both in and out of the workplace, ask how best to teach international student groups and question how successful learning can best take place. Charlesworth (2007) suggests that one step in this direction might be to look at the learning styles of individuals of different cultural backgrounds. Based on research that analysed the learning style preferences of international students studying hospitality and tourism management in Australia, Barron (2006) argues that many international students have learning style preferences that differ from those of other international and domestic students. From this, Barron (ibid.) raises the question of whether such students should fit into a system very different from their prior experience or whether it should be more sensitive and accommodating to their needs.

Airey and Tribe (2007) suggest that the over-supply of programmes and graduates globally has been a constant strand of criticism of hospitality education. The criticism may be justified when this is looked at in narrow terms of programmes providing training and education for specific entry positions in the industry. Indeed, some of the early programmes may have had such a narrow orientation. However, today there is little excuse for programmes confined to narrow vocationalism. The knowledge base about hospitality is extensive and provides a rich basis for developing programmes and providing quality education at all levels (Hsu et al., 2017). In addition, well-designed hospitality management programmes provide graduates with career and personal development opportunities (Lee et al., 2022). Dredge et al. (2014) argue that after an intense period of growth and development, hospitality education is now in an excellent position to do this: to provide new insights into the operation and management of a significant activity in the global economy; to contribute to the effective stewardship of scarce resources used by hospitality; to ensure that those who leave their courses have a range of knowledge and competencies for their career, whether it be in hospitality or elsewhere. It is these features that will make hospitality education relevant in the future.

Curriculum Design and Quality Assurance

The increasing global competition in HE closely relates to adopting and applying quality assurance management practices (Gross et al., 2017). The demand for quality assurance became inseparable from the development and facilitation of hospitality management programmes (Frawley et al., 2019); this occurred due to an increasing number of HE hospitality programme providers who are pursuing internationalisation to cater for student and faculty mobility and increase their international competitiveness (Kim & Jeong, 2018). The increased number of international collaborations in hospitality management programs has raised the issue of creating a valid international quality instrument to ensure standardisation, homogenisation, and academic recognition (Barron, 2014). Using any recognised quality assessment instrument indicates the quality of a hospitality management programme itself. As a result, students can be more confident in their qualifications from programmes assessed via such instruments (Stierand & Zizka, 2015). Furthermore, quality assurance practices referred to using this instrument appear relevant to increasing the recognition of foreign qualifications.

Among the various quality assurance forms in HE, external validation and accreditation are preferred in the US and Europe for global programmes (Hobson, 2010). Validation is the process through which a university determines that a new programme is academically viable, that academic standards have been adequately specified, and that all students are provided with the best opportunity to learn (Kis, 2005). Revalidation is only necessary when programs have undergone major changes or to satisfy the needs of an external entity. Revalidation ensures continuous fitness for purpose; HE providers in the UK revalidate their programmes every four years. On the other hand, accreditations are offered by HE institutes and professional bodies. An institution or programme can be accredited if it meets a threshold standard and qualifies for a certain status. Major programme accrediting agencies and professional bodies, such as the *International Council on Hotel, Restaurant and Institutional Education* (ICHRIE) and the *Institute of Hospitality* (IoH), have assumed the role of gatekeeper for the quality of hospitality education. Despite the increasing globalisation and internationalisation of hospitality management programs, the validation and accreditation systems are primarily restricted to Western countries and collaborating HE institutes worldwide.

The standardisation of hospitality management programmes appeared necessary, especially in the UK higher education establishments (Wood, 2015). As a response, hospitality education should overcome its traditional focus and be designed based on standards with a structured approach to curriculum development (Hatipoglu et al., 2014). The curriculum should be context-related and not context-bound (Smith & Cooper, 2000). Its planning should focus on philosophical questions relevant to the aims of education in addition to other sociological analyses (Wattanacharoensil, 2014). Still, it should be developed in such a way as to produce work-ready graduates capable of making future innovations (Morrison & O'Mahony, 2003) and university programmes relevant both for the present and future (Hawkins et al., 2012). Therefore, a well-balanced approach is required to create hospitality programmes that emphasise the industry's needs, location, and other local stakeholders' views.

The Use of ICT and AI in Hospitality Education

Over the past four decades, *Information and Communication Technology* (ICT) has transformed teaching and learning practices and shaped the curriculum design in hospitality management programmes (Goh & King, 2020). ICT integration in hospitality education refers to incorporating digital technologies and tools into the teaching and learning process within the hospitality industry (Fotiadis & Sigala, 2015). This integration aims to enhance the educational experience, increase student satisfaction, and prepare students for the technological demands of the modern hospitality sector (Frawley et al., 2019). With the exponential growth of ICT in classrooms, lecturers have a unique opportunity to enhance students' learning experiences through more engaging, interactive, student-centred instructional practices that boost students' motivation and learning outcomes while reducing problematic classroom behaviors (Sigala, 2013). During the COVID-19 pandemic, the technology adoption in hospitality education accelerated, enabling educators to experience both the advantages and limitations of working online (i.e., online teaching, e-conferences, virtual meetings, and online student supervision) (Sigala, 2021).

Furthermore, the use of Artificial Intelligence (AI), particularly in the form of ChatGPT, has a disruptive effect on the entire educational system and scientific research. As AI technology advances, it offers various opportunities to enhance the learning experience and improve the overall efficiency of education and research in the hospitality industry (Ivanov & Soliman, 2023). The disruptive nature of AI brings several challenges for HE institutes and hospitality educators, that is, students have used it since it was released to write summaries, essays, and even full theses, raising questions about academic degrees and their validity. As a result, HE institutes must redesign their teaching and assessment strategies and incorporate generative language models in teaching. In addition, we are not far from the first virtual teaching and research assistants, taking over many of the hospitality educators' cognitive tasks (Dwivedi et al., 2023). Researchers and scholars have also embraced the use of AI-generated content in all disciplines; this raises the question of whether publishers should be more receptive to manuscripts partially generated by artificial intelligence (Stokel-Walker, 2023). The key aspects of ICT and AI integration into hospitality education are presented below:

E-Learning Platforms: Implementing online learning platforms, such as Learning Management Systems (LMS) or Virtual Learning Environments (VLE), allows students to access course materials, assignments, and resources from anywhere at any time (Marinakou & Giousmpasoglou, 2015). This flexibility enables them to study at their own pace and facilitates distance learning. Furthermore, these platforms integrate multimedia elements, such as videos, interactive presentations, and animations, making learning more engaging and enjoyable, improving student retention and understanding of complex topics.

Personalised Learning: AI-powered platforms like ChatGPT can offer personalised learning experiences to students. By individually analysing the student's strengths, weaknesses, and learning pace, the AI can tailor educational content and resources to meet each student's specific needs (Ali and OpenAI Inc, 2023). Personalisation can improve performance and engagement and improve student retention rates. Furthermore, offering digital certifications and badges for completing specific tasks or acquiring skills can motivate students and showcase their achievements to potential employers.

Virtual Simulations: ICT can create virtual simulations and augmented reality of hospitality environments, such as online booking platforms, hotel operations, or restaurant management (Fotiadis & Sigala, 2015). This virtual learning environment enables students to gain practical experience in a controlled, risk-free setting, enhancing their skills and decision-making abilities (Price-Howard & Lewis, 2022).

Mobile Learning: Utilising mobile devices and applications allows students to access learning materials and resources *anytime-anywhere*, promoting continuous learning and engagement beyond traditional classroom settings (Tu & Hwang, 2020). In addition, mobile technologies can intensify learning and enhance students' motivation, interest, and learning achievements (Wang et al., 2017). Most VLEs can now be accessed from mobile devices (i.e., smartphones and tablets), providing great flexibility for students and staff.

Online Assessments and Data Analytics: The facilitation of online assessments enables immediate student feedback and allows hospitality educators to monitor progress effectively (Xiao et al., 2019). AI platforms and VLEs can help automate administrative tasks, such as grading assignments and providing feedback on basic assessments. This can save educators time, allowing them to focus on more personalised and interactive aspects of teaching. Different types of online assessments include quizzes, essay questions, debates, online polls, peer evaluation and review, and game-type activities (Kearns, 2012). This data-driven approach helps identify areas where students might need additional support. Furthermore, leveraging data analytics in hospitality education through VLEs can help educators, and HE institutions track student performance, identify trends, and make data-informed decisions to improve teaching strategies.

Language Learning: Hospitality education often involves learning multiple languages to cater to international guests. AI language models like ChatGPT can support language learning, helping students practice and improve their language skills through conversations and real-life scenarios (Ali and OpenAI Inc, 2023).

Continuous Learning and Upskilling: The hospitality industry is ever-evolving, and professionals and academics must continuously update their skills and knowledge (Chaudhuri et al., 2023). ICT can offer ongoing training and upskilling opportunities to hospitality professionals, ensuring they stay up-to-date with the latest trends and best practices (Giousmpasoglou et al., 2021). In addition, several faculty staff training courses (i.e., fire safety, data security, and health and safety) are now offered online with multiple benefits for the HE institutions and their employees.

Cloud Computing and Online Collaboration: Storing and accessing educational resources in the cloud provides easy scalability and cost-effectiveness for educational institutions, staff, and students. In addition, cloud computing facilitates virtual teamwork, allowing students to collaborate with peers and professionals worldwide, enhancing cross-cultural understanding and communication skills (Yadegaridehkordi et al., 2019).

It also allows academics and researchers to establish collaborations and work in real time, regardless of their location.

Industry Insights: Integrating ICT tools can enable access to real-time industry trends, best practices, and case studies, helping students and educators stay updated with the latest developments in the hospitality sector (Goh & Sigala, 2020).

Overall, the ICT and AI integration in hospitality education provides numerous benefits, including improved learning outcomes, increased student satisfaction and engagement, better employability, and enhanced graduate competitiveness in the evolving hospitality job market. HE institutions must stay abreast of technological advancements and adapt their curricula, teaching methodologies, and assessment strategies to prepare students for successful careers in the hospitality industry. It is also essential to understand the sweeping changes AI brings: despite its numerous benefits, AI should not replace human interaction and instruction in hospitality education. Instead, it should complement traditional teaching methods to create an efficient and inclusive learning environment.

The Importance of Hospitality Internships

Most hospitality and tourism courses offer student internship programmes, which are considerably promoted during student recruitment. This experiential form of learning is viewed as an excellent opportunity for students to integrate their thinking and action (Petrillose & Montgomery, 1997), apply theory taught in the classroom to real-world situations (Stansbie et al., 2016), develop skills such as decision-making and critical thinking (Marinakou & Giousmpasoglou, 2013), improve students' self-confidence (Ko, 2008), improve adaptability and become familiar with the industry (Robinson et al., 2016). Various definitions and different perspectives exist on what constitute internships. Agheorghiesei and Prodan (2011) propose that an internship is a systematic way for students to learn at work by interacting with others and learning by observation, reflection, analysis, and communication. Zopiatis and Constanti (2012: 34) view internships as "a short-term period of practical work experience wherein students receive training as well as gaining valuable job experiences in a specific field." Students learn in a professional context where they understand the theoretical concepts and how they apply them in practice (Beggs et al., 2008). There are three key stakeholders in the internship process: students, employers, and higher education institutions, and all contribute to the internship program and experience (Marinakou & Giousmpasoglou, 2013).

Many studies on hospitality internships have been conducted in different countries, including Australia (Nguyen et al., 2021), China (Chen et al., 2021), Cyprus (Farmaki, 2018), Greece (Christou & Chatzigeorgiou, 2019), Hong Kong (Lam & Ching, 2007), Malaysia (Pusiran et al., 2020), Taiwan (Wang & Hsieh, 2022), South Korea (Kim & Park, 2013), the Netherlands (Zhang & Eringa, 2022), Turkey (Collins, 2002), the UK (Jenkins, 2001), and the US (Hussien & La Lopa, 2018). The existing studies indicate that hospitality students, regardless of their backgrounds, have been found to face common challenges during their placements at hotels. In general, hospitality students are concerned with the capitalisation of their internship to find jobs (Collins, 2002), working conditions (Robinson et al., 2016), their relationships with their co-workers and supervisors (Kim & Park, 2013), and preparing themselves for the reality of work in the industry (Zopiatis et al., 2021). The positive and negative aspects of hospitality internships are discussed in the following sub-sections.

Factors That Lead to Internship Dissatisfaction

Several studies criticise the effectiveness of internships as an experiential approach to learning. Various factors have been found to create dissatisfaction and decreased motivation. Studies suggest that factors such as the ineffective design of an internship programme, wage discrepancies, and poor treatment of students may cause them to leave the industry after their internships (i.e., Ko, 2008; Richardson, 2008; Stansbie et al., 2016). Internship programmes that fail to meet students' expectations discourage them from entering the industry after graduation (Chen et al., 2021). This experience should provide students with suitable career factors, such as job satisfaction, job security, and reasonable salaries and workloads

(Kim & Park, 2013). In addition, the literature suggests that a successful internship program should be structured, planned, and organised to provide students with a challenging experience (Farmaki, 2018). It should also allow students to feel they play a significant role in the organisation and, thus, have a sense of fulfilment (Edwards, 2010). Zopiatis and Constanti (2007) argue that the interns' hosting organisations should be aware of adult learning styles and share their knowledge and skills while encouraging them to learn about and solve problems.

Discrepancies are found between student and industry expectations of an internship. Hospitality organisations expect students to demonstrate an understanding of the industry, interpersonal skills, a work ethic, teamwork, problem-handling, and good communication (Giousmpasoglou & Marinakou, 2021). Some scholars suggest that students are not appropriately prepared to meet the industry requirements and have unrealistic expectations regarding work and employment in the sector (i.e., Dickerson, 2009; Farmaki, 2018). Zopiatis and Constanti (2007) propose that students often find discrepancies between what they are taught in the classroom and what is practiced in hotels. Nevertheless, they suggest that some educational institutions still adequately prepare students to adapt to actual work environments by confronting them with operational issues and practices during their studies. Dickerson (2009) stated that students have high expectations of working in hotels, with a gap between their expectations and satisfaction. Agheorghiesei and Prodan (2011) and Zopiatis and Constanti (2007) propose that universities should prepare students with the required knowledge. The level of training prior to the internship is vital in forming expectations (Singh & Dutta, 2010), while host organisations should help develop skills and competencies and motivate the students to learn and engage. They add that a perceived fit should exist between students' and organisations' expectations and the provision of an internship programme.

Moreover, Kim and Park (2013) suggest that unfair promotions, unsatisfactory pay and benefits, and inappropriate behaviour of co-workers can contribute to unfavourable conditions that negatively shape students' perceptions of the industry. Jaszay and Dunk (2003) claim that if the mentor-managers or supervisors lack experience and efficiency, students' experience will be limited. Similarly, Zopiatis and Constanti

(2012) argue that supervisors directly influence student internship satisfaction. Furthermore, Taylor (2004) proposes that students assign a share of responsibility for problems at their internships to the employers and the receiving company. Their main concern is that they are used as cheap labour. Others claim that companies are unprepared to enhance and contribute to the student experience (Roney & Oztin, 2007). Thus, employers are faced with the challenge of offering projects to keep students challenged and interested.

Factors That Lead to Internship Satisfaction

Incorporating practical experiences in the hospitality curriculum provides numerous advantages (Hussien & La Lopa, 2018). Internships are found to prepare students for successful and fulfilling careers (Chen et al., 2021). Internships contribute to students' learning in a real working environment where they can reflect on the knowledge acquired during their studies (Self et al., 2016). Interestingly, internships allow students to understand the context of work in the hospitality industry and be aware of all the realities. Mihail (2006) in his study proposes that internships help students develop critical skills required for a career in hospitality, such as communication, time management, and self-motivation.

For many students, an internship is the first step in their careers (Kauffman, 2010) and a way to test their strengths and weaknesses in the workplace (Busby, 2005). It is also a process that requires students to be flexible and adaptable. Hussien and La Lopa (2018) found that the following factors contributing to internship satisfaction: feedback, autonomy, university supervisor support, academic preparedness, flexible working hours, student self-initiatives, location, and skills variety. Yoonjoung Heo et al. (2018) investigated hospitality student internship satisfaction based on generational differences. They found that fostering good relationships among colleagues can increase millennials' internship satisfaction and eventually reduce their intentions to leave the industry. In addition, critical factors such as gender, personality, and nationality were found to regulate student satisfaction (Chen et al., 2021) and career intention (Lugosi & Jameson, 2017).

In conclusion, the facilitation of well-planned internship programmes as an integral part of hospitality education programmes contributes towards creating high-quality, work-ready graduates for the global hotel industry. Managers and host organisations in the industry should add value to the internship programmes offered at their hotels by considering and meeting the students' expectations. They should not treat students as a solution to a labour-shortage problem. Furthermore, HR managers should investigate the factors influencing students' intention to stay at the organisation rather than what makes them leave. The main purpose of these hospitality organisations is to retain talented students; retaining interns provides them with a good pool of potential employees and managers.

Chapter Summary

Hospitality education is more than a century old, but as an academic discipline appears in the 1980s. The vocational nature of the hospitality curricula and the industry focus have created controversies and debates that are still in effect today. On the other hand, the rapid internationalisation of the hotel industry has pushed hospitality education globally, beyond the Western world boundaries. The need for standardisation and quality assurance created internationally recognised programmes and highly qualified work-ready graduates. Furthermore, the use of ICT and AI in hospitality curricula design and delivery has brought significant developments in the past 40 years. Finally, when designed and implemented correctly, internships can provide students with a smooth transition to the world of work and help employers attract talented graduates.

References

Agheorghiesei, D., & Prodan, A. (2011). The need for an internship model for the students of master in tourism and hotel management in Romania: Some conclusions and directions. *EuroCHRIE Proceedings*, 58–71.

Airey, D. (2015). 40 years of tourism studies—A remarkable story. *Tourism Recreation Research, 40*(1), 6–15.

Airey, D., & Tribe, J. (Eds.). (2007). *Developments in tourism research*. Routledge.

Ali, F., & ChatGPT OpenAI, Inc. (2023). Let the devil speak for itself: Should ChatGPT be allowed or banned in hospitality and tourism schools? *Journal of Global Hospitality and Tourism, 2*(1), 1–6. https://doi.org/10.5038/2771-5957.2.1.1016

Ayikoru, M., Tribe, J., & Airey, D. (2009). Reading tourism education neoliberalism unveiled. *Annals of Tourism Research, 36*(2), 191–221.

Barron, P. (2006). Stormy outlook? *Journal of Teaching in Travel & Tourism, 6*(2), 5–22.

Barron, P. (2014). International issues in curriculum design and delivery in tourism and hospitality education. In D. Dredge, D. Airey, & M. J. Gross (Eds.), *The Routledge handbook of tourism and hospitality education* (pp. 181–194). Routledge.

Baum, T. (2019). Does the hospitality industry need or deserve talent? *International Journal of Contemporary Hospitality Management, 31*(10), 3823–3837.

Baum, T., & Nickson, D. (1998). Teaching human resource management in hospitality and tourism: A critique. *International Journal of Contemporary Hospitality Management, 10*(2), 75–79.

Beggs, B., Ross, C. M., & Goodwin, B. (2008). A comparison of student and practitioner perspectives of the travel and tourism internship. *Journal of Hospitality, Leisure, Sport & Tourism Education, 7*(1), 31–39.

Bowen, J. T. (2005). Managing a research career. *International Journal of Contemporary Hospitality Management, 7*(7), 633–637.

Busby, G. (2005). Work experience and industrial links. In D. Airey & J. Tribe (Eds.), *An international handbook of tourism education* (pp. 93–107). Routledge.

Casado, M. A. (2003). Hospitality education: Prevalent perceptions. *FIU Hospitality Review, 21*(1), 83–92.

Charlesworth, Z. (2007). Educating international hospitality students and managers: The role of culture. *International Journal of Contemporary Hospitality Management, 19*(2), 133–145.

Chaudhuri, R., Chatterjee, S., Vrontis, D., Galati, A., & Siachou, E. (2023). Examining the issue of employee intentions to learn and adopt digital technology. *Worldwide Hospitality and Tourism Themes, 15*(3), 279–294.

Chen, T. L., Shen, C. C., & Gosling, M. (2021). To stay or not to stay? The causal effect of interns' career intention on enhanced employability and retention in the hospitality and tourism industry. *Journal of Hospitality, Leisure, Sport & Tourism Education, 28.* https://doi.org/10.1016/j.jhlste.2021.100305

Chipkin, H. (2004). Schools of thought. *Lodging Magazine*, 28–32.
Christou, E., & Chatzigeorgiou, C. (2019). Experiential learning through industrial placement in hospitality education: The meat in the sandwich. *Journal of Contemporary Education Theory & Research (JCETR), 3*(2), 31–35.
Collins, A. (2002). Gateway to the real world, industrial training: Dilemmas and problems. *Tourism Management, 23*(1), 93–96.
Deale, C. S., & Lee, S. H. (2019). Time is of the essence: A descriptive study of hospitality and tourism faculty members' perceptions of their jobs regarding time spent and activities pursued. *Journal of Hospitality & Tourism Education, 31*(2), 61–73.
Devonport, T., Biscomb, K., & Lane, A. (2008). Sources of stress and the use of anticipatory, preventative and proactive coping strategies by higher education lecturers. *Journal of Hospitality, Leisure, Sport & Tourism Education, 7*(1), 70–81.
Dickerson, J. P. (2009). The realistic preview may not yield career satisfaction. *International Journal of Hospitality Management, 28*(2), 297–299.
Dredge, D., Airey, D., & Gross, M. J. (2014). Creating the future: Tourism, hospitality and events education in a post-industrial, post-disciplinary world. In D. Dredge, D. Airey, & M. J. Gross (Eds.), *The Routledge handbook of tourism and hospitality education* (pp. 535–550). Routledge.
Dwivedi, Y. K., Pandey, N., Currie, W., & Micu, A. (2023). Leveraging ChatGPT and other generative artificial intelligence (AI)-based applications in the hospitality and tourism industry: Practices, challenges and research agenda. *International Journal of Contemporary Hospitality Management*. https://doi.org/10.1108/IJCHM-05-2023-0686
Edwards, J. (2010). Young professionals pave their own path to development. *American Water Works Association Journal, 102*(8), 36–41.
EHL. (n.d.). Our history. https://www.ehl.edu/en/about-ehl/our-history
Farmaki, A. (2018). Tourism and hospitality internships: A prologue to career intentions? *Journal of Hospitality, Leisure, Sport & Tourism Education, 23*, 50–58.
Felisitas, C., Molline, M., & Clotildah, K. (2012). The hospitality and tourism honours degree programme: Stakeholders' perceptions on competencies developed. *Journal of Hospitality Management and Tourism, 3*(1), 12–22.
Fidgeon, P. R. (2010). Tourism education and curriculum design: A time for consolidation and review? *Tourism Management, 31*(6), 699–723.
Fotiadis, A. K., & Sigala, M. (2015). Developing a framework for designing an Events Management Training Simulation (EMTS). *Journal of Hospitality, Leisure, Sport & Tourism Education, 16*, 59–71.

Frawley, T., Goh, E., & Law, R. (2019). Quality assurance at hotel management tertiary institutions in Australia: An insight into factors behind domestic and international student satisfaction. *Journal of Hospitality & Tourism Education, 31*(1), 1–9.

Giousmpasoglou, C. (2012). *A contextual approach to understanding managerial roles and competencies: The case of luxury hotels in Greece.* Unpublished Ph.D. thesis, University of Strathclyde.

Giousmpasoglou, C., & Marinakou, E. (2021). Hotel internships and student satisfaction as key determinant to career intention. *Journal of Tourism Research, 25*, 42–67. http://jotr.eu/pdf_files/V25.pdf

Giousmpasoglou, C., Marinakou, E., & Zopiatis, A. (2021). Hospitality managers in turbulent times: The COVID-19 crisis. *International Journal of Contemporary Hospitality Management, 33*(4), 1297–1318.

Goh, E., & King, B. (2020). Four decades (1980–2020) of hospitality and tourism higher education in Australia: Developments and future prospects. *Journal of Hospitality & Tourism Education, 32*(4), 266–272.

Goh, E., & Sigala, M. (2020). Integrating Information & Communication Technologies (ICT) into classroom instruction: Teaching tips for hospitality educators from a diffusion of innovation approach. *Journal of Teaching in Travel & Tourism, 20*(2), 156–165.

Grey, M. (2002). Drawing with difference: Challenges faced by international students in an undergraduate business degree. *Teaching in Higher Education, 7*(2), 153–166.

Gross, M. J., Benckendorff, P., Mair, J., & Whitelaw, P. A. (2017). Hospitality higher education quality: Establishing standards in Australia. *Journal of Hospitality and Tourism Management, 30*, 4–14.

Grubb, N. W., & Lazerson, M. (2005). Vocationalism in higher education: The triumph of the education gospel. *The Journal of Higher Education, 76*(1), 1–26.

Hatipoglu, B., Ertuna, B., & Sasidharan, V. (2014). A referential methodology for education on sustainable tourism development. *Sustainability, 6*(8), 5029–5048.

Haviland, D., Alleman, N. F., & Cliburn Allen, C. (2017). 'Separate but not quite equal': Collegiality experiences of full-time non-tenure-track faculty members. *The Journal of Higher Education, 88*(4), 505–528.

Hawkins, D. E., Ruddy, J., & Ardah, A. (2012). Reforming higher education: The case of Jordan's hospitality and tourism sector. *Journal of Teaching in Travel & Tourism, 12*(1), 105–117.

Hearns, N., Devine, F., & Baum, T. (2007). The implications of contemporary cultural diversity for the hospitality curriculum. *Education + Training, 49*(5), 350–363.

Hewitt, T. W. (2006). *Understanding and shaping curriculum: What we teach and why*. Thousand Oaks.

Hobson, J. P. (2010). Ten trends impacting international hospitality and tourism education. *Journal of Hospitality & Tourism Education, 22*(1), 4–7.

Hospitalitynet.org. (2012). Cornell School of Hotel Administration turns 90. https://www.hospitality net.org/news/4057820.html

Hsu, C. H., Xiao, H., & Chen, N. (2017). Hospitality and tourism education research from 2005 to 2014: "Is the past a prologue to the future?". *International Journal of Contemporary Hospitality Management, 29*(1), 141–160.

Hussien, F. M., & La Lopa, M. (2018). The determinants of student satisfaction with internship programs in the hospitality industry: A case study in the USA. *Journal of Human Resources in Hospitality & Tourism, 17*(4), 502–527.

ICHRIE. (2021). Guide to college programs in hospitality, tourism, & culinary arts. https://www.chrie.org/assets/2021_GuideToCollegePrograms_Final.pdf

Ivanov, S., & Soliman, M. (2023). Game of algorithms: ChatGPT implications for the future of tourism education and research. *Journal of Tourism Futures, 9*(2), 214–221.

Jaszay, C., & Dunk, P. (2003). *Training design for the hospitality industry*. Thomson-Delmar Learning.

Jayawardena, C. (2001). Challenges in international hospitality management education. *International Journal of Contemporary Hospitality Management, 13*(6), 310–315.

Jenkins, A. K. (2001). Making a career of it? Hospitality students' future perspectives: An Anglo-Dutch study. *International Journal of Contemporary Hospitality Management, 13*(1), 13–20.

Kauffman, R. (2010). *Career development in recreation, parks, and tourism: A positioning approach*. Human Kinetics.

Kearns, L. R. (2012). Student assessment in online learning: Challenges and effective practices. *Journal of Online Learning and Teaching, 8*(3), 198.

Kim, H. B., & Park, E. J. (2013). The role of social experience in undergraduates' career perceptions through internships. *Journal of Hospitality, Leisure, Sport & Tourism Education, 12*(1), 70–78.

Kim, H. J., & Jeong, M. (2018). Research on hospitality and tourism education: Now and future. *Tourism Management Perspectives, 25*, 119–122.

Kis, V. (2005). *Quality assurance in tertiary education: Current practices in OECD countries and a literature review on potential effects*. OECD. https://www.oecd.org/education/skills-beyond-school/38006910.pdf

Ko, W. H. (2008). Training, satisfaction with internship programs, and confidence about future careers among hospitality students: A case study of universities in Taiwan. *Journal of Teaching in Travel and Tourism, 7*(4), 1–15.

Ladkin, A. (2005). Careers and employment. In D. Airey & J. Tribe (Eds.), *An international handbook of tourism education* (pp. 437–450). Elsevier.

Ladkin, A., & Weber, K. (2009). Tourism and hospitality academics: Career profiles and strategies. *Journal of Teaching in Travel & Tourism, 8*(4), 373–393.

Lam, T., & Ching, L. (2007). An exploratory study of an internship program: The case of Hong Kong students. *International Journal of Hospitality Management, 26*(2), 336–351.

Larson, L. R., Duffy, L. N., Fernandez, M., Sturts, J., Gray, J., & Powell, G. M. (2019). Getting started on the tenure track: Challenges and strategies for success. *SCHOLE: A Journal of Leisure Studies & Recreation Education, 34*(1), 36–51.

Lee, P. C., Yoon, S., & Lee, M. J. (2022). Are you ready? Perceived career readiness attributes of the hospitality management students. *Journal of Hospitality & Tourism Education, 34*(3), 157–169.

Lugosi, P., & Jameson, S. (2017). Challenges in hospitality management education: Perspectives from the United Kingdom. *Journal of Hospitality and Tourism Management, 31*, 163–172.

Marinakou, E., & Giousmpasoglou, C. (2013). An investigation of student satisfaction from hospitality internship programs in Greece. *Journal of Tourism and Hospitality Management, 1*(3), 103–112.

Marinakou, E., & Giousmpasoglou, C. (2015). M-learning in the Middle East: The case of Bahrain. In *Assessing the role of mobile technologies and distance learning in higher education* (pp. 176–199). Hershey.

Marinakou, E., & Giousmpasoglou, C. (2019). Talent management and retention strategies in luxury hotels: Evidence from four countries. *International Journal of Contemporary Hospitality Management, 31*(10), 3855–3878.

McKercher, B. (2002). The future of tourism education: An Australian scenario. *Tourism and Hospitality Research, 3*(3), 199.

Mihail, D. M. (2006). Internship at Greek universities: An exploratory study. *Journal of Workplace Learning, 18*(1), 28–41.

Morrison, A., & O'Mahony, G. B. (2003). The liberation of hospitality management education. *International Journal of Contemporary Hospitality Management, 15*(1), 38–44.

Nguyen, I., Goh, E., & Murillo, D. (2021). Living through the lives of hospitality students during work-integrated learning (WIL) internships: An application of the critical incident technique to explore factors affecting students' WIL experience. *Journal of Hospitality & Tourism Education.* https://doi.org/10.1080/10963758.2021.1963755

Petrillose, M., & Montgomery, R. (1997). An exploratory study of internship practices in hospitality education and industry's perception of the importance of internships in hospitality curriculum. *Journal of Hospitality & Tourism Education, 9*(4), 46–51.

Powell, J. J., & Finger, C. (2013). The Bologna process's model of mobility in Europe: The relationship of its spatial and social dimensions. *European Educational Research Journal, 12*(2), 270–285.

Price-Howard, L. K., & Lewis, H. (2022). Perceived usefulness of simulation learning in hospitality education. *International Hospitality Review.* https://doi.org/10.1108/IHR-05-2022-0028

Pusiran, A. K., Janin, Y., Ismail, S., & Dalinting, L. J. (2020). Hospitality internship program insights. *Worldwide Hospitality and Tourism Themes, 12*(2), 155–164.

Ricci. (2022). The shifting landscape of hospitality and tourism education. https://www.hotelmanagement.net/operate/shifting-landscape-hospitality-and-tourism-education

Richardson, S. (2008). Undergraduate tourism and hospitality students attitudes toward a career in the industry: A preliminary investigation. *Journal of Teaching in Travel & Tourism, 8*(1), 23–46.

Riley, M., Ladkin, A., & Szivas, E. (2002). *Tourism employment: Analysis and planning.* Channel View Publications.

Robinson, R. N., Ruhanen, L., & Breakey, N. M. (2016). Tourism and hospitality internships: Influences on student career aspirations. *Current Issues in Tourism, 19*(6), 513–527.

Roney, S. A., & Oztin, P. (2007). Career perceptions of undergraduate tourism students: A case study in Turkey. *Journal of Hospitality, Leisure, Sport & Tourism Education, 6*(1), 4–17.

Rutherford, D. G., & Samenfink, W. (1992). Most frequent contributors to the hospitality literature. *Hospitality Research Journal, 16*(1), 23–39.

Schmidgall, R. S., & Woods, R. H. (1994). CHRIE member perceptions of tenure requirements in hospitality education programs. *Hospitality Research Journal, 18*(1), 101–120.

Self, T. T., Adler, H., & Sydnor, S. (2016). An exploratory study of hospitality internships: Student perceptions of orientation and training and their plans to seek permanent employment with the company. *Journal of Human Resources in Hospitality & Tourism, 15*(4), 485–497.

Sigala, M. (2013). Using and measuring the impacts of geovisualisation on tourism education: The case of teaching a service management course. *Journal of Hospitality, Leisure, Sport & Tourism Education, 12*(1), 85–98.

Sigala, M. (2021). Rethinking of tourism and hospitality education when nothing is normal: Restart, recover, or rebuild. *Journal of Hospitality and Tourism Research, 45*(5), 920–923.

Singh, A., & Dutta, K. (2010). Hospitality internship placements: Analysis for United Kingdom and India. *Journal of Services Research, 10*(1), 85–99.

Slater, J. (2013). How Cook found the right recipe for Swiss travel. https://www.swissinfo.ch/eng/ pioneering-spirit_how-cook-found-the-right-recipe-for-swiss-travel/36758830

Small, J., Arris, C., Wilson, E., & Teljevic, I. (2011). Voices of women: A memory-work reflection on work-life dis/harmony in tourism academia. *Journal of Hospitality, Leisure, Sport & Tourism Education, 10*(1), 23–36.

Smith, G., & Cooper, C. (2000). Competitive approaches to tourism and hospitality curriculum design. *Journal of Travel Research, 39*, 90–95.

Stansbie, P., Nash, R., & Chang, S. (2016). Linking internships and classroom learning: A case study examination of hospitality and tourism management students. *Journal of Hospitality, Leisure, Sport & Tourism Education, 19*, 19–29.

Stierand, M., & Zizka, L. (2015). Reflecting on hospitality management education through a practice lens. *Quality Assurance in Education, 23*(4), 353–363.

Stokel-Walker, C. (2023). ChatGPT listed as author on research papers: Many scientists disapprove. *Nature, 613*, 620–621.

Taylor, S. (2004). Cooperative education in emerging economies. In R. K. Coll & C. Eames (Eds.), *International handbook for cooperative education* (pp. 207–214). World Association for Cooperative Education.

Tribe, J. (2014). The curriculum: A philosophic practice? In *The Routledge handbook of tourism and hospitality education* (pp. 17–29). Routledge.

Tu, Y. F., & Hwang, G. J. (2020). Trends and research issues of mobile learning studies in hospitality, leisure, sport and tourism education: A review of academic publications from 2002 to 2017. *Interactive Learning Environments, 28*(4), 385–403.

Velo, V., & Mittaz, C. (2006). Breaking in to emerging international hotel markets: Skills needed to face this challenge and ways to develop them in hospitality management students. *International Journal of Contemporary Hospitality Management, 18*(6), 496–508.

Wang, C. J., & Hsieh, H. Y. (2022). Effect of deep learning approach on career self-efficacy: Using off-campus internships of hospitality college students as an example. *Sustainability, 14*(13). https://doi.org/10.3390/su14137594

Wang, H. Y., Liu, G. Z., & Hwang, G. J. (2017). Integrating socio-cultural contexts and location-based systems for ubiquitous language learning in museums: A state of the art review of 2009–2014. *British Journal of Educational Technology, 48*(2), 653–671.

Wattanacharoensil, W. (2014). Tourism curriculum in a global perspective: Past, present, and future. *International Education Studies, 7*(1), 9–20.

Wood, R. (2015). 'Folk' understandings of quality in UK higher hospitality education. *Quality Assurance in Education, 23*(4), 326–338.

Xiao, C., Qiu, H., & Cheng, S. M. (2019). Challenges and opportunities for effective assessments within a quality assurance framework for MOOCs. *Journal of Hospitality, Leisure, Sport & Tourism Education, 24*, 1–16.

Yadegaridehkordi, E., Shuib, L., Nilashi, M., & Asadi, S. (2019). Decision to adopt online collaborative learning tools in higher education: A case of top Malaysian universities. *Education and Information Technologies, 24*, 79–102.

Yoonjoung Heo, C., Kim, S., & Kim, B. (2018). Investigating the impact of relationship quality during an internship on millennials' career decisions and gender differences. *Journal of Hospitality & Tourism Education, 30*(2), 71–84.

Zhang, R., & Eringa, K. (2022). Predicting hospitality management students' intention to enter employment in the hospitality industry on graduation: A person–environment fit perspective. *Research in Hospitality Management, 12*(2), 103–113.

Zopiatis, A., & Constanti, P. (2007). And never the Twain shall meet: Investigating the hospitality industry-education relationship in Cyprus. *Education + Training, 49*(5), 391–407.

Zopiatis, A., & Constanti, P. (2012). Managing hospitality internship practices: A conceptual framework. *Journal of Hospitality and Tourism Education, 24*(1), 44–51.

Zopiatis, A., Papadopoulos, C., & Theofanous, Y. (2021). A systematic review of literature on hospitality internships. *Journal of Hospitality, Leisure, Sport & Tourism Education, 28*. https://doi.org/10.1016/j.jhlste.2021.100309

8

Diversity and Gender Issues in Hotel Management

Photo Credits: *Ketut Subiyanto* (*Free to use under the Pexels License*). (Source: https://www.pexels.com/photo/happy-diverse-colleagues-working-on-laptop-4350084/)

Introduction

The hospitality and tourism industry constantly evolves, with fast-paced changes, multidimensional challenges, fierce competition, generational and cultural differences, and crises. This volatile environment requires hotel leaders to be resilient and able to adapt. (Giousmpasoglou et al., 2021). Moreover, one of the key challenges for hoteliers globally is the high labour turnover, which costs the industry £274 million per annum (People 1st, 2017), as well as skills shortages (McKinsey & Company, 2020). As a result of the COVID-19 pandemic, many hotels closed down and had difficulty reopening. In addition to causing cultural diversity and inclusion challenges, the post COVID-19 crisis negatively affected the gender wage gap, negatively affecting women disproportionately in the workplace (Madera et al., 2023).

This chapter explores diversity and diversity management, focusing on gender issues in hotel management. Despite the profound benefits of an inclusive working environment, the global hotel industry is slow in adopting best practices in diversity management. In addition, the challenging working conditions and the masculine occupational culture are the key challenges for women to pursue a career in hotels. The #metoo campaign and other recent developments have brought to light issues, including sexual harassment and widespread gender segregation in the hotel sector, particularly in senior management and board positions. The organisational barriers preventing women from progressing in their careers, the structural barriers in the hotel sector, and the pay differences between male and female managers are discussed in the chapter. For this purpose, the chapter presents some key success stories from existing hotels and proposes ways to benefit from the existing talent of women and other diverse groups.

Diversity and Diversity Management

Only as late as in the 90s, the United Nations Universal Declaration on Cultural Diversity (1995) provided a description of diversity which is considered to widen "the range of options open to everyone; it is one of the roots of development, understood not simply in terms of economic growth, but also as a means to achieve a more satisfactory intellectual, emotional, moral and spiritual existence" (Article 3). The Society for Human Resource Management (cited in Kalargyrou & Costen, 2017: 69) defined diversity as "the collective mixture of differences and similarities that include, for example, individual and organisational characteristics, values, beliefs, experiences, backgrounds, preferences and behaviours." Van Knippenberg and Schippers (2007: 156) defined diversity as "a characteristic of social grouping that reflects the degree to which objective or subjective differences exist between group members." Research on diversity in hospitality has increased, and diversity has been viewed as a multidimensional concept (Mistry et al., 2021), proposing that it refers to groups with particular characteristics (Hsiao et al., 2015), either named *primary characteristics* (i.e., age, nationality, ethnicity, and gender) or *secondary characteristics* (i.e., educational level, personality, social and economic backgrounds). In general, diversity encompasses not only observable dimensions such as gender, age, and race but also non-observable dimensions such as beliefs and values (Madera et al., 2023). Kreitz (2008: 102) proposed four groups of diversity characteristics: (1) *personality* (e.g., traits, skills, and abilities); (2) *internal characteristics* (e.g., gender, race, ethnicity, and sexual orientation); (3) *external characteristics* (e.g., national culture, religion, and marital or parental status); and (4) *organisational characteristics* (e.g., position, department, or union/non-union).

Inclusion is a concept incorporated into diversity, which refers to the level of employee engagement and integration within the organisation. Inclusion plays a vital role in managing diversity as it fosters a sense of value and respect; employees feel included and contribute with their unique characteristics and talents to creativity, innovation, and productivity (Madera et al., 2023). Diversity management is a complex and challenging process as it requires addressing inequality, stereotypes, and discrimination based on the characteristics already provided, such as age, gender, and disability (Manoharan et al., 2021). Diversity management practices in the hotel industry have been in place for over two decades to address workforce diversity and its characteristics. Malik et al. (2017) found that a diverse and inclusive climate in hospitality organisations positively impacts employee performance. Diversity management refers to all policies and practices related to human resources management to address differences among the workforce. The effectiveness of diversity management depends on the employees' perceptions of diversity management practices (Garcıa-Rodrıguez et al., 2020). Such practices in hotel management are discussed in this chapter.

Diversity and Diversity Management in Hotels

Hotels are characterised by a high level of diversity among employees and customers because the hospitality and tourism industry is one of the most diverse context where employees from different backgrounds serve customers of different age groups, gender, ethnicity, culture, and, in general, from diverse geographic locations. In this multicultural context, hotel managers must proactively pursue diversity and diversity management, especially if they want fresh ideas, growth, a strong brand image, and high performance (Madera et al., 2023). The hotel sector relies on a culturally diverse workforce with an influx of migrant labour and minority employees, challenging human resources management and staff retention (Giousmpasoglou et al., 2021). Corporate success in the global economy depends on stakeholders respecting diversity, yet, 51% of countries have no laws to protect workers from discrimination (Boogaard, 2021). There are various dimensions where people may experience discrimination, just as there are various dimensions and qualities for diversity. Age, disability, origin/colour, sexual orientation, and gender are some of the most prevalent factors in hotel management.

Age Differences

There is evidence of age differences among employees in hotels. Although age discrimination at the workplace is prohibited by law and recognised as poor industry practice, it still occurs in hotels. Research is limited in this area, as most studies focus more on young generations than elderly groups (Goh & Lee, 2018). Evidence suggests that only 3% of hotels in the US hire employees older than 65, and less than 20% of employees are above 50, suggesting that organisational cultures, operating practices, and HR policies are designed to suit the younger generations' needs (TalentHive, 2022).

Disabilities

Most of the studies in hospitality and tourism on disabilities focus on customers rather than employees (Madera et al., 2023). Several policies, practices, and legislation refer to the legal obligations of hotels to effectively meet the needs of customers with mobility impairments or other disabilities. The studies on employees with disabilities used exploratory and conceptual approaches focusing on policy and regulations (Kalargyrou & Costen, 2017). People with disabilities represent 15% of the global population (World Health Organization, 2023b). People with disabilities face employment and career development challenges in hotels, as managers have concerns regarding their abilities and capability of working, including high costs, low productivity, and a lack of qualified trainers (Kalargyrou & Costen, 2017). Interestingly, Nickson et al.'s (2005) assertion that the hotel business needs workers with aesthetic and self-representation skills presents a barrier to career opportunities for individuals with disabilities when emphasis is placed on physical appearance. Nevertheless, studies demonstrate that employees with disabilities are reliable, loyal, and provide quality service (Madera et al., 2023) (Box 8.1).

> **Box 8.1 Accor Group's Commitment to People with Disabilities**
>
> Accor is the world's leading hotel operator, with 470,000 rooms in 3600 hotels in 92 countries across 14 trusted brands such as Sofitel, Pullman, Novotel, Mercure and Ibis. Accor is a place that welcomes, integrates and respects individuals from diverse backgrounds and knows how to appeal to them. The Group's internal efforts to encourage diversity are based on four pillars: diversity of origin; gender equality; the inclusion of people with disabilities; and diversity of age. These pillars were formalised within the Group in 2011 by way of an International Diversity Charter, released in 15 languages. With regard to people with disabilities, the Charter states clearly that the Group is "committed to an active policy for the inclusion and retention of each legislation locally."
>
> The Group's commitment to people with disabilities can be seen through efforts at international and national levels. In addition to a diversity charter, Accor raises awareness and, importantly, increases contact between hiring managers and people with disabilities through annual celebrations of the International Day of Persons with Disabilities. In 2013, for example, meetings between business managers (including Operations Managers and Department Heads), team members with disabilities and guests from the Brazilian Rede Empresarial de Inclus o Social (Corporate Network for Social Inclusion) were organised to learn about and discuss the recruitment and inclusion needs of people with disabilities.
>
> A number of hotels adapted their kitchen following Novotel Saclay's example. Pullman Paris Montparnasse is the only hotel that requires more than 50 trolleys to restock in-room minibars. To reduce the strain involved in pushing and pulling the trolleys along carpeted corridors, motorised trolleys have been introduced. This was a major investment for the hotel and made possible by additional financing contributed by the Disability Team on behalf of the Group. This adjustment helps reducing the risk of musculoskeletal disorders and other types of disabilities related to handling heavy objects and using repetitive gestures.
>
> Source: ILO (2014: 15)

Origin / Colour

Employees' ethnicity and skin tone constitute another form of discrimination in the hotel industry. Ethnic segregation in the workplace is due to differences in language between black and white employees or people from different countries. Many employees have experienced discrimination on these grounds in five-star hotels, either from managers in the hiring process or customers (Lashley, 2022). Although the notion of beauty differs per culture, managers still discriminate when hiring people in hotels, as employees are the face of the company and often feel that skin colour variations do not match the company's profile. The Castell Project report (2022) highlights the key issues regarding colour representation in hotel leadership positions. More specifically, the report states that in 2021, only 11% of the 671 hotel companies included in the study had Black executives showing a decline from 2019. The pandemic also had an impact, as black hotel employees' representation dropped to 13.6% in 2021 from 18.8% in 2019. In the US, racial diversity is evolving as immigrants continue to enter the country (Kalargyrou & Costen, 2017). Similarly, migrants were the primary source of labour for hotels in the UK which has been reduced dramatically after BREXIT (McKinsey & Company, 2020). The 2020 movement *#blacklivesmatter (BLM)*, set off by the murder of George Floyd, has rippled through various industries, including hotels. The movement urged for scrutiny of discrimination endemic in the sector, as people of colour are more likely to experience higher unemployment levels, lower quality education and housing, reduced health outcomes, "*leading to lower economic opportunities, weaker social networks, and reduced chances of economic mobility*" (ROC, 2015: 20). Consequently, hotel managers must be aware of racial and cultural diversity to manage diverse teams effectively.

Many discrimination cases have been reported in hotels, including sexual harassment, racial discrimination, and age discrimination. For instance, The Washington Post reported on a hotel employee at the Country Inn & Suites by Radisson in Newport News who referred to a black guest as a "monkey" and was subsequently dismissed (Glusac, 2018). In 2015 the hospitality industry received the most complaints of discrimination of any other sector, with the hotel sector being prevalent in incidents related to racial bias (Malik et al., 2017). Such discrimination cases negatively impact staff job satisfaction, retention, and brand publicity, making it more challenging for such organisations to attract and retain talent (Ouyang et al., 2020). Diversity and inclusion are paramount for the hotel industry, where it is important to appreciate the connections between guests and employees. Studies suggest that certain groups (i.e., white men in US organisations) have less positive attitudes towards diversity management practices and the inclusion of minority groups, such as women and people with disabilities (Madera et al., 2023). One factor to consider when fostering an inclusive working environment is resistance to diversity. The hotel sector is a unique, diverse context with employees from different backgrounds. While multiple barriers exist, cultural diversity can help managers facilitate innovative and creative practices, improving the hotel's performance and reputation.

Therefore, diversity is not only recognising and valuing differences but also understanding how these differences influence the individual experience in hotels. In this case, employees are satisfied, and customers enjoy inclusive services that meet or exceed their expectations. With the continued labour market challenges, more women aged 30–44 are entering the workforce, millennials, and Generation Zs, forcing hotels to offer more flexibility to attract employees from this pool of talent (Goldfischer, 2023).

Sexual Orientation

The employee's sexual orientation is another area of discrimination in hotels. Although it is difficult to measure the global population of lesbian, gay, bisexual, transgender, or queer (LGBTQQ) groups, some data is available. For example, 1.6% of people in the US and 1.5% of people in the UK are members of this minority group. (Catalyst, 2015). Members of this group face institutionalised prejudice, social exclusion, and anti-homosexual hatred and violence (World Health Organization, 2023a). Kalargyrou and Costen (2017) suggest that most countries do not provide legal protection for this group; however, the number of hotel companies introducing LGBTQ policies in their diversity programmes is rising. Sexual harassment is a problem plaguing the hospitality industry, including hotels, profoundly affecting the employee psyche and increasing employee burnout (Pearlman & Bordelon, 2022). For example, *#MeToo* has become an international movement against sexual harassment and assault, mainly in the workplace, a movement that empowers marginalised voices such as the LGBTQ community. In their study, Pearlman and Bordelon (2022) found that male guests approached 44 out of 46 room attendants inappropriately. Understanding the problem and taking action to stop discriminatory practices are crucial for combating sexual harassment and bias. The Equal Employment Opportunity Commission (EEOC) is the federal agency in the US to eliminate sexual harassment in the workplace. They emphasise the benefit of prevention and urge organisations to communicate and train employees not to tolerate harassment and highlight the need to establish an effective complaint or grievance process for immediately taking action in case of a complaint (Pearlman & Bordelon, 2022).

Gender and Gender Diversity in Hotel Management

Gender is another key dimension of diversity in hotels. The hospitality industry, including the hotel sector, has been traditionally male-dominated, where employment opportunities are versatile (Marinakou, 2012). The concept of gender has been broadly studied, taking a more diffuse set of meanings. In early studies, gender was not separated from sex (Davis et al., 2006), referring to the differences between men and women. Nevertheless, studies proposed that a separation between sex and gender was required in order to study gender in leadership and management. Gherardi (1994) suggested that gender is a symbol that embodies the biological differences in culture; she further proposed that masculinity and femininity are socially constructed. As a result, people are born with a particular sex. For example, a man may be born as a male but not naturally manly; instead, via his social interactions, he develops masculinity and therefore becomes a man (Connell, 2009). Gender is defined by West and Zimmerman (1987: 126) as:

> *the activity of managing situated conduct in the light of normative conceptions or attitudes and activities appropriated for one's sex category. Doing gender involves a complex of socially guided perceptual, interactional and micropolitical activities that cast particular pursuits as expressions of masculine and feminine natures.*

Based on the above, gender refers to social expectations and social roles attributed to people, and gender roles may change depending on the situation (Marinakou, 2012). People's attitudes towards female managers are gradually changing and, with traditional masculine stereotypes regarding leadership traits, tend to become extinct in the workplace (Pardal et al., 2020). Nevertheless, issues still hinder women's careers in hotel management like the glass ceiling, as jobs require senior executives to be flexible with relocation options and based on other stereotypical issues discussed in the following sections. The hospitality and tourism industry suffers from significant *occupational segregation* (Hutchings et al., 2020), where men hold most managerial positions and earn more than their female counterparts (UNWTO, 2019). For example, women's Australian full-time hourly earnings in the hospitality industry were 10.9% less than men's (WGEA, 2016).

Occupational segregation by sex (or gender) is defined as when "the jobs that women do are different from those done by men (horizontal segregation) and women work at lower levels than men in the occupational hierarchy (vertical segregation)" (Stockdale, 1991: 57). There is *vertical and horizontal gender segregation* in hotels, indicating gender differences in the positions held, pay, promotions, as well as corporate management strategies (Xiong et al., 2022). Gender stereotypes impact the hospitality business; for example, there is a presumption that most women have seasonal or part-time jobs in hotels. Purcell (1996: 20) identified three types of jobs in her study; these are:

- *contingently gendered jobs*, where women do jobs that include a role mainly gender-neutral;
- *sex-typed jobs*, where roles are sex related; and
- *patriarchal practice jobs*, where roles are identified and specified by beliefs and practices that reflect gender attributes.

Therefore, most female hotel employees hold mainly positions in the front office, food and beverage, and housekeeping. These jobs do not allow them to progress to senior managerial positions (Mistry et al., 2021). In 2019 the position of women in managerial and executive positions was 13% in hotels, although women account for 53% of the hospitality workforce (Russen et al., 2021). Interestingly, "little effort has been made to correct the male domination of higher positions and marginalisation of women in hospitality" (Gebbels et al., 2019). Xiong et al. (2022) argue that many female hotel employees encounter sexism, discrimination, and gender stereotypes. Gender is not a simple property of people but an activity and a social dynamic (Marinakou, 2012). Although gender is socially constructed (Liu et al., 2020), it is still a key dimension in organisations, constraining the behaviour of both men and women and limiting them to contribute to diversity based on their perspectives.

As already discussed, gender is a system of beliefs that creates a distinction between females and males; it is also used to define social roles and coerce women and men to individual paths (Segovia-Perez et al., 2019). Risman (2004) in his "Gender as a Social Structure" theory, proposed three levels of gender. First, the individual level is linked with the construction of gender at an individual level; it investigates how individuals see their gendered selves, thus creating cognitive images of femininity and masculinity. Second, the interactional level refers to reinforcing gender roles and expected behaviours. Third, the institutional level refers to the different attitudes towards women and men. At this level, there are gaps in opportunities, contractual differences, and the glass ceiling because of the diverse organisational systems where males preserve control, replicating gender and gender differences. Therefore, the experience of either gender at work is governed by gender roles in organisations, which reflect the socially constructed image of maleness and femaleness and specify power relations among them. Therefore, gender roles in organisations identify gender differences and determine how individuals interact and who dominates the group.

The Glass Ceiling in Hotels

Today's hospitality and tourism environment is characterised by uncertainty and unpredictability; the most recent challenges such as the COVID-19 pandemic and Brexit in the UK have caused a massive exodus of employees in the industry creating shortage of skills and adding more challenges for women to occupy positions in hotel management and leadership. Studies propose that gender is present in organisations, as it is difficult for people to leave their "gender" at the door when entering the workplace (Martin, 2006), making gender relevant to work.

Although the industry shows growth and there is need to cover all positions in hotels, the position of women in management is low and only few women are found in high managerial positions. ILO (2015) reports that 60–70% of employees in the hospitality and tourism industry are women. Nevertheless, Castell Project (2022) suggests that only 11% of women hold senior management or executive positions (e.g., Managing Director, President, CEO). The report even proposes that only one woman out of eight men reaches a top leadership position. The founder of Women in Hospitality (WOHO), Julia Campbell claimed that 55.5% of employees in the US hospitality sector are women. People 1st (2017) in their study of the UK hospitality and tourism industry found that there were 1.05 million women working in the hospitality industry, 49% working in operational roles and only 11% in managerial roles. Evidently there is a paradox, women form the majority of employees in hospitality and tourism, but yet they are one of the most vulnerable groups in terms of career progression and working conditions.

The barriers for women to progress in hotel management and leadership are best described by a phenomenon known as the "glass ceiling." The glass ceiling is defined as "the invisible, generally artificial barriers that prevent qualified individuals—in this case women—from advancing within their organisation and reaching their full potential" (Knutson & Schmidgall, 1999: 64). This phenomenon is socially constructed from social expectations and beliefs and is based on attitudinal and/or organisational bias (Ragins et al., 1998) that undermine women's managerial positions (Marinakou, 2012). Eagly et al. (2007) provided another concept, namely, the "labyrinth effect," which refers to the difficulties women face in progressing in their career. Pasquerella and Clauss-Ehlers (2017: 7) added the concept of the "broken rung," which "refers to one aspect of the proverbial glass ceiling, where women are missing the first step to the ladder of leadership or the stages in the promotion process."

There are many different views of the barriers that exist and account to the phenomenon of the glass ceiling. Interestingly, most studies on the phenomenon are descriptive and do not differentiate by industry

(Marinakou, 2012). This section provides an overview of the glass ceiling phenomenon in hotel management.

Studies propose that the most prominent barrier to women's advancement in hotel management are stereotypes and preconceptions of women's roles and abilities (WiH, 2020; Mihail, 2006). Helgesson (2005) described gender stereotypes as generalisations to differentiate groups of people (women and men) and she identified the features people assign to women and men in societies, not due to social roles or biological sex. Eagly (2007) included prejudice, which exists when people have certain beliefs about each gender's social roles, and how each gender should behave including certain distinct traits and abilities. Such stereotypes may be experienced without being aware of it. For example, gender stereotypes reinforce the view that women are nurturing and child bearers and men are focusing on the task and take control (Hoyt, 2012). Hence, such stereotypes spill at the workplace, where men are considered to be the leaders and women the followers. Hotels are male-dominated and reflect a masculine culture; women in hotel management face fierce competition with their male counterparts as they should also work harder than males to prove themselves (Elhoushy & El-Said, 2020).

The glass ceiling falls within the organisational culture and practices in organisations. Occupational segregation has already been discussed, which is evident in hotel management. As stereotypes spill in the workplace, the organisational culture may influence the perceptions about women's and men's roles. There are organisational cultures that favour men such as hotels (Metcalfe, 2008). Women's opportunities are limited by structural organisational barriers. The "old boys network" an informal system where people with similar background support each other. Lack of networking and mentoring limits women's opportunities as due to domestic responsibilities they find it difficult to take part at the old boys network and relevant activities. Women in hotel management suggested that they developed their network when they changed jobs, they mentored other women supporting them for greater work success and job satisfaction (Marinakou, 2012). There are organisational cultures that support women to advance their careers and diversity, hence they erect barriers that prevent women from advancing, but still the glass ceiling persists with working family conflict and poor childcare support (Gebbels et al., 2019; Mistry et al., 2021), lack of human capital investment in recruiting female managers, and insufficient career planning including lack of appropriate organisational approaches to career development and advancement for women. Within this environment, "social structures, systems and arrangements channel and define gender differences due to discrepancies in status and power" (Russen et al., 2021). Poor working conditions, pay inequality, and few opportunities for promotion are other issues women face in hotel management (Elhoushy & El-Said, 2020). Often women are not considered for hiring or promotion on the grounds they will get married, will get pregnant, and will be less productive (Elhoushy & El-Said, 2020). Due to the difficult working practices, irregular and long working hours, many women either leave their career or choose to work in another industry. In view to this evidence, Martin (2006) proposed that if people believe that gender matters, then they will behave according to the gender roles ascribed to their gender and they will interpret this with routinised engagements in verbal and body actions and interactions. On this note, the personal cost for female hotel managers is high and usually at the expense of their family (Marinakou, 2014; Narayanan, 2017).

Such gender roles and stereotypes and the consequence of gender discrimination include the *gender pay gap*. Although the pay gap between women and men is narrowing in hospitality, women still earn less than men with many variations of this pay difference at different levels, positions, and roles (People 1st, 2017). For example, women earn on average 21 percent less an hour than their male counterparts (Fig. 8.1).

Although many hospitality organisations transmit positive discourses and images promoting gender equality, the gender gap and the barriers for women's progression in the career ladder persist. The glass ceiling phenomenon and such barriers are summarised in Fig. 8.2.

Interestingly, Boone et al. (2013) suggested that the glass ceiling is no longer evident in the hospitality industry. They claim that it is only the failure of organisations to assist women with their self-imposed barriers to success. On the contrary, when female managers were interviewed, they simply proposed that "if you manage your time, then you can

Annual Income

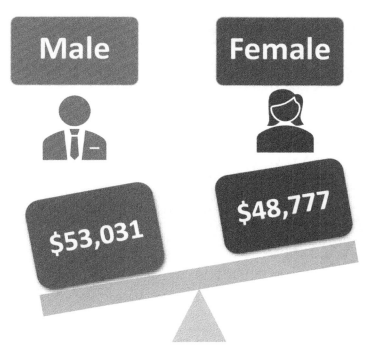

Fig. 8.1 Hospitality manager pay gap in the US. (Source: www.zippia.com)

balance work with family… and pursue a career in hotel management" (Marinakou, 2014: 20). Hence, we argue that hotel management is male-dominated, is a highly gendered sector (Baum, 2013) with clear evidence of strong segregations of occupations and prevalence of men in senior management positions. The career for women is a complex journey, but as the concept supports, it is not necessary to view these obstacles as discouraging, as women may be aware of these challenges and find ways to overcome these barriers. Studies on the position of women in hotel management propose that women's own personal drive, ambition, and talent helped them climb the career ladder successfully (Carvalho et al., 2018; Marinakou, 2014).

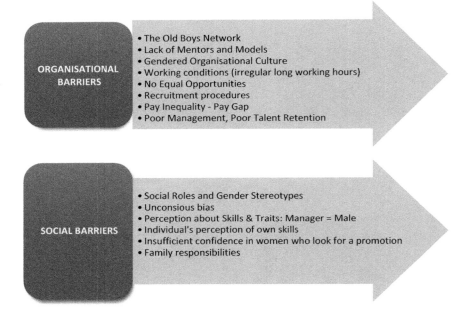

Fig. 8.2 Glass ceiling dimensions in hotel management. (Source: Authors' creation)

Diversity Management Practices in Hotels

Diversity and inclusion are important for employees' wellbeing, job satisfaction, and business success. Hotels—as any other business—have a social responsibility to provide equal opportunities and fair treatment to all individuals regardless their background (Mistry et al., 2021). Organisations that embrace diversity management practices are found to gain the competitive advantage. Effective diversity management includes practices to manage a diverse workforce to ensure inclusivity and requires employees' positive perceptions of such practices (García-Rodríguez et al., 2020).

Recent studies have focused on diversity management practices in hotels. Iverson (2000) developed a model of diversity management practices which include the following:

- Taking all employees seriously;
- Recognising the capabilities of all employees;
- Supporting all employees;
- Communicating effectively with all employees;
- Valuing a diverse work group;
- Respecting the cultural beliefs and needs of employees; and
- Accepting non-English-speaking employees.

She recommended practices such as effective communication, respect and inclusion, and respect for different cultures and languages. Madera et al. (2023) further included training programmes to be offered to all employees on diversity and the encouragement of diversity councils within hotels to enhance and promote cultural awareness. Furthermore, emphasis should be placed on supporting minority groups, including women and the LGBTQ community, or even include intergenerational programmes, disability benefits, and veteran benefits (Mistry et al., 2021).

In terms of people with disabilities, various examples of diversity management practices are proposed. For example, for employees with Down syndrome, detailed tasks and processes should be provided with repetitive tasks. Since this group has issues with impersonal objects, machines such as vacuum cleaners are given names. For people with reading issues, colours and symbols describing the task can be used (Kalargyrou & Costen, 2017). They also propose other practices such as developing partnerships with social services to provide support and training to educate non-disabled employees on how to interact and collaborate with people with disabilities. Training may help managers and employees remove physical and social barriers from indifference, ignorance, and fear of people with disabilities. Similarly, training should be provided to address social injustice and marginalisation of the LGBTQ group. Interventions to reduce bias and practices which are person-environment fit influence how employees perceive their organisation (Madera et al., 2023).

Gender diversity has been found to have a positive impact on hotels' performance (Deiana & Fabbri, 2020). Marinakou (2014) suggests that gender-diverse organisations where women occupy operational positions and/or have executive roles are outperforming similar businesses with less women in management, hence hotels should ensure they implement practices that reduce the gender gap and reach gender balance. Women's qualities and leadership style are found to be a success factor for hotels, hence their qualities should be valued.

Women should be aware of the barriers they face in their career and develop self-esteem and self-confidence on dealing with such challenges. Women should engage with female role models to be inspired to succeed. Work-life balance practices can also support women's career progression. For example, new technologies (i.e., videoconferencing) support work from home and flexible working hours, hence women can use new technologies to balance work with family responsibilities. Hotels should support such practices for positions and roles where flexible work practices are feasible, that is, HR (Deiana & Fabbri, 2020). Family leave should also be available especially for managers who occupy leadership roles to encourage more women to accept such roles. Other practices are proposed by People 1st (2017), for example, to introduce job sharing even at management level or redesign job roles to adjust working hours to women returning from maternity leave; meetings could also be held in this case to discuss and understand women's needs due to come back from maternity leave; balancing childcare commitments could also be part of discussions at exit interviews. One example is Omni Hotels in the US that take the lead in providing more flexible schedules to accommodate working parents and careers (Goldfischer, 2023) (Box 8.2).

Box 8.2   IHG diversity example

InterContinental Hotel Group's (IHG) COO Karin Sheppard was recently featured by hotel management stating that underlying changes in workplace environment and culture are necessary to drive improved gender diversity at upper management levels. Following the implementation of a generous paid parental leave program (for both men and women) IGH has achieved a 95% return to work after parental leave from its female talent. It's an impressive figure by any account, particularly in these days of steadily decreasing employee loyalty and retention rates. A sense of loyalty, in turn, has an impact on engagement, motivation, and productivity.

Source: Pinnacle People (2016)

Hotels should encourage the participation of women to different organisations and associations that foster women's leadership and empower women in hotel management. For example, the non-profit Women in Hospitality Leadership Alliance was launched in the US in 2022. It started with 18 members and has grown to 27 groups around the globe. Such organisations provide knowledge exchange, information sharing, and opportunities to connect and network with other women gaining strength. Suggestions on gender inclusivity in hotel management are made by different organisations and businesses, for example, they propose to:

- Make gender diversity a priority in the hiring process;
- Introduce clear policies that are gender inclusive;
- Create zero tolerance policy to discrimination;
- Promote openness to tackle microaggressions;
- Reward employees who succeed in implementing such policies;
- Provide gender diversity training to employees and educate the leadership team.

A lot has been discussed about women's attitudes to pursuing a career in hotel management, implying that societal roles and gender stereotypes refrain women from climbing the career ladder. Female hotel managers could adopt strategies to increase their opportunities to be hired for higher managerial positions. For example, they may develop leadership skills, advocate for themselves, build a support network, challenge gender bias, and be visible. Nevertheless, we propose that fixing women is not the solution to underrepresentation of women in hotel management. It is important to create a systemic inclusion environments where women are allowed to succeed in their own authentic way. Promoting diversity does not ensure inclusion.

Diversity management practices should encourage hotel managers to build one-to-one relationships with employees, especially from minority groups. An understanding of employees' needs can be developed through increased interaction, through social events, to bridge the communication gap with such minority groups and build an environment of mutual understanding, respect, trust, and loyalty (Malik et al., 2017).

Summarising the above, we argue that the hospitality and tourism industry and the hotel sector specifically focus on four key areas for developing and implementing diversity management initiatives; these are training, career development and planning, flexible and supportive organisational culture, and corporate strategies and materials. A supportive work environment and leadership commitment positively impact diversity management initiatives. Such working environments result in self-motivated employees, increasing productivity, and employees' differences are respected and utilised as strength (Malik et al., 2017). Workforce diversity can be seen as an asset, where positive attitudinal and behavioural outcomes are generated. Hotel managers may create a succession plan to identify and develop a diverse pool of talent providing them with an opportunity to develop future leaders.

Chapter Summary

The hotel sector operates in a multicultural environment, with customers and employees from diverse backgrounds. Diversity in hotels should be recognised for valuing and celebrating differences among employees. Equal opportunities are a mandate to manage diversity following a novel approach to diversity management efforts in order to generate positive outcomes, job satisfaction, high productivity, reduced staff turnover, enhanced brand image, and staff loyalty. A passive approach to diversity is not beneficial, as all practices should be embraced by both employees and managers within hotels. Diversity management should be included in hotels' strategic plans to fully benefit from a diverse workforce. All employees should be included in diversity management policies and practices including women. Hotels with high representation of women managers are found to be successful and perform better financially (McKinsey & Company, 2020).

Furthermore, the existence of anti-discrimination practices is seen as a form of "reverse racism" within hotels (Madera et al., 2023). Some employees or managers see diversity as a threat, believing that such practices only benefit a small group of employees while neglecting the rest. In this case, training should be provided to eliminate such beliefs that spill at the workplace. In addition, there should be a connection between what the companies say and what they do to provide credibility inside and outside the organisation and contribute to authentic inclusion. Those lacking diversity face steeper penalties as they are outperformed by more diverse companies, which include more women in management. Progress has been slow, however, actions should be taken to tackle gender diversity in hotel management. The barriers that women face to career advancement are invisible, where women create their own barriers to professional growth. Social roles and stereotyping influence women's attitudes to hotel management, hence mentoring programmes may support the representation of women and encourage them to challenge traditional gender roles and balance work with life. Women can lead the hotel sector into sustainability as female managers are keen on implementing sustainable practices in operations. Women can break the glass ceiling, transform the perceptions about leadership, bring difference perspectives in decision-making and solutions, bring empathy and collaboration. Women can thrive as leaders in hotel management, as long as the gender bias is challenged, equal opportunities are adopted, and inclusive environments are fostered to ensure the glass ceiling is the past. Further work should be done to ensure that the U.N. Sustainable Goals 10 (*Reduced Inequalities*) and 5 (*Gender Equality*) will be a reality by 2030.

References

Baum, T. (2013). *International perspectives on women and work in hotels, catering and tourism*. Bureau for Gender Equality Working Paper 1/2013, Sectoral Activities Department Working Paper No. 289, International Labour Office, Sectoral Activities Department, Geneva.

Boogaard, K. (2021). *Is your hospitality company an equal opportunity employer?* https://employers.hosco.com/blog/is-your-hospitality-company-an-equal-opportunity-employer

Boone, J., Veller, T., Nikolaeva, K., & Keith, M. (2013). Rethinking a glass ceiling in the hospitality industry. *Cornell Hospitality Quarterly, 54*(3), 230–239.

Carvalho, I., Costa, C., Lykke, N., & Torres, A. (2018). Agency, structures and women managers' views of their careers in tourism. *Women's Studies International Forum, 71*, 1–11.

Castell Project. (2022). *Black representation in hospitality leadership 2022*. https://www.hospitalitynet.org/news/4109352.html

Catalyst. (2015). Quick take: Lesbian, gay, bisexual and transgender workplace issues. *Catalyst*, May.

Connell, R. (2009). *Short introduction in gender* (2nd ed.). Policy Press.

Davis, K., Evans, M., & Lorber, J. (2006). *Handbook of gender and women's studies*. SAGE.

Deiana, M., & Fabbri, C. (2020). Barriers to the success of female leaders in the hospitality industry. *Research in Hospitality Management, 10*(2), 85–89.

Eagly, A. H. (2007). Female leadership advantage and disadvantage: Resolving the contradictions. *Psychology of Women Quarterly, 31*(1), 1–12.

Eagly, A. H., Carli, L. L., & Carli, L. L. (2007). *Through the labyrinth: The truth about how women become leaders* (Vol. 11). Harvard Business School Press.

Elhoushy, S., & El-Said, O. A. (2020). Hotel managers' intentions towards female hiring: An application to the theory of planned behaviour. *Tourism Management Perspectives, 36*, 100741.

Garcia-Rodriguez, F. J., Dorta-Afonso, D., & Gonzalez-de-la-Rosa, M. (2020). Hospitality diversity management and job satisfaction: The mediating role of organisational commitment across individual differences. *International Journal of Hospitality Management, 91*, 102698.

Gebbels, M., Cai, W., & Gao, X. (2019). Gender issues in tourism and hospitality organisations: How to bridge the gap between gender awareness and organisational support? *Critical Tourism Studies Proceedings, 2019*, Article 62.

Gherardi, S. (1994). The gender we think, the gender we do in our everyday organisational lives. *Human Relations, 47*(6), 591–610.

Giousmpasoglou, C., Marinakou, E., & Zopiatis, A. (2021). Hospitality managers in turbulent times: The COVID-19 crisis. *International Journal of Contemporary Hospitality Management, 33*(4), 1297–1318.

Glusac, E. (2018). Hotels grapple with racial bias. *The New York Times*, August. https://www.nytimes.com/2018/08/01/travel/hotels-diversity-training.html

Goh, E., & Lee, C. (2018). A workforce to be reckoned with: The emerging pivotal generation Z hospitality workforce. *International Journal of Hospitality Management, 73*, 20–28.

Goldfischer, E. (2023). *2023 predictions for women in the hotel industry*. https://womenleadingtravelandhospitality.com/2023-predictions-for-women-in-the-hotel-industry/

Helgesson, V. S. (2005). *Psychology of gender* (2nd ed.). Prentice Hall.

Hoyt, C. L. (2012). Women and leadership. In P. G. Northouse (Ed.), *Leadership: Theory and practice*. Sage Publications.

Hsiao, A., Auld, C., & Ma, E. (2015). Perceived organisational diversity and employee behavior. *International Journal of Hospitality Management, 48*, 102–112.

Hutchings, K., Moyle, C., Chai, A., Garofano, N., & Moore, S. (2020). Segregation of women in tourism employment in the APEC region. *Tourism Management Perspectives, 34*. https://doi.org/10.1016/j.tmp.2020.100655

ILO. (2014). *Business as usual: Making workplaces inclusive of people with disabilities*. https://www.ilo.org/wcmsp5/groups/public/%2D%2D-ed_emp/%2D%2D-ifp_skills/documents/publication/wcms_316815.pdf

ILO. (2015). *Sectorial brief: Hotels, catering and tourism. Gender*. https://www.ilo.org/wcmsp5/ groups/public/%2D%2D-ed_dialogue/%2D%2D-sector/documents/briefingnote/wcms_162188.pdf

Iverson, K. (2000). Managing for effective workforce diversity. *Cornell Hotel and Restaurant Administration Quarterly, 41*(2), 31–38.

Kalargyrou, V., & Costen, W. (2017). Diversity management research in hospitality and tourism: Past, present and future. *International Journal of Contemporary Hospitality Management, 29*(1), 68–114.

Knutson, B. A., & Schmidgall, R. S. (1999). Dimensions of the glass ceiling in the hospitality industry. *Cornell Hotel and Restaurant Administration Quarterly, 40*(6), 64.

Kreitz, P. A. (2008). Best practices for managing organisational diversity. *The Journal of Academic Librarianship, 34*(2), 101–120.

Lashley, C. (2022). *Prejudice and discrimination in hotels, restaurants and bars*. Routledge.

Liu, T., Shen, H., & Gao, J. (2020). Women's career advancement in hotels: The mediating role of organisational commitment. *International Journal of Contemporary Hospitality Management, 32*(8), 2543–2561.

Madera, J. M., Yang, W., Wu, L., Ma, E., & Xu, S. (2023). Diversity and inclusion in hospitality and tourism: Bridging the gap between employee and customer perspectives. *International Journal of Contemporary Hospitality Management*. https://doi.org/10.1108/IJCHM-04-2023-0450

Malik, R., Madappa, T., & Chitranshi, J. (2017). Diversity management in tourism and hospitality: An exploratory study. *Foresight, 19*(3), 323–336.

Manoharan, A., Sardeshmukh, S. R., & Gross, M. J. (2021). Informal diversity management practices and their effectiveness: In the context of ethnically diverse employees in hotels. *International Journal of Hospitality Management, 82*, 181–190.

Marinakou, E. (2012). *An investigation of gender influences on transformational leadership style in the Greek hospitality industry*. PhD Thesis, Business School, University of Strathclyde.

Marinakou, E. (2014). Women in hotel management and leadership: Diamond or glass? *Journal of Tourism and Hospitality Management, 2*(1), 18–25.

Martin, P. Y. (2006). Practicing gender at work: Further thoughts on reflexivity. *Gender, Work and Organisation, 13*(3), 254–276.

McKinsey & Company. (2020). *Diversity wins. How inclusion matters*. https://www.mckinsey.com/~/media/mckinsey/featured%20insights/diversity%20and%20inclusion/diversity%20wins%20how%20inclusion%20matters/diversity-wins-how-inclusion-matters-vf.pdf

Metcalfe, B. (2008). Women, management and globalisation in the Middle East. *Journal of Business Ethics, 83*, 85–100.

Mihail, D. (2006). Gender-based stereotypes in the workplace: The case of Greece. *Equal Opportunities International, 25*(5), 373–388.

Mistry, T. G., Okumus, F., & Orlowski, M. (2021). Employee perceptions of diversity management in the hospitality industry. *International Hospitality Review*. https://doi.org/10.1108/IHR-05-2021-0041

Narayanan, E. (2017). Women in management: Breaking barriers on female career advancement in the hospitality industry. *Journal of Hospitality and Tourism, 14*(1), 1–17.

Nickson, D., Warhurst, C., & Dutton, E. (2005). The importance of attitude and appearance in the service encounter in retail and hospitality. *Managing Service Quality, 15*(2), 195–208.

Ouyang, Z., Zhang, Y., & Hu, X. (2020). Negative publicity and potential applicants' intention to apply amid a discrimination scandal: A moderated mediation model. *Personnel Review, 50*(1), 129–142.

Pardal, V., Alger, M., & Latu, I. (2020). Implicit and explicit gender stereotypes at the bargaining table: Male counterparts' stereotypes predict women's lower performance in dyadic face-to-face negotiations. *Sex Roles, 83*(5), 289–302.

Pasquerella, L., & Clauss-Ehlers, C. S. (2017). Glass cliffs, queen bees, and persistent barriers to women's leadership in the academy. *Liberal Education, 103*(2), 6–13.

Pearlman, D. M., & Bordelon, B. M. (2022). How the #MeToo movement affected sexual harassment in the hospitality industry: A US case study. *International Journal of Hospitality Management, 101*, 103–106.

People 1st. (2017). *Insight report. Women working in the hospitality and tourism sector.* https://www.people1st.co.uk/getattachment/Insight-opinion/Latest-insights/Female-talent/Women-working-in-the-hospitality-sector-report-Oct-2017.pdf/?lang=en-GB

Pinnacle People. (2016). *Gender diversity—Facts and effects in the hospitality industry.* https://www.pinnaclepeople.com.au/news/gender-diversity-in-hospitality/14180/

Purcell, K. (1996). The relationship between career and job opportunities: Women's employment in the hospitality industry as a microcosm of women's employment. *Women in Management Review, 11*(5), 17–24.

Ragins, B. R., Townsend, B., & Mattis, M. (1998). Gender gap in the executive suite: CEOs and female executives report on breaking the glass ceiling. *Academy of Management Executive, 12*(1), 28–42.

Restaurant Opportunities Centers United. (2015). *Ending Jim Crow in America's restaurants: Racial and gender occupational segregation in the restaurant industry.* ROC United.

Risman, B. J. (2004). Gender as a social structure: Theory wrestling with activism. *Gender and Society, 18*(4), 429–450.

Russen, M., Dawson, M., & Madera, J. M. (2021). Gender diversity in hospitality and tourism top management teams: A systematic review of the last 10 years. *International Journal of Hospitality Management, 95*, 102942.

Segovia-Perez, M., Figueroa-Domecq, C., Fuentes-Moraleda, L., & Munoz-Mazon, A. (2019). Incorporating a gender approach in the hospitality industry: Female executives' perceptions. *International Journal of Hospitality Management, 76*, 184–193.

Stockdale, J. E. (1991). Sexual harassment at work. In J. Firth-Cozens & M. A. West (Eds.), *Women at work: Psychological and organisational perspectives.* Open University Press.

Talent Hive. (2022). *Why is hospitality so great for older workers?* https://www.talenthive.co.uk/blog/view/186/index7/Why-Is-Hospitality-So-Great-For-Older-Workers-#:~:text=Hospitality%20has%20a%20culture%20of,path%20of%20progression%20to%20follow

United Nations. (1995). *Universal declaration on cultural diversity, global agreement.* Mexico City.

UNWTO. (2019). *Global report on women in tourism* (2nd ed.). World Tourism Organisation. https://doi.org/10.18111/9789284420384

Van Knippenberg, D., & Schippers, M. C. (2007). Work group diversity. *Annual Review of Psychology, 58*, 515–541.

West, C., & Zimmerman, D. (1987). Doing gender. *Gender and Society, 1*(2), 125–151.

Women in Hospitality. (WiH). (2020). *Women in Hospitality, Travel, and Leisure 2020, WiH2020 Review.* Available at: https://www.pwc.co.uk/hospitality-leisure/documents/women-in-hospitality-traveland-leisure-final-report.pdf

Workplace Gender Equality Agency, (WGEA). (2016). Gender equity insights 2016 Inside Australia's gender pay gap. Available at: https://www.wgea.gov.au/sites/default/files/documents/BCEC_WGEA_Gender_Pay_Equity_Insights_2016_Report.pdf

World Health Organization. (2023a). *Improving LGBTIQ+ health and well-being with consideration for SOGIESC.* https://www.who.int/activities/improving-lgbtqi-health-and-well%2D%2Dbeing-with-consideration-for-sogiesc

World Health Organization. (2023b). *Fact sheets: Disability and health.* www.who.int/mediacentre/factsheets/fs352/en/

Xiong, W., Chen, S., Okumus, B., & Fan, F. (2022). Gender stereotyping and its impact on perceived emotional leadership in the hospitality industry: A mixed-methods study. *Tourism Management, 90*, 104476.

zippia.com. (n.d.). Hospitality manager demographics and statistics in the U.S. https://www.zippia.com/hospitality-manager-jobs/demographics/

9

Current Challenges and Future Perspectives

Photo Credits: *Polina Zimmerman (Free to use under the Pexels License)*. (Source: https://www.pexels.com/photo/sticky-notes-on-board-3782235/)

Introduction

In 2022, a new word was introduced to describe our era: Permacrisis. This new word comes from the merge of the words "permanent" and "crisis," which accurately portray the current situation globally from an economic, social, and political perspective (Turnbull, 2022). Global and regional events such as the COVID-19 pandemic, the implementation of BREXIT, and the war in Ukraine that triggered an unprecedented energy crisis have created a challenging business environment difficult to operate in, regardless of the company's size, structure, location, and available resources. The service industries that rely heavily on front-line employees have suffered the consequences of the above-described situation. More specifically, the global hotel industry has experienced radical changes and challenges concerning five people management areas: staff shortages; talent management; managerial resilience; work-life balance and employee wellbeing; and fair work and worker exploitation-related issues.

This final chapter aims to explore hotel management's current challenges and future perspectives, focusing on people management. In particular, the effect of Permacrisis is critically investigated in the context of the global hotel industry's workforce. It also provides actionable recommendations for improving people management in the industry.

The Permacrisis Impact on People Management

The continuous and ongoing changes in the global business environment in the past decade have profoundly impacted people management in the global economy, especially in labour-intensive industries such as hospitality and tourism. This impact is explored and summarised below in five different people management areas. Regardless of the company's size, structure, business type, and location, all five areas are critical for successful hotel operations.

Staff Shortages

Staff shortages were not unknown to the global hotel industry, especially during periods of high demand. The massive redundancies and businesses closure due to the impact of COVID-19 in the market has caused unprecedented damage to the hotel industry labour supply. Although the post-COVID era has brought a high demand for hospitality services and products, the industry struggles to fill the existing vacancies at all levels, seniority, and specialisations. The latest ONS (2023) data in the UK reveal that the available vacancies in January 2023 increased to 83% compared to the same period in 2019; it is estimated that there are approximately 17,400 hospitality jobs that UK-based employers struggle to fill. During the same period, in the US, there were nearly 2 million vacant posts in hospitality jobs (Bhattarai & Penman, 2023). Similar reports arrive from European countries with developed hospitality and tourism industries; according to the WTTC (2022), one in five vacancies in the accommodation sector will remain unfilled, creating a deficit of 842,000 workers.

It is argued that several causes triggered this phenomenon. Many workers have changed sectors during or after the pandemic (Kwok, 2022). The unpopular working conditions in the hotel industry, including low pay, shift working, long working hours, and limited career progression opportunities, have pushed many hospitality workers (especially the younger ones) to seek office jobs in professional or business services (e.g., law, accounting, and engineering firms). In contrast, others sought opportunities in transportation, construction, and warehousing (Bhattarai & Penman, 2023). Other reasons hospitality workers decided to leave the industry were to retire early or stop working to reduce health-related risks caused by their exposure to customers and other employees (Forsythe et al., 2022). It is also suggested that part of the "lost" workforce died during the pandemic (Bhattarai & Penman, 2023). The unprecedented number of employees quitting their jobs during or after the pandemic has been described as "The Great Resignation" (Ellerbeck, 2023). The hotel industry has been the leader in employee resignations in the US since 2017. Similar phenomena are observed in the UK and Europe, where the hospitality workforce shrinks without signs of recovery soon.

Another critical factor that contributed to staff shortages is the dramatic drop in the migrant workforce in hospitality jobs; during the pandemic, migrant workers in Europe, Great Britain, and the US decided to return homes to reunite with their families and cope with the financial hurdles. According to the WTTC (2022), the migrant workforce in Europe and the UK was estimated to be up to 16% of the total hospitality workforce before the pandemic, whereas, in the US, it was nearly 20%. The migrant workforce in the UK originates predominantly from EU countries (Ioannou & Dukes, 2021); the combination of BREXIT and COVID-19 resulted in a mass exodus of hospitality EU workers despite the creation of nearly 300,000 new jobs and the sector's ongoing growth (Big Hospitality, 2022). Staff shortages also hit the wider tourism industry hard, with a significant disruption caused during the summer of 2022 in Europe and the US; the chaotic scenes at major European and UK airports due to the staff shortages (Pole, 2022) indicate this problem's magnitude. The above discussion suggests that the global hospitality and tourism industry was unprepared for returning to normality in the post-COVID era. The long-term and well-known pathogenies in hospitality led a significant part of the workforce to other industries and sectors with better remuneration and working conditions.

Talent Management

The hotel industry has always suffered from a deficit in talented employees and managers. This deficit has grown disproportionally during and after the COVID-19 pandemic: as already discussed above, the hotel industry has been unable to stop its people from moving to other sectors with better remuneration and working conditions (Liu-Lastres et al., 2023). The Talent Management debate in the hospitality context is long-standing and received several researchers' attention (Baum, 2019). Despite its popularity, it is challenging to define and frame Talent Management in contemporary hospitality settings and its shifting boundaries (D'Annunzio-Green & Ramdhony, 2019). The existing empirical research and the industry's requirements provide many ambiguous interpretations of talent management.

Jooss et al. (2022) describe talent management as the process through which organisations meet their talent requirements. Furthermore, talent management is often defined as unique skills, attributes, and capabilities contributing to achieving broader organisational goals (Kruesi & Bazelmans, 2023). Based on the "unique" proposition, talent is viewed as a strategic resource for organisations critical for creating or reestablishing the organisation's competitive position (Marinakou & Giousmpasoglou, 2019). In addition, the inclusive and exclusive approaches are hospitality organisations' dominant strategies regarding talent management (Jooss et al., 2022). The former identifies all employees as potential talent, which can be nurtured through the organisation's training and development programmes (Johnson et al., 2019). The latter approach views talent as a small exclusive group of individuals who can make a difference to the organisation (Mousa et al., 2022).

Regardless of the approach followed, it is argued that the difficulty in understanding talent management is created by emphasising organisational or managerial needs rather than individual ones (Goh & Okumus, 2020). The fact that the current talent management approaches and industry practices primarily address organisational needs raises several issues experienced on a global scale. The existing research on talent management practices focuses on three key areas: talent acquisition, learning and development, and retention (Kravariti et al., 2022). The main criticism of these studies is that they were conducted in Western multinational hotel chains ignoring the independent local businesses that occupy approximately 80% of the global hospitality sector (Jooss et al., 2022; Transparency Market Research, 2022). Another fundamental weakness appears to be the lack of understanding of the talented employees' needs, especially the younger ones (Generation Z) that just entered or will enter the labour market soon (Goh & Okumus, 2020). Baum (2019) argues that we need to redefine how we educate and train future hospitality leaders; he also suggests that the current occupational culture and working conditions may not be suitable for attracting and retaining talent. Overall, the literature indicates that the hospitality industry in the post-COVID-19 era is losing the "War for Talent" (Benedet & Nikolov, 2022), especially in younger generations who choose more attractive jobs in other industries or sectors. A recent survey by People 1st (2021) identifies the top

The Top 3 factors to attract and retain future talent

The Top 3 most important factors in a work environment

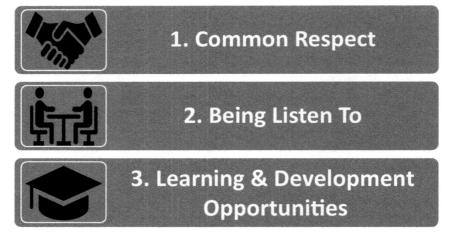

Fig. 9.1 Future talent retention factors in hospitality. (Source: Adapted from People 1st [2021])

three areas related to future talent retention: Work-Life Balance, Pay, and Learning and Development. In addition, the top three factors identified in relation to a good working environment are Common Respect, Being Listen To, and Learning and Development Opportunities (Fig. 9.1).

Managerial Resilience

Any significant event that can cause adverse effects that threaten the viability of organisations, companies, or industries and is characterised by cause ambiguity can be defined as a crisis (Paraskevas & Quek, 2019). The critical element to overcoming and managing a crisis is resilience; in the hotel industry, resilience is regarded as a fundamental approach to responding, adapting, and surviving organisational or external environment changes (Hall et al., 2023). Brown et al. (2018: 69) define resilience as the capacity to "assess, innovate, adapt, and overcome possible disruptions that are triggered by disaster." Resilience is linked to extraordinary and incremental change, whereas *crisis management* is linked to change due to extraordinary circumstances (Prayag, 2018). Key resilience indicators include learning, risk identification, vulnerability assessment, proactive posture, planning strategies, and recovery priorities (Paraskevas & Quek, 2019).

During the COVID-19 pandemic, the general managers (GMs) in hotels and restaurants were responsible for implementing contingency and crisis management plans. The existing research (i.e., Ghaderi et al., 2022; Giousmpasoglou et al., 2021; Filimonau et al., 2020; Lombardi et al., 2021) demonstrates their pivotal role in business recovery. A qualitative study among 50 luxury hotel GMs in 45 countries (Giousmpasoglou et al., 2021) revealed that luxury hotel GMs are vital in coping with changes and leading their hotel units to recovery. GMs' resilience and renewed role and abilities enabled them to adapt rapidly to external changes in their business environment. It should be noted that the best-performing GMs were the ones employed by multinational hotel chains, which provided them with adequate support and resources to deal with this mega-crisis. Those GMs employed in independent operators (mainly family businesses) reported that despite their efforts, the results to support their staff and restart the business were poor, mainly due to luck or resources and the unwillingness of the owners to support their plans. Another study by Ghaderi et al. (2022) identified the importance of crisis preparedness concerning managerial resilience. A proactive approach to crisis and organisational-level plans helps managers prepare for unforeseen circumstances and better respond to contingencies. This study also suggests that organisational resilience and culture play a significant role in developing effective strategies for different crisis types, considering their severity and urgency. Filimonau et al. (2020) argue that establishing and facilitating Corporate Social Responsibility (CSR) practices at the organisational level help managers become resilient and respond better to crises. Finally, a study in Italian hotels during the COVID-19 crisis identified the importance of resilient leadership and improvisation (Lombardi et al., 2021). The latter is used as a response by managers in the absence of planning using the available resources rather than the optimal ones; this is a common practice in smaller businesses or when the existing plans are inadequate to respond to a contingency or crisis.

Work-Life Balance and Employee Wellbeing

The discussion regarding the impact of *work-life balance* (WLB) and wellbeing on hospitality workers has taken a different turn during and after the COVID-19 pandemic. It is argued that the role of WLB is more decisive in hospitality than in any other sector (Andrade et al., 2021); nevertheless, this is an area where poor practice is still observed, especially in independent operators. Work is a primary constituent of personal wellbeing, providing income, and signifies social status (Chandran & Abukhalifeh, 2021). Nevertheless, balancing work demands and family-related responsibilities has always posed significant challenges for hospitality workers and organisations. Blake (2014) suggests that work-life balance includes the employees' ability to successfully amalgamate work and family domains, functions, and demands. It is, therefore, significant to investigate how easy it is for the hotel industry to achieve WLB for its workforce.

It is well evidenced (i.e., Baum, 2019; Brown et al., 2015; Kusluvan et al., 2010) that the hotel industry has always suffered a poor image mainly to the sub-standard working condition (i.e., long working hours, shift work, and health and safety-related concerns), low remuneration, and limited career progression opportunities (mainly in independent operators). As a result, organisations that fail to create and implement successful WLB programmes experience low employee (job) satisfaction (Andrade et al., 2021). Kong et al. (2018) suggest that hospitality organisations failing to facilitate a positive work environment and job satisfaction experience high employee turnover, burnout, absenteeism, and low productivity. According to Chandran and Abukhalifeh (2021), balancing the employees' career and life goals is imperative. As a result, introducing family-friendly practices that include healthcare and childcare programmes and flexible working patterns for both parents can positively impact hospitality workers' wellbeing (Kim et al., 2023). The recent lessons learned from the pandemic demonstrated that the companies who invested money and time in their employees' wellbeing enjoyed high employee retention, contributing to successful businesses' reopening (Kipping, 2023). The existing research suggests that most businesses that could support their furloughed or redundant staff during the pandemic were multinational or national hotel chains (Giousmpasoglou et al., 2021). It is therefore argued that the rest of the industry, dominated by independent and family businesses (Jooss et al., 2022), has a long way to go in facilitating effective WLB and employee wellbeing policies.

Fair Work and Worker Exploitation

The Fair Work Agenda has played a significant role in improving working conditions for the hospitality industry over the years in refining the industry's image and reputation (Baum, 2019). On the other hand, one of the most significant barriers to adopting better work-related practices and creating a sustainable work environment is the precarious nature of work (Alberti, 2014).

Robinson et al. (2019) suggest that this precarity creates the conditions for worker exploitation in different contexts. Among other things, worker exploitation refers to underpayment and poor working conditions that are internationally criminalised (FRA, 2019). Specifically, according to the European Union Agency for Fundamental Rights (ibid.: 10), worker exploitation refers to "working conditions significantly different from the standard working conditions as defined by legislation." These conditions include remuneration, working hours, leave entitlements, Health and Safety standards, and decent treatment. Loyens and Paraciani (2021) state that this phenomenon is surrounded by moral and legal ambiguity due to the blurred boundaries between victim and perpetrator. Hence, it is often difficult to determine the criminal threshold limits for worker exploitation from a people management perspective.

These practices are covered by the Modern Slavery Act (2015) in the UK, and similar legislation exists in the US. According to ILO (2017), worker exploitation and modern slavery are more prevalent than ever in human history across many service and production industries, including restaurant and food services, domestic work, agriculture, nail bars, and car washes. In these industries, disadvantaged populations such as minorities and migrants are given preference for lower-level manual occupations that need little or no specialisation. According to Mooney and Baum (2019), migrants are less expensive to hire, have a strong work ethic, are easy to control, and are pliable, making it easier for employers to manipulate and abuse the migrant workforce. A good example is the recent phenomenon of Dark Kitchens, which introduced a new form of precarity through the algorithmic management of the temporary workforce ("gig workers") in working conditions that barely meet the minimum standards (Giousmpasoglou et al., 2023). Governments, industry bodies, and NGOs recognise these issues and try to minimise the impact of precarious work in vulnerable groups. For example, the Sustainable Hospitality Alliance (2022a) has recently issued ethical recruitment guidelines for temporary migrant worker recruitment; these guidelines identify the risks of unethical recruitment (Fig. 9.2), guarantee the temporary workers' fundamental rights, and prevent forced labour. Forced or compulsory labour is a human rights violation (ILO, n.d.) that "can result from unethical employment and recruitment practices affecting the global supply chains of many goods and services across multiple industries." As a result of the above discussion, it is argued that key stakeholders and decision-makers in the industry need to prioritise actions related to worker exploitation and the Fair Work Agenda.

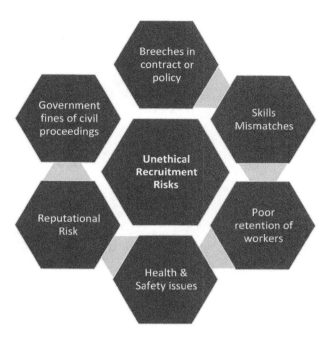

Fig. 9.2 Risks from unethical recruitment. (Source: Adapted from Sustainable Hospitality Alliance [2022a])

Required Action Towards the Industry's Recovery

So far, we identified and discussed five areas in people management that have been heavily affected by the prolonged period of crisis in the global economy. It is argued that these areas should draw the attention of the global hotel industry's key stakeholders and policymakers. These areas are the fundamental building blocks for creating a blueprint to bring hospitality back on track on the road to recovery and help restore its poor image. Undoubtedly, policies and initiatives must be prioritised to address the challenge of staff shortages and people management within the sector (Fig. 9.3).

Fig. 9.3 Required actions towards the industry's recovery. (Source: Author's creation)

- *Encourage flexible and remote work opportunities.* A short-term action that can help hospitality employers reduce staff shortages is offering flexible and remote work opportunities when this is possible. The hotel industry is traditionally known as a "people's industry" that requires most of the job conducted on-site. However, with technological advancements and changing work dynamics, flexible and remote work opportunities are becoming more prevalent in this industry. Some benefits from flexible and remote work opportunities include improved work-life balance and job satisfaction for employees, cost savings for the business, access to a broader pool of talent, and environmental benefits (Liu-Lastres et al., 2023). On the other hand, hotel businesses need to assess their specific needs, consider the nature of their operations, and establish policies and guidelines that balance flexibility and maintaining operational efficiency. Flexible and remote working patterns hinder challenges such as communication and collaboration issues that must be addressed promptly by the company's management. In addition, remote workers, mainly for back-office and admin support roles, cannot easily fit into the organisational culture as they are seen as an "external body" (Wang et al., 2021). To conclude, flexible and remote working patterns can solve part of the existing staff shortage issues currently experienced in the global hotel industry.

- *Encourage labour mobility.* Encouraging labour mobility is another short-term action that can help employers attract a wider pool of talented candidates. The benefits from labour mobility in the hotel industry positively impact both the employees and the industry: it fosters skill development, career advancement, job satisfaction, and retention while promoting knowledge sharing, innovation, and building a strong talent pool (Duncan et al., 2013). The most significant barrier to labour mobility is working visa-related restrictions. BREXIT is a characteristic example of what happens when labour mobility is restricted; service industries in the UK now experience unprecedented staff shortages due to the difficulty attracting EU workers (Big Hospitality, 2022). On the other hand, European countries like Italy, Spain, and Portugal have eased their migration policies to attract seasonal workers for their hospitality and tourism industry (Carbonaro, 2023).
- *Use of technology.* Furthermore, technology has already been applied in the global hotel industry to respond to COVID-19 restrictions and staff shortages. Big multinational hotel chains operators like Marriott International, Hilton Hotels, and the Accor Group invest in many different areas to further develop the existing technologies and platforms that replace or assist humans in performing their tasks (Shiwen et al., 2022). A good example is the implementation of self-service kiosks or mobile apps for tasks such as check-ins, reservations, and ordering food and beverages in budget hotels and quick-service restaurants (i.e., Ibis Hotels, Premier Inn, McDonald's); this reduces the need for staff members to handle these transactions, allowing them to focus on other

critical service areas (Shin & Perdue, 2019). Another example the industry currently focuses on is using Artificial Intelligence (AI) and chatbots on websites or mobile apps to handle customer inquiries and provide basic assistance. Chatbots can answer frequently asked questions, provide recommendations, and assist with bookings, freeing staff members to handle more specialised tasks (Pillai & Sivathanu, 2020). The use of AI rapidly expands to other functions such as online bookings, recruitment and selection, digital marketing and social media, and big data analytics. On the other hand, implementing new technologies can be expensive, especially for small- and medium-sized hotel businesses. The cost of acquiring, implementing, and maintaining technology solutions, such as *Property Management Systems* (PMS), customer relationship management software, or self-service kiosks, can be a significant barrier. Additionally, measuring the *return on investment* (ROI) and determining the tangible benefits of these investments can be difficult. Other challenges regarding the use of technology include systems integration and compatibility issues, staff training, data security and privacy, technical issues and downtime, and the overall impact on the customer's experience (Law et al., 2014). Overcoming these challenges requires careful planning, investment, and a strategic approach to technology adoption. Hotel businesses must conduct thorough research, seek expert advice, and continuously evaluate and adapt their technology strategies to sustain their competitive advantage. By leveraging technology, the hotel industry can alleviate the impact of staff shortages by optimising operations, automating tasks, and empowering staff members to focus on delivering exceptional guest experiences.

- *Develop a skilled workforce.* Moving on to the long-term required action, addressing the skills gap in the hospitality industry is crucial for ensuring the industry's growth and success. Hospitality professionals and academics have debated how to address the skills gap in the industry for a long time (Baum, 2019). The starting point to bridge the skills gap is the industry collaboration with educational institutions to develop courses that meet the market's current and future needs. These courses should focus on developing hard and soft skills beyond the technical ones, like emotional intelligence, resilience, communication, leadership, and problem-solving (Brown et al., 2015). Furthermore, implementing well-designed apprenticeship and internship programmes to provide practical, hands-on training opportunities can help students gain real-world experience while working under the guidance of experienced professionals (Bakkevig Dagsland et al., 2015). The industry-academia collaboration can ensure that educational programmes align with industry requirements and produce work-ready graduates. The role of professional hospitality associations can play a crucial role in creating and maintaining recognised standards in education and training; for example, the Institute of Hospitality provides accreditations globally for a wide variety of courses (https://www.instituteofhospitality.org/ accreditation/). Another strategy to address the skills gap is facilitating upskilling and reskilling courses for existing hotel employees; by providing opportunities to learn new skills, they stay updated with the latest industry trends and technologies (Huang et al., 2021). These courses can be conducted in-house, remotely (online), or by partnering with external training providers. Successfully implementing strategies to bridge the skills gap requires the broader collaboration and contribution of key stakeholders such as the industry, higher education and vocational training providers, industry associations, government agencies, and the local community.

- *Develop Retention Strategies.* The industry's problems have been known for decades; however, factors such as low-profit margins, high operational costs, and many independent or family businesses operating in a volatile environment have always driven down labour costs. On the other hand, the permacrisis phenomenon in global markets has intensified the war for talent in the post-COVID-19 era. Therefore, hotel businesses must implement effective retention strategies for their talented and skilled employees. A combination of strategies can be used by hotel businesses to improve their high turnover rates and loss of talent. Retention strategies require long-term planning and implementation of organisation-wide changes, such as creating a positive work environment, fostering inclusivity, offering competitive compensation and benefits packages, recognising and rewarding employee achievements, and providing opportunities for career development (Marinakou

& Giousmpasoglou, 2019). Corporate hotel businesses have already established strategies to encourage employee mobility within the company limits at local, regional, national, and international levels. For example, graduate development programmes like the *Marriott Voyage* and the *Hilton Elevator* are part of a broader strategy for talent retention in multinational hotel and restaurant chains. Unfortunately, this is not the case for most small and medium enterprises (SMEs) in the sector who either cannot financially support the implementation of such practices/policies or do not have the expertise to design and facilitate these (Johnson et al., 2019). It should be noted that the UK and most EU countries provide employee training and development programmes through job centres or other related government agencies; for example, large companies in the UK are funding apprenticeships through a levy, which is set at a rate of 0.5% of their total annual pay bill (Gov.UK, 2023). Although hotel SMEs employees can benefit from these programmes, there are not always facilitated successfully for various reasons, such as bureaucracy, poor communication, and inability to address the market needs. In conclusion, talent retention in permacrisis market conditions is an ongoing process, and it is vital to regularly review and adjust strategies based on feedback and the employees' changing needs. By implementing these strategies, hotel businesses can create a positive and supportive work environment that fosters employee loyalty and satisfaction, which will help to achieve talent retention.

- *Promoting the Fair Work Agenda.* Promoting and implementing the Fair Work Agenda in the hotel industry is vital to ensure fair treatment, improved working conditions, and better employment practices for workers. It is also a unique opportunity to improve the damaged industry reputation and image, contributing to staff retention and talent attraction. It will take a multi-stakeholder approach, including the public sector, education providers, industry representatives, Trade Unions, and hospitality associations, to achieve this goal. The starting point is to establish fair wages for workers regardless of their contract type and role. Governments can push this agenda through the minimum wage that must be negotiated and agreed upon with industry and workers' representatives. Ensuring fairness regarding working hours and shifts is another area where employers and the public sector share responsibility. Employers are obliged by law to establish and monitor policies that address reasonable working hours, rest periods, and limitations on consecutive shifts, to prevent overworking and burnout among hospitality workers. Governments, on the other hand, should ensure through the use of related authorities and law enforcement that employers comply with legislation and provide fair working conditions for all staff members. Health and Safety at the workplace is another critical area where despite the strict legislation and regulations, many violations are observed predominantly in SMEs. The industry and the public sector must work together to regulate sub-sectors or niches like dark kitchens with poor working conditions and questionable hygiene standards (Giousmpasoglou et al., 2023). On the other hand, celebrating good practices and publicising these to the general public is also important. Hotel chains like Hyatt are often listed as "best places to work" in national and global table leagues (Sczepanski, 2023); there are also excellent hotel SMEs at local and regional levels who adopt best practices in people management. Industry associations facilitate prestigious recognition awards for the best employers, projecting a positive industry image to printed and electronic media (Fig. 9.4). Therefore, businesses in the hotel industry should work with associations, trade unions, and other stakeholders to implement and improve the Fair Work Agenda. This collaboration on initiatives such as wage benchmarking, sharing best practices, and advocating for policy changes will benefit workers and improve the industry's reputation.

Conclusion

The final chapter of this book discussed the people management areas affected mainly by the permacrisis phenomenon in the global hotel industry. It also recommended six specific actions for the industry's recovery regarding staff retention. It is evident from the above discussion that Permacrisis has significant implications for people management's future in the hotel industry.

Fig. 9.4 Examples of Hospitality Awards. (Source: Author's creation)

From a practical perspective, the industry needs to focus on building a resilient workforce, promoting sustainability, fostering diversity and inclusion, prioritising employee wellbeing, facilitating continuous learning and adaptability, and engaging with various stakeholders to address the challenges posed by the Permacrisis. On the other hand, education providers should contribute to the colossal task of creating a resilient workforce equipped with a skillset suitable to survive the fast pace of changes at the workplace. Governments also play a vital role in ensuring that employees are paid fair wages under the minimum wage legislation and industry-specific agreements. Furthermore, industry associations should focus on assisting hotel SMEs in adopting standards and best practices. The theoretical implications suggest that more research is required in this relatively new field. Our current knowledge is limited to empirical and conceptual studies conducted in the past three years since the outbreak of the COVID-19 pandemic. The long-term effects of Permacrisis in people management require longitudinal studies and a multidisciplinary approach due to the complexity of this phenomenon.

In conclusion, it can be argued that Permacrisis must be viewed as an opportunity to reinvent the global hotel industry. It is also suggested that the industry's stakeholders are morally obligated to future generations to create a sustainable workforce in a truly global industry.

References

Alberti, G. (2014). Mobility strategies, 'mobility differentials' and 'transnational exit': The experiences of precarious migrants in London's hospitality jobs. *Work, Employment and Society, 28*(6), 865–881.

Andrade, M. S., Miller, D., & Westover, J. H. (2021). Job satisfaction in the hospitality industry: The comparative impacts of work-life balance, intrinsic rewards, extrinsic rewards, and work relations. *American Journal of Management, 21*(2), 39–56.

Bakkevig Dagsland, Å. H., Mykletun, R. J., & Einarsen, S. (2015). "We're not slaves—we are actually the future!" A follow-up study of apprentices' experiences in the Norwegian hospitality industry. *Journal of Vocational Education and Training, 67*(4), 460–481.

Baum, T. (2019). Does the hospitality industry need or deserve talent? *International Journal of Contemporary Hospitality Management, 31*(10), 3823–3837.

Benedet, P., & Nikolov, I. (2022). Winning the war for talent in product development. https://www.mckinsey.com/capabilities/operations/our-insights/operations-blog/winning-the-war-for-talent-in-product-development

Bhattarai, A., & Penman, M. (2023). Restaurants can't find workers because they've found better jobs. https://www.washingtonpost.com/business/2023/02/03/worker-shortage-restaurants-hotels-economy/

Big Hospitality. (2022). Staff shortages in hospitality hit record high. https://www.bighospitality.co.uk/Article/2022/06/14/Staff-shortages-in-hospitality-hit-record-high

Blake, J. (2014). Work-family fit. In A. C. Michalos (Ed.), *Encyclopedia of quality of life and wellbeing research* (pp. 7219–7221). Springer.

Brown, E. A., Thomas, N. J., & Bosselman, R. H. (2015). Are they leaving or staying: A qualitative analysis of turnover issues for generation Y hospitality employees with a hospitality education. *International Journal of Hospitality Management, 46*, 130–137.

Brown, N. A., Orchiston, C., Rovins, J. E., Feldmann-Jensen, S., & Johnston, D. (2018). An integrative framework for investigating disaster resilience within the hotel sector. *Journal of Hospitality and Tourism Management, 36*, 67–75.

Carbonaro, G. (2023). Thinking of moving to Europe? Here are the easiest countries to get a work visa. https://www.euronews.com/travel/2022/10/02/thinking-of-moving-to-europe-here-are-the-easiest-countries-to-get-a-work-visa

Chandran, K. S., & Abukhalifeh, A. N. (2021). Systematic literature review of research on work-life balance in hospitality industry since millennium. *Review of Integrative Business and Economics Research, 10*(1), 14–33.

D'Annunzio-Green, N., & Ramdhony, A. (2019). It's not what you do; it's the way that you do it: An exploratory study of talent management as an inherently motivational process in the hospitality sector. *International Journal of Contemporary Hospitality Management, 31*(10), 3992–4020.

Duncan, T., Scott, D. G., & Baum, T. (2013). The mobilities of hospitality work: An exploration of issues and debates. *Annals of Tourism Research, 41*, 1–19.

Ellerbeck, S. (2023). The Great Resignation continues. Why are U.S. workers continuing to quit their jobs? https://www.weforum.org/agenda/2023/01/us-workers-jobs-quit/

Filimonau, V., Derqui, B., & Matute, J. (2020). The COVID-19 pandemic and organisational commitment of senior hotel managers. *International Journal of Hospitality Management, 91.* https://doi.org/10.1016/j.ijhm.2020.102659

Forsythe, E., Kahn, L. B., Lange, F., & Wiczer, D. (2022). Where have all the workers gone? Recalls, retirements, and reallocation in the COVID recovery. *Labour Economics, 78.* https://doi.org/10.1016/j.labeco.2022.102251

FRA. (European Union Agency for Fundamental Rights). (2019). Protecting migrant workers from exploitation in the E.U.: Workers' perspectives. https://fra.europa.eu/en/publication/2019/protecting-migrant-workers-exploitation-eu-workers-perspectives

Ghaderi, Z., King, B., & Hall, C. M. (2022). Crisis preparedness of hospitality managers: Evidence from Malaysia. *Journal of Hospitality and Tourism Insights, 5*(2), 292–310.

Giousmpasoglou, C., Ladkin, A., & Marinakou, E. (2023). Worker exploitation in the gig economy: The case of dark kitchens. *Journal of Hospitality and Tourism Insights.* https://doi.org/10.1108/JHTI-10-2022-0477

Giousmpasoglou, C., Marinakou, E., & Zopiatis, A. (2021). Hospitality managers in turbulent times: The COVID-19 crisis. *International Journal of Contemporary Hospitality Management, 33*(4), 1297–1318.

Goh, E., & Okumus, F. (2020). Avoiding the hospitality workforce bubble: Strategies to attract and retain generation Z talent in the hospitality workforce. *Tourism Management Perspectives, 33*. https://doi.org/10.1016/j.tmp.2019.100603

Gov.UK. (2023). How are apprenticeships funded and what is the apprenticeship levy? https://educationhub.blog.gov.uk/2023/03/10/how-are-apprenticeships-funded-and-what-is-the-apprenticeship-levy/

Hall, C. M., Safonov, A., & Naderi Koupaei, S. (2023). Resilience in hospitality and tourism: Issues, synthesis and agenda. *International Journal of Contemporary Hospitality Management, 35*(1), 347–368.

Huang, A. Y., Fisher, T., Ding, H., & Guo, Z. (2021). A network analysis of cross-occupational skill transferability for the hospitality industry. *International Journal of Contemporary Hospitality Management, 33*(12), 4215–4236.

International Labor Organisation (ILO). (2017). Global estimates of modern slavery: Forced labor and forced marriage. https://www.ilo.org/global/publications/books/WCMS_575479/lang%2D%2Den/index.htm

International Labor Organisation (ILO). (n.d.). What is forced labour, modern slavery and human trafficking. https://www.ilo.org/global/topics/forced-labour/definition/lang%2D%2Den/index.htm

Ioannou, G., & Dukes, R. (2021). Anything goes? Exploring the limits of employment law in U.K. hospitality and catering. *Industrial Relations Journal, 52*(3), 255–269.

Johnson, K. R., Huang, T., & Doyle, A. (2019). Mapping talent development in tourism and hospitality: A literature review. *European Journal of Training and Development, 43*(9), 821–841.

Jooss, S., Lenz, J., & Burbach, R. (2022). Beyond competing for talent: An integrative framework for coopetition in talent management in S.M.E.s. *International Journal of Contemporary Hospitality Management, 35*(8), 2691–2707.

Kim, M. S., Ma, E., & Wang, L. (2023). Work-family supportive benefits, programs, and policies and employee wellbeing: Implications for the hospitality industry. *International Journal of Hospitality Management, 108*. https://doi.org/10.1016/j.ijhm.2022.103356

Kipping, D. (2023). COVID-19: Strategies and solutions. https://www.linkedin.com/pulse/attracting-retaining-hotel-employees-wake-covid-19-daniel-p-kipping/

Kong, H., Jiang, X., Chan, W., & Zhou, X. (2018). Job satisfaction research in the field of hospitality and tourism. *International Journal of Contemporary Hospitality Management, 30*(5), 2178–2194.

Kravariti, F., Voutsina, K., Tasoulis, K., Dibia, C., & Johnston, K. (2022). Talent management in hospitality and tourism: A systematic literature review and research agenda. *International Journal of Contemporary Hospitality Management, 34*(1), 321–360.

Kruesi, M. A., & Bazelmans, L. (2023). Resources, capabilities and competencies: A review of empirical hospitality and tourism research founded on the resource-based view of the firm. *Journal of Hospitality and Tourism Insights, 6*(2), 549–574.

Kusluvan, S., Kusluvan, Z., Ilhan, I., & Buyruk, L. (2010). The human dimension: A review of human resources management issues in the tourism and hospitality industry. *Cornell Hospitality Quarterly, 51*(2), 171–214.

Kwok, L. (2022). Labor shortage: A critical reflection and a call for industry-academia collaboration. *International Journal of Contemporary Hospitality Management, 34*(11), 3929–3943.

Law, R., Buhalis, D., & Cobanoglu, C. (2014). Progress on information and communication technologies in hospitality and tourism. *International Journal of Contemporary Hospitality Management, 26*(5), 727–750.

Liu-Lastres, B., Wen, H., & Huang, W.-J. (2023). A reflection on the Great Resignation in the hospitality and tourism industry. *International Journal of Contemporary Hospitality Management, 35*(1), 235–249.

Lombardi, S., Cunha, M. P., & Giustiniano, L. (2021). Improvising resilience: The unfolding of resilient leadership in COVID-19 times. *International Journal of Hospitality Management, 95.* https://doi.org/10.1016/j.ijhm.2021.102904

Loyens, K., & Paraciani, R. (2021). Who is the ('Ideal') victim of labor exploitation? Two qualitative vignette studies on labor inspectors' discretion. *The Sociological Quarterly, 64*(1), 27–45.

Marinakou, E., & Giousmpasoglou, C. (2019). Talent management and retention strategies in luxury hotels: Evidence from four countries. *International Journal of Contemporary Hospitality Management, 31*(10), 3855–3878.

Mooney, S., & Baum, T. (2019). A sustainable hospitality and tourism workforce research agenda: Exploring the past to create a vision for the future. In R. Sharpley & D. Harrison (Eds.), *A research agenda for tourism and development* (pp. 189–205). Edward Elgar Publishing.

Mousa, M., Arslan, A., & Szczepańska-Woszczyna, K. (2022). Talent management practices in the extreme context of hospitality sector: An exploratory study. *International Journal of Organisational Analysis.* https://doi.org/10.1108/IJOA-07-2022-3356

ONS. (2023). U.K. job vacancies (thousands)—Accommodation & food services activities. https://www.ons.gov.uk/employmentandlabourmarket/peopleinwork/employmentandemployeetypes/

Paraskevas, A., & Quek, M. (2019). When Castro seized the Hilton: Risk and crisis management lessons from the past. *Tourism Management, 70*, 419–429.

People 1st. (2021). Future talent in hospitality. https://www.people1st.co.uk/insights-resources/research-intelligence/future-talent-in-hospitality/

Pillai, R., & Sivathanu, B. (2020). Adoption of AI-based chatbots for hospitality and tourism. *International Journal of Contemporary Hospitality Management, 32*(10), 3199–3226.

Pole, G. (2022). Europe's airports struggle with mass staff shortages as travel sector faces 'summer of discontent'. https://www.euronews.com/travel/2022/06/22/europes-airports-struggle-with-mass-staff-shortages-as-travel-sector-faces-summer-of-disco

Prayag, G. (2018). Symbiotic relationship or not? Understanding resilience and crisis management in Tourism. *Tourism Management Perspectives, 25*, 133–135.

Robinson, R., Martins, A., Solnet, D., & Baum, T. (2019). Sustaining precarity: Critically examining tourism and employment. *Journal of Sustainable Tourism, 27*(7), 1008–1025.

Sczepanski, A. (2023). Hyatt celebrates a decade on Fortune's "100 Best Companies to Work For" list. https://www.hospitalitynet.org/news/4115791.html

Shin, H., & Perdue, R. R. (2019). Self-service technology research: A bibliometric co-citation visualisation analysis. *International Journal of Hospitality Management, 80*, 101–112.

Shiwen, L., Kwon, J., & Ahn, J. (2022). Self-service technology in the hospitality and tourism settings: A critical review of the literature. *Journal of Hospitality and Tourism Research, 46*(6), 1220–1236.

Sustainable Hospitality Alliance. (2022a). Establishing ethical recruitment practices in the hospitality industry. https://sustainablehospitalityalliance.org/wp-content/uploads/2022/02/Guidance-note-for-hospitality-sector-on-ethical-recruitment_FINAL.pdf

Transparency Market Research. (2022). Hotels market. https://www.transparencymarketresearch.com/hotels-market.html

Turnbull, N. (2022). Permacrisis: What it means and why it's word of the year for 2022. https://theconversation.com/permacrisis-what-it-means-and-why-its-word-of-the-year-for-2022-194306

Wang, B., Liu, Y., Qian, J., & Parker, S. K. (2021). Achieving effective remote working during the COVID-19 pandemic: A work design perspective. *Applied Psychology, 70*(1), 16–59.

WTTC. (2022). Staff shortages. https://wttc.org/Portals/0/Documents/Reports/2022/WTTC-Staff%20Shortages-August22.pdf

Index

A

Abilities, 74
Absenteeism, 97, 221
Academic discipline, 164
Accommodation, 4
Accreditation, 169
Adaptability, 75, 173
Administration, 42, 166
Administrative management, 44
Age differences, 191
Age discrimination, 193
Age gaps, 150
Agency staff, 151
Anthropology, 52
Apprenticeship, 227
Artificial intelligence (AI), 6, 150, 170, 226
Asset-light business, 14
Assistant General Manager, 26
Asynchronous, 140
Authentic leadership, 107
Authoritarian, 100
Autonomy, 106, 115, 176

B

Behavioural Management movement, 44
Brand, 146
Brexit, 148
Broken rung, 198
Bureaucratic states, 42
Burnout, 221
Business ethics, 54
Business recovery, 219
Business strategy, 68

C

Capital expenditure, 71
Career competencies, 168
Career development, 84, 227

Career ladder, 200
Career progression, 215
Change agents, 2, 77
Change management, 56
Characteristics, 74
Charismatic leadership, 110
Chatbots, 226
Classical Management thinking, 44
Classified, 20
Cloud computing, 172
Code of practice, 54
Cognitive competencies, 83
Collection-style brands, 18
Command, 45
Communication, 52
  skills, 85
Compensation, 53, 141
Competencies, 3, 51, 66, 78, 168
Competencies frameworks, 5, 77
Competing Values Framework (CVF), 84
Competitive advantage, 5, 226
Complaint, 195
Complexity, 74
Compliance, 53
Contemporary hospitality organisations, 97
Contingency plans, 115
The contingent reward, 103
Continuous learning, 172
Control, 45
Convergence, 75
Coordination, 45
Corporate governance, 54
Corporate philanthropy, 54
Corporate planning, 67
Corporate Social Responsibility (CSR), 54

COVID-19, 2
Creating Shared Value (CSV), 54
Creativity, 96
Crisis management, 4, 57, 72, 219
Crisis management plans, 219
Crisis preparedness, 219
Critical thinking, 173
Cross-cultural management, 55
Cross-cultural skills, 75
Cultural context, 163
Cultural diversity, 188, 193
Cultural sensitivity, 75
Curriculum development, 160
Curriculum planning, 165
Customer satisfaction, 97

D

Dark kitchens, 229
Data analytics, 172
Decision-makers, 71
Decision-making, 52, 69, 173
Democratic, 100
Demographic changes, 150
Demographic features, 148
Depersonalisation, 102
Devolution, 50
Differentiating competencies, 79
Digital distribution, 12
Disabilities, 191
Discrimination, 55, 190
Diverse forms of employment, 151
Diversification, 148
Diversity, 188
Diversity management, 6, 188, 189
Diversity training, 55
Downsizing, 57

E

Eco-friendly, 152
Economics, 52
Educational experience, 170
Educational system, 170
Effective teams, 53
E-learning platforms, 171
Electronic HRM (eHRM), 150
Emotional exhaustion, 102
Emotional intelligence, 116
Emotional maturity, 75
Empathy, 116
Empirical research, 165
Empirical studies, 66, 105
Employee burnout, 148
Employee diversity, 3
Employee engagement, 53, 102
Employee performance, 96
Employee practices, 146
Employee relations, 5, 53, 130, 142, 146
Employee retention, 30, 97
Employee turnover, 53, 221
Empowering leadership, 106
Empowerment, 146
Engaging work environments, 53
Entry positions, 168
Environmental footprint, 58
Environmentally-specific servant leadership, 115
Environmental sustainability, 54
Ethical behaviour, 54, 105, 108
Ethical leadership, 108
Ethical recruitment, 222
Ethics and Corporate Social Responsibility, 4
Ethnicity, 192
Ethnic segregation, 192
EU workers, 148

Evaluation, 144
Event planning, 163
Exclusive approach, 145
Experience, 68
Exploitative leadership, 113
External recruitment methods, 135
External validation, 169

F

Faculty staff, 165
Fair treatment, 105
Fair wages, 228
Fair Work, 7
Fair Work Agenda, 228
Feedback, 176
Female leaders, 114
Financial management, 71
Financial performance, 66
Flexibility, 75
Flexible working hours, 176, 204
Flexible working patterns, 221
Food and beverage management, 163
Franchise, 14
Franchising, 18
Front-line managers, 66
Functional competencies, 83
Future perspectives, 214

G

Gamification, 151
Gender, 195
 issues, 188
 pay gap, 200
 roles, 197
 segregation, 6, 188
 stereotypes, 199
 wage gap, 188

General manager (GM), 25, 67
Generation Zs, 194, 217
Gig economy, 151
Gig workers, 222
Glass ceiling, 198
Globalisation, 117
Globalised business environment, 55
Graded, 20
Graduate development, 228
Great Resignation, 148, 215
Green accommodation, 152
Green human resource management (GHRM), 152
Green Key International, 20
Grievance, 195
Group dynamics, 52
Guest expectations, 27–29
Guest-facing staff, 26
Guest satisfaction, 66

H

Hard HRM, 132
Health and Safety, 53, 222
Higher Education (HE), 6
Homogenisation, 168
Honesty, 105
Horizontal segregation, 196
Hospitality, 10
    education, 3, 6, 160
    management curriculum, 160
    management degree, 161
    management education, 84
    management students, 160
    operations, 163
    professional bodies, 22
    and tourism management, 3
    workers, 160
Hotel industry, 7

Hotel management, 2, 7, 188
Hotel managers, 66
Hotel operations, 148, 163
Hotel school, 6, 160
Hotel sector, 13
HR planning, 53
Human behaviour, 46
Human Relations movement, 44
Human Resources (HR) planning, 133
Human resources management (HRM), 3–5, 53, 130, 132
Humble leadership, 113
Hybrid approach, 145

I

Idealised influence, 101
Incentives, 142
Inclusion, 188, 189, 193
Inclusive approach, 145
Inclusive leadership, 113
Inclusive work environment, 54, 188
Increased competition, 27–29
Independence, 106
Individualised consideration, 101
Induction, 137
Industrial relations, 143
Industrial revolution, 4
Industry engagement, 166
Industry experience, 75
Industry insights, 173
Information and Communication Technologies (ICT), 6, 170
Information networks, 78
Information sharing, 205
Information technology, 71, 83
Inspirational motivation, 101
Integrity, 116

Intellectual stimulation, 101
Internal recruitment methods, 135
International etiquette, 75
International hospitality managers, 77
International hospitality operations, 77
Internationalisation, 66, 160, 167
Internet-based methods, 136
Internship programmes, 173
Internships, 160, 227
Interpersonal skills, 75

J

Job demands, 69
Job descriptions, 80
Job functions, 66
Job insecurity, 148
Job requirements, 3
Job satisfaction, 52, 102, 108
Job sharing, 204
Job stress, 166

K

Knowledge, 68, 168
   exchange, 205

L

Labour exploitation, 7
Labour mobility, 225
Labour supply, 215
Labyrinth effect, 198
Laissez-faire, 100, 103
Language learning, 172
Leader, 97
Leader-Member Exchange theory (LMX), 111

Leadership, 3, 5, 52, 71, 96
   skills, 5, 96
   styles, 3, 5, 100, 103
Learning and development, 217, 218
Leased, 14
Legal compliance, 131
Legislation, 152, 222
Liaison, 71
Low pay, 215
Loyalty, 205
Luxury hotels, 160

M

Male managers, 114
Male-dominated, 195
Managed, 14
Management, 40, 51
   contract, 14
   development, 78
   functions, 78
   practices, 4, 202
The management-by-exception (active), 103
The management-by-exception (passive), 103
Managerial competencies, 77
Managerial resilience, 7
Managerial roles, 68
Managerial work, 3, 40, 66
Managerial work requirements, 5
Managers, 51
Managing, 51
   change, 4
   diversity, 54
Managing Diversity and Cross-Cultural Management, 4
Managing Quality and Service Quality, 4

Index

Market fluctuations, 29–30
Marketing, 71
Meta-competencies, 83
Migrant labour, 190
Millennials, 194
Minimum wage, 228
Minority employees, 190
Minority groups, 194
Mobile learning, 171
Mobility, 84
Modern management, 43
Monetary rewards, 146
Moral principles, 54
Motivation, 46, 52, 166
Multicultural context, 190
Multifactor Leadership Questionnaire (MLQ), 102

N

National culture, 87
Needs analysis, 138
Networking, 71, 84

O

Occupational culture, 6, 188
Occupational hierarchy, 196
Occupational segregation, 196
Off-the-job, 140
Old boys network, 199
Onboarding (induction), 53, 137
Online assessments, 172
Online collaboration, 172
Online platforms, 20
Online Reputation Management, 31–32
Online teaching, 170
On-the-job, 140

Open communication culture, 55
Operational costs, 227
Operational HR planning, 134
Operations Manager, 26
Organisation, 5, 45
Organisational barriers, 188
Organisational behaviour (OB), 4, 52
Organisational bias, 198
Organisational charts, 23
Organisational commitment, 97, 108
Organisational culture, 52, 107, 199
Organisational stability, 71
Organisational structure, 23
Outsourcing, 151
Owner, 25
Ownership, 14

P

Package holidays, 160
Pay, 218
Pay inequality, 200
People management, 2, 3, 7, 66
People with disabilities, 203
Performance, 53
    appraisal, 53, 140
    management, 140
Performance and Reward, 5, 130
Permacrisis, 7, 214
Personal attributes, 75
Personalised learning, 171
Personality characteristics, 75
Personality traits, 66, 74
Personnel management, 53, 131
Planning, 5, 45, 130
Policymaking, 67
Poor working conditions, 221
Power and influence, 52

Practice-based definitions of
    hospitality, 10
Practices, 53
Precarious work, 222
Precarity, 221
Preconceptions, 199
Preparedness, 176
Primary characteristics, 189
Principles of management, 45
Privately owned and operated, 14
Processes, 53, 55
Productivity, 53
Products, 55, 66
Professional background, 165
Professional practice, 166
Profitability, 55
Profit margins, 227
Programmes, 53
Promotion, 166
Psychology, 52, 115

Q

Qualifications, 165
Quality assessment, 168
Quality assurance, 168
Quality management, 55
Quantitative Management
    Movement, 44

R

Racial discrimination, 193
Recruitment, 135
Recruitment and Selection (R&S),
    5, 53, 130
Redundancies, 215
Relations, 142
Relationships, 55

Remote work, 148, 151, 224
Remuneration, 141
Repetitive tasks, 203
Reputation, 58, 84, 152, 221
Research, 166
Resilience, 72, 219
Resilient leadership, 114
Respect, 205
Restructuring cases, 57
Retention, 217
Retention strategies, 227
Revalidation, 169
Revenue Management, 29
Reward systems, 141
Risk-taking, 116

S

Scientific management, 4, 44
Seasonal demand, 29–30
Secondary characteristics, 189
Security and safety, 32–33
Selection, 135
Self-confidence, 75, 173, 204
Self-esteem, 204
Self-service kiosks, 225
Semantic definitions of
    hospitality, 10
Senior management, 6, 66, 198
Servant leadership, 104
Service Quality Management, 56
Services, 55, 66
    excellence, 5
    quality, 66, 71
Sexual harassment, 6, 188, 193
Sexual orientation, 194
"7-star" hotels, 21
Shift working, 215
Single-parent families, 151

Skills, 3, 5, 66
  gap, 226
Social competencies, 83
Social interaction, 148
Social media, 151
Social sustainability, 54
Society, 54
Sociology, 52, 115
Soft HRM, 133
Specialisations, 163, 215
Spiritual leadership, 112
Staffing shortages, 7
Staff performance, 166
Staff shortages, 215
Staff turnover, 97
Stakeholders, 2, 54
Standardisation, 168
Standards, 54, 66
Star classification, 20
Stereotypes, 196, 199
Strategic approach, 54
Strategic HR Planning, 134
Strategic HRM, 140
Strategic objectives, 53
Strategic planning, 67
Strategic vision, 111
Strategy, 53
Stress, 52, 74
Student satisfaction, 170
Student's expectations, 164
Succession planning, 143
Superior performance, 79
Sustainability, 71
  management, 4, 58
Sustainable HRM, 152
Synchronous, 140
Systems, 53
Systems and Contingency
    approach, 44

T

Talent, 145
  acquisition, 217
  retention, 146
  retention strategies, 150
Talent management (TM), 3, 5, 7, 72, 144, 216
Teaching, 166
Technical skills, 75, 165
Technology, 150
  integration, 30–31
Tenure, 166
Theoretical concepts, 174
360-degree feedback, 141
Threshold competencies, 79
Tolerance, 75
Total Quality Management (TQM), 56
Tourism education, 163
Tourism industry, 160
Training and Development (T&D), 5, 53, 130, 138
Training programme, 109
Transactional leadership, 103
Transformational leadership, 101
Trust, 55, 105, 205

U

Underpayment, 221
Unionisation, 143
Upskilling, 172

V

Values, 68
Vertically disintegrated, 13
Vertical segregation, 196
Virtual simulations, 171

Vocationalism, 164
Vulnerable groups, 222

W
Wellbeing, 97, 166, 220
Wisdom leadership, 110
Workforce, 143, 214
Working conditions, 6, 151, 188
Work-life balance (WLB), 7, 71, 146, 218, 220
Workload, 166
Work-ready graduates, 177